Scribe Publications
THE WRECK OF WESTERN CULTURE

John Carroll is professor of sociology at La Trobe University in Melbourne. His books include *The Western Dreaming, Terror: a meditation on the meaning of September 11, The Existential Jesus, Ego and Soul: the modern west in search of meaning,* and *Greek Pilgrimage.*

THE WRECK OF WESTERN CULTURE

Humanism Revisited

JOHN CARROLL

SCRIBE

Melbourne • London

Scribe Publications
18–20 Edward St, Brunswick, Victoria 3056, Australia
2 John St, Clerkenwell, London, WC1N 2ES, United Kingdom

First published by Scribe 2004
New edition published 2010
This edition published 2014

Typeset in Dante by the publishers.
Printed and bound in England by CPI Group (UK) Ltd.

National Library of Australia
Cataloguing-in-Publication data

Carroll, John, 1944-

The Wreck of Western Culture: humanism revisited

New ed.

9781921640223 (Australian edition)
9781922247766 (UK edition)
9781921753886 (e-book)

1. Humanism. 2. Renaissance. 3. Civilisation, Western.

144

scribepublications.com.au
scribepublications.co.uk

Contents

ILLUSTRATIONS

PREFACE

The first incarnation of this book, which was published in 1993, was titled *Humanism* and subtitled *The Wreck of Western Culture*. Consideration was given at the time to reversing the order—my own preference, if weakly held. This new, substantially revised edition now pitches the grand theme and driving thesis as its title, while transposing the concrete matter at hand to the subtitle.

The single structural modification has been to take out a section on Poussin from a chapter on 'The Battle of the Artists' and develop it into an independent chapter, 'The Alternative Reformation', adding it as the fourth leg to the Foundation story. I have also taken account of September 11, 2001, arguing that it has deep metaphysical implications for the West, ones that relate to the core of the humanism question. I draw here on a short book I wrote in 2002— *Terror: a meditation on the meaning of September 11* (Scribe).

New account has been taken of music. Bach has been added to an analysis of the bourgeois cultural form, and Mozart to Enlightenment and Romance. Also, the revised edition has given stronger acknowledgment to the achievements of liberal democracy.

The first edition elicited a common response to this effect: given that you have diagnosed what has gone wrong with Western culture, and the gravity of its current malaise, what is the remedy? Where do we go now? It was never the mission of *The Wreck of*

Western Culture to move into that vast new terrain. Piecing together the logic of the dominant old culture, the path of its rise and fall, is a task unto itself, and necessary in order to understand what has failed, and why. Doctors cannot recommend a cure if they are blind to the disease. I have begun the subsequent task—of 'Where to now?'—in later work, principally *Ego and Soul: The Modern West in Search of Meaning* (HarperCollins, 1998) and *The Western Dreaming* (HarperCollins, 2001).

I wish to thank a number of people. Justin Wintle edited the first edition, and Philip Gwyn Jones at HarperCollins in London published it. Anthony Flew, Andrew Riemer and Agnes Heller alerted me to flaws. With the revised edition, I have taken note of points made by Eva Stewart, Don Watson and Katie Wright. Peter Murphy provided a considered response to the Marx section, and Russ Radcliffe at Scribe made substantive suggestions that I have implemented. Henry Rosenbloom, Scribe's publisher, has been his usual cheerful, critically intelligent, and helpful self.

Philip Rieff delivered a lecture on 'Authority and Culture' at La Trobe University in 1980 which stimulated two of the book's lines of thought. Rieff used Holbein's *The Ambassadors* to show that culture works indirectly, and that, when no prohibitions remain, and there are no moral limits, death rules.

PROLOGUE

We live amidst the ruins of the great, five-hundred-year epoch of humanism. Around us is that 'colossal wreck'. Our culture is a flat expanse of rubble. It hardly offers shelter from a mild cosmic breeze, never mind one of those icy gales that regularly return to rip us out of the cosy intimacy of our daily lives and confront us with oblivion. Is it surprising that we are run down? We are desperate, yet don't care much any more. We are timid, yet we cannot be shocked. We are inert underneath our busyness. We are destitute in our plenty. We are homeless in our own homes.

What should be there to hold our hand, is not. Our culture has absented itself. It has left us terribly alone. In its devastation it cannot even mock us any more or sneer at the lost child whimpering for its mother. That stage, too, is over. Our culture is like a dying god, its altar untended, past retribution at this insolence, its rage turned to indifference.

What are we to do? Is it a time to lament, complain, or laugh? Is it a time to seize hold of some fine marble fragment and dream it whole? Is it a time to close our eyes and try to lose ourselves in our own tiny back-gardens? Or is it a time to embrace one of the lingering ghosts, squeeze it for its warmth, and pretend we are alive? No! It is the time for a new beginning ... but not quite yet. First, the old must be buried, and with due rites. A requiem must be sung, one that gets the story right, in all its magnificence and its meanness. We come less to honour Caesar than to bury him, that there be no mistaking that he is dead, that we understand him so as not to choose him again. The occasion is grave; our own sorry state makes that plain. There shall be honour, too.

We are gathered here to bury a myth, a myth that failed. This myth has held us Westerners in thrall—through its long and struggling foundation, through its middle period when it systematically demolished all competitors, and finally through its autumn when it turned against itself and, in its insatiable hunger, devoured its own entrails. It drove our ancestors relentlessly on as it worked through an inexorable logic. In the process it created a huge and brilliantly lit metropolis of a culture, next to which all that had gone before seemed but a handful of small towns. It put everything in question in the most revolutionary and categorical either-or in human history. It set its converts so much on edge that they were, for a half-millennium, driven into the most sustained bout of philosophical, literary, artistic and musical wrestling ever known. What was at stake was the future of the Western soul.

Humanism sought to turn the treasure-laden galleon of Western culture around. It attempted to replace God by man, put humans at the centre of the universe—to deify them. Its ambition was to found an order on earth in which freedom and happiness prevailed, without any transcendental or supernatural supports—an entirely human order. The challenge facing it and, with it, modernity, had been put graphically by Archimedes in a quite different time, 'Give me somewhere to stand and I shall move the earth.' To place the human individual at the centre meant that he or she had to become the Archimedean point around which everything revolved. A world without such a point is relativity and chaos, without direction, bearings or sense—a world in which humans cannot live and stay sane. But if

humans were to become the still-point in the universe, they had to
have somewhere to stand that would not move under their feet.

Humanism had to build a rock. It had to create out of nothing
something as strong as the faith of the New Testament that could
move mountains. Luther, whose instinct about these matters was
sure, whose lifelong battle was really against humanism and not the
Catholic Church, could assert at his decisive moment, 'Here I stand,
I can do no other.' In his choice of words Luther was taunting his
time and, above all, humanists such as Erasmus, challenging them
to see if they could find a place to stand. We can imagine him,
under his breath, answering his own rhetorical question, 'That'll be
the day!'

The axiom on which the humanist rock was to be forged was put
as well by Pico della Mirandola in 1486 as by anyone, 'We can
become what we will.' It is more complete than Alberti's earlier and
more celebrated formulation, 'Men can do all things if they will.' So
the fathers put their founding axiom: humans are all-powerful, if
their will is strong enough. They can create themselves. They can
choose to be courageous, honourable, just, charitable, rich, influential, or not. They are creator and creature in one. Out of their own
individual wills they can move the earth. The great individual stands
alone; under his or her feet the earth does not move.

Here is a radical inflation of the power of the human will, conjoined with a new conception of being, of what it is to exist, of
what it is that exists. All religions predicate being in the way the
Lord God of the Old Testament, Hebrew Bible did to Moses, 'I am
that I am.' The divinity, whether single or multiple, is primal and all-
encompassing Being. It is first cause and source of all life and spirit.
There are no questions to be asked about primal being: it simply *is*.
Moreover, in that everything derives from it, the rallying cry, 'We
can become what we will', is highly problematic, if not absurd. In
fact, humanism had to undermine the 'I am that I am' if it was

going to establish its rock. It had to replace it with 'I am', where the *I* is the individual human being. This was the central task of the Renaissance. It attempted it in the only way possible—by example.

Its examples were formidable, a procession of great men, men of awesome character who, by their deeds and their creations—works of statecraft, ideas, art, and science—demonstrated that it is possible to *be*. And they were all men, with no women enshrined in the original humanist pantheon—with the indirect exception of Queen Elizabeth of England. Their implicit boast was, 'I have made myself what I am, and that is good, even more, it is great. *I* am!' The world of ordinary mortals looking at the Renaissance man, astride his destiny, composed, knowledgable, secure, an authority unto himself, could cry out in spontaneous wonder, 'He is!' That, at least, was the theory, and for a time it seems to have worked. After all, the West has chosen to live for five hundred years under the humanist credo. We *can* become what we will.

The early men of the Renaissance were not aware that they would have to choose. They were Christians. The most instructive example, Erasmus himself, tried in his moderate Christian humanism to adapt his religion to the methods of the new secularism. It took Luther to smell a rat, and in his rejection of free-will to establish the metaphysical either-or which was, from behind the scenes, to dominate the humanist epoch. When Luther said to Erasmus with uncharacteristic politeness, 'You are not devout!', he had, philosophically speaking, hit the nail on the head. He had prophesied the inevitable path of humanism once it had chained itself, as it must, to a belief in free-will. This simple and direct, uncouth German peasant had told the most refined, best educated, wittiest and most eloquent man of his time, a man he admired, 'You stand on nothing.'

Three hundred and fifty years later, the last great humanist philosopher, Nietzsche, staked his entire work on defending the pre-eminence of the human will. By this time, however, the battle had been lost, as he knew, and his twilight struggle is consequently feverish, full of wild gesticulation and despair, by the end demented. Nietzsche, too, was German, and shared Luther's directness and sureness of instinct. He repeatedly ranted against his great predecessor as 'that German barbarian'. He knew that it was Luther or him. The last line of Nietzsche's last work reads 'Dionysus versus the Crucified', by which he meant, myself or Christ, one or the other, either-or. When he typed these words in 1888 he was already far down the slide into catatonic madness. His words were mad. They are the dying cry of humanist philosophy.

What is so admirable about Nietzsche is that he saw clearly what was at stake, and refused to give up the hopeless struggle. Humans had to be able to move the earth by their own will, or they would be paralysed. The philosopher's job was to remove all mental impediments to the will, especially the moral ones. The Renaissance was for Nietzsche the last era of wilful men. Since then humanity had progressively lost its still-point. It had become more and more at the mercy of any fickle breath of wind, at the mercy of what the ancients called Necessity. The material forces of birth and death, of disease and war, of this fate or that, could once again play with human life as if it were a bit of flotsam in the cosmic void. Will meant the conquest of necessity, of fate. Individuals had to be able to make their fortune, to get hold of fate by the scruff of the neck and force it to bow to their will. When Goya in the humanist waning was to paint the fates hovering over human life, remorseless, dark, directing by whim, he was painting against the bright confidence of Pico and the founding fathers.

Necessity reduces ultimately to one thing—death. When necessity rules, humanity finds that it has subjected itself to the most severe of all metaphysics, that life is under the command of death, that mortality rules. Christianity had focused itself in all its formative intensity on the crucifixion, on one tragic image of death and its transcendence. Humanism had to find a credible alternative to Christ crucified. Otherwise it would leave its own pilgrims helplessly vulnerable, gone the moment they relaxed their control—one careless instant would do it, and they would be staring into the eyes of their Medusa.

The weakening of Christian faith would lead the West back into the arms of the other parent of its culture, the ancient Greek one. The Greek tragedians had known all about the eyes that would freeze humans in their tracks, turn them to stone. They had found their own means of countering that cold stare out of eternity, one that humanism would have to recapture if it were to survive. Archimedes, too, knew the Medusa, for 'Give me somewhere to stand and I shall move the earth' has as its implicit corollary, 'If I don't find a place to stand, I shall not be able to move even myself.' Thus, from the outset, humanism was confronted with the metaphysical challenge of neutralising the fear of death. It had to give individuals enough support, a reliable enough hand to hold, so that when they caught the whiff of a corpse they would not go weak at the knees, and collapse in pale terror. It had to give them enough gravity in themselves, enough I, to be able to withstand the gale of mortality.

Kierkegaard had already seen the cracks in 1846. He told the anecdote of the wager. Two English lords were riding along when a man whose horse had bolted galloped past shouting for help. One lord said to the other, 'A hundred pounds he falls off!' 'Taken,' was the immediate reply, at which they wheeled their horses, spurred them on, galloping past the runaway horse to open the gates and prevent anything getting in its way. Kierkegaard concludes scornfully that his own age lacked even the stylish sporting zest of the aristocracy. The dismal message in the story is that the humanist will has atrophied to nothing, it has lost its higher conscience, the I having degenerated into that of a chronic invalid watching life from a hospital window. The advice to the few active ones is: don't go riding, lest your horse bolt and you need help.

The cracks in the humanist edifice were to be seen from the beginning. The mortar was still damp between the foundation stones when the hairline fissures appeared. Luther saw them with his conscious eye, and wrote his *Enslaved Will*. Holbein and Shakespeare saw them, in their cases unconsciously and therefore with special force. It will be one of the main theses of the work to follow that humanism was doomed from the start, that it carried within its own seed the elements of its destruction.

There is another side to the story. For the humanists, the age that had come before, what we know as the Middle Ages, had been an age of darkness. The darkness had been both mental and physical. Medieval thinking was steeped in superstition, a phantasmagoria of devils and sorcerers, of saints and relics, of the threat of a ghastly hell inhabited by demonic hybrids, part-human and part-monster. Most people, most of the time, experienced everyday life as a miserable struggle to survive. It was unremitting, cheerless toil, further cursed by endemic warfare, famine, disease and, from the fourteenth century, plague of such virulence that almost entire cities were periodically wiped out. The Hobbesean epithet of the life of man being solitary, poor, nasty, brutish, and short was a realistic description of the European Middle Ages. The humanists' response to this nightmare was necessary and correct—to use everything in their power to change their infernal condition. The medieval slum was to be replaced by a new city, planned and built by confident, rational men of fine character. The clarity and light of reason, of precise, classical forms, would drive out the darkness of superstition and squalor.

This image of human progress was to prove so persuasive that, to counter it, Luther had to preach a new darkness, that of faith—that of the dark night of faith.

Humanism succeeded in building its city of light. Today, it is culture's metropolis that is in ruins, not the metropolis itself. The wreck of humanist culture is in stark contrast to the physical edifice that its drive to know, channelled into science and technology, and applied in factories, has produced. Humanism's lasting achievement has been industrial civilisation and its brilliant triumph over most of the trials inflicted by age-old necessity—poverty, starvation, disease and brute labour. The material comfort enjoyed by Western societies in the last century represents a giant advance in human experience, and we are duty-bound to acknowledge the fact. Who in their right mind would give up clean water, sanitation and sewers, antibiotics, reliable supplies of varied foodstuffs, civic police, the jumbo jet, computers, and skyscrapers, in exchange for what came before—the filth, contagion and stench of medieval Europe?

On September 11, 2001, this ground shifted. A terrorist attack, by means of hijacked passenger jets, on the West's most cosmopolitan city—the exemplar of its civilisation's technological prestige and might—destroyed New York's tallest skyscrapers, and succeeded in turning humanist philosophy against its own material triumph. Usama bin Laden mocked America as 'the camp of unbelief', proclaiming that his God, Allah, has 'elevated the skies without pillars'. The subtext was chilling in its clarity, 'If material comfort is all you Western infidels believe in, as symbolised by these spectacular twin towers—your pillars—then I will bring your culture down.' The casual pace of the humanist going under had, on the instant, been electrified.

***

The subject matter of this book is, in essence, the spiritual history of the modern West. I have set myself the task of finding the beacons lighting that history, and of distinguishing what they represent at each key stage. During the humanist half-millennium, the spirit's finest projection has been high culture. High culture has its own hierarchy, with a few supreme masterpieces at the top. This study concentrates on those masterpieces. They are worked for all their worth. In other words, this is not a cultural history in the sense of looking comprehensively at all major theorists and artists of a period. It seeks the best, and neglects the rest.

Such an unorthodox method rests on the assumption that the rare masterpieces of culture are so because they have tapped the deepest truths of their time. They are illuminated by what they have touched, and gain timeless surety and clarity thereby. As such, they stand as signposts. If we manage to read them we shall know the path along which we have come, and what we have alternatively lost and gained along the way.

There is such difference in quality between the exceptional works and the rest that more is to be learned from sitting day after day with them than in taking a broad sweep of the whole field. The story those few works tell is deceptively simple, and yet they never reveal all. There are many veils. Even the most concentrated devotion leaves penitents with the feeling that they have found the only path that matters, yet are not permitted to see it clearly.

Within the great works there is a division. This is an elite with two factions. Some works are in touch with the eternal powers and their laws, and they are oriented to their own time according to them, in obedience, striving above all to represent them. They judge their contemporary world by the light of those higher truths. The other works do not have this special virtue, and they are, as a consequence, unsettling. They rattle their times, imposing on them a commanding turmoil. This distinction will gain major significance as our story unfolds.

Part One

FOUNDATION

Chapter Two

THE GLORY OF THE RENAISSANCE

The Gattamelata and Brutus

For over five hundred years now, the small square in front of the Cathedral of San Antonio in Padua has worshipped a different god than he who rules inside the church doors, where one plunges into the dark. There is awe in that square, open to the heavens. To come in sight of it—and it is best to do so at noon in the full light of day, and to lift the eyes and look—from that moment on, one is in the thrall of humanism. True, it is possible to sidle up to the cathedral with head lowered, the first signs being the stalls for tourists and pilgrims selling plastic knick-knacks, garish red charms and crudely painted virgins, all the paraphernalia of modern Italian Catholicism. They can crowd out the square.

What does command here, set on a high and massive stone pedestal, is the Gattamelata (see fig. 1). He is the Venetian general Erasmo de Narni, on horseback, immortalised in bronze a few years after his death in 1443, by Donatello. His form is that of the medieval *condottiere*, the warrior who by means of his own singular, brute strength and courage could win any war. The *condottiere* was the hero of the earlier epoch, one embodying subhuman fantasies of the monstrous force of animal nature, at times sublimated into the chivalrous ideal of the Christian knight. The most brilliant representation of the medieval *condottiere* stands fewer than thirty miles from Padua, in the Campo of Saints Giovanni and Paolo in

Venice—that is, Verrocchio's equestrian statue of Il Colleoni. A mountain of a man, rearing up erect in his stirrups, Il Colleoni thrusts his huge armour-clad left shoulder up and forward, shielding his massive torso and neck, his thick and crude features glowering from under a steel helmet like those of an enraged beast. He is a hulk of indomitable power.

The Gattamelata belongs to another species. Already in the late 1440s Donatello could anticipate the Renaissance ideal, the 'We can become what we will', and project it in three-dimensional visual form. The genius of Donatello presents a new measure of human force.

The Gattamelata is mounted on a strong, square warhorse, formidably serviceable, with stocky legs, the neck and chest of a bull, and a fierce head. It is neighing and tossing, chafing at the bit, as it strides forward. This charger has the attributes that Verrocchio was to give to his warrior. The Gattamelata himself is the epitome of balance, and confidence of a different order—its source is inward. He sits lightly in the saddle, his posture straight and relaxed. He looks ahead, without helmet. In his right hand, which is forward over the horse's mane, he delicately holds a baton. Whereas his charger strives, he is composed. Donatello underscores the point by making the rider proportionately small in relation to the bulk of his horse. The human individual is master of powerful forces surging beneath him: they champ, they pull, they are vastly stronger yet, through his own will, his own force of character, nothing to do with physical strength only to do with balance, and a clear and concentrated mind, he is master. The baton is also suggestive of a scroll, symbol of knowledge, of the rational human mind conquering the volcanic chaos of nature. The Gattamelata is Renaissance man.

He has nothing to obey but himself; he needs nothing above or beyond the *I*. He is the value-creating individual—on the move. There is such intensity focused between the brows, such inviolable purpose buried in the eyes, that the head itself, bare to the heavens, becomes the sacred site. A concentrated mind may move the very earth.

Humanism, nevertheless, needed an ethic, a central moral axiom, to secure its foundation. The clarity and steady vision with which the Gattamelata looks straight ahead, taking in the world, is not enough. Neither is his commanding will. He is so superbly in form because he embodies the humanist *ethos*. He does obey one external—he is a gentleman, or in the Italian characterisation of Castiglione, a courtier. And, as a gentleman, he is under the command of honour.

The humanist ethos was founded on a character ideal. If humanism was going to find its place to stand, it had to enshrine the value of honour, and without any higher transcendental backing. For the preceding epoch, the Middle Ages, it had been easier: its ideal, the *saint*, including the warrior-saint (St Joan of Arc; Sir Galahad), was the direct human representative of the divinity, from whom it derived its authority. For humanism, honour had to stand alone, by itself. Then everything else would follow. The principal role of the humanist hero was therefore to become so awesomely noble that the rest of common humanity would believe in the culture he exemplified.

The ease and grace of the Gattamelata is predicated on the knowledge that he is right, doing what he has to do. The great political realist of Renaissance thought, Machiavelli, was keenly aware of the challenge, placing *virtu* at the core of his ideal politics—*vir*, the stem of the word, simply meaning 'man'. Contained in one word was an entire philosophy of what it is to be a man, an entire conception of male being. However, to learn of the significance of the struggle to enshrine honour, of just what was at stake, and of the enormity of the task, we need to move on to the last period of Renaissance humanism, to Shakespeare. It is fitting that humanism's quintessential genius should have provided the key text, *Julius Caesar*.

As the most perceptive character in the play puts it at the start, 'honour is the subject of my story'. In particular, the aim of *Julius Caesar* is to honour the name of Brutus. Brutus is cast as the highest example of man, and Shakespeare sets out to examine what it means to be Brutus. The 'hallowed be Thy name' of the Lord's Prayer is almost explicitly transposed here onto the humanist hero. What is really at stake is the replacing of Christ crucified by Brutus. The structure of the play works in simple obedience to this plan, with the defeat and death of Brutus constituting the climax; its significance is articulated in the funeral oration by Mark Antony, his enemy:

> This was the noblest Roman of them all;
> All the conspirators save only he
> Did that they did in envy of great Caesar;
> He only, in a general honest thought
> And common good to all, made one of them.
> His life was gentle, and elements
> So mix'd in him that Nature might stand up
> And say to all the world, 'This was a man!'

'This was a man!' is a deliberate and heavily charged displacement of Pilate's public acknowledgment of Jesus, 'Behold the man!' or '*Ecce homo!*'

Even Mark Antony's earlier funeral oration for Caesar, in Act III, the best-known speech in the play, opening with 'Friends, Romans, countrymen ...' relates to the climax. It has the surface function of turning the people against Brutus, and starting the chain of events that will lead to his defeat. It has the deeper function of anticipating the second oration as the significant one. It is only in the second speech that Mark Antony is sincere.

The main aim of the stirring rhetoric of 'Friends, Romans, countrymen' is less grief for Caesar than a crafty eloquence to move the mob for Antony's own political ends, to avenge Caesar's murder. The argument hinges on Brutus' character. It will succeed if the repeated, increasingly bitter and satirical, 'And Brutus is an honourable man', can get through. It does. Brutus is destroyed because the master orator succeeds in impugning his honour. Without honour he is nothing. He is worse than nothing: he is a betrayer and a murderer.

Henry V and *Julius Caesar* are Shakespeare's most idealistic plays outside the comedies. *Henry V* projects the strongest representation in literature of the 'good king'. It is a simple and telling drama. In *Julius Caesar* little is simple. It is a true late-Renaissance work. The drama opens zestfully with the cobbler, the mender of bad soles, and a string of puns. But he is merely the bright foreground setting off the reality of grave politics. The day is the feast of Lupercal, a Roman festival of expiation; however, what is being celebrated is the greatness of Caesar, whose pride and ambition, many fear, are about to break all limits.

Enter Brutus. Who is he? What ideal does Shakespeare paint? Brutus loves principle, and always seeks to act by it. He is a poor politician, lacking the capacity for expedient action. He is contrasted with Cassius, who has good political and military judgment, and few qualms about employing evil means for a necessary end, but who is a malicious and envious man. Brutus rejects Cassius' advice to kill Mark Antony while they can; later, he rejects his military advice. In each case he is disastrously wrong, in terms of the practical consequences, in terms of politics. In terms of honour, certainly on the first occasion, he is right. Brutus is also rational and prudent, at least early in the drama. On another front, he says of himself that he lacks Antony's quick spirit. He loves his wife, and she him. In fact, almost everybody in the play loves Brutus. He is a good man.

Brutus is the hero of just action, in the tradition of Antigone. He is no Hamlet, who will dither around while the state falls apart. His cogitations lead him to the conclusion, after many sleepless nights, that Caesar is abusing his high office. Power has gone to his head. It has lost its necessary tie to compassion. Liberty is under threat. Brutus decides to kill Caesar, who is his friend, a reasonable man and a great leader, for the good of the state. His mind is now clear, his character firm. When the conspirators next meet, Cassius urges them to swear to their resolution. Brutus opposes him, arguing that an oath is unnecessary and that it is only men with a bad or doubtful cause who need to swear. They are above this. Their promise is enough—their word. They are gentlemen. Brutus later uses the same noble argument to oppose the killing of Mark Antony:

> Let's be sacrificers, not butchers, Cassius
> … purgers, not murderers.

Brutus justifies his having killed Caesar, to Antony, by saying:

> … so pity, pity—
> Hath done this deed on Caesar.

In other words, he has acted not only to save Rome from tyranny, but also for Caesar, to save him from himself, to save *his* honour. Brutus has acted out of friendship, tragic friendship. Here is the burden carried by the man of honour. As Brutus puts it to the people in his oration over the corpse of Caesar:

> As Caesar loved me, I weep for him; as he was fortunate, I rejoice at it; as he was valiant, I honour him; but, as he was ambitious, I slew him. There is tears for his love; joy for his fortune; honour for his valour; and death for his ambition.

The words 'honour' and 'noble' litter the text of *Julius Caesar*. In response to Caesar's judicious concern about Cassius, 'Yond Cassius has a lean and hungry look ... such men are dangerous', Antony counters, 'He is a noble Roman.' Decius talks Caesar into going to the Capitol by playing on his honour:

> If Caesar hide himself, shall they not whisper
> 'Lo, Caesar is afraid'?

The crowd responds to the orations, 'There's not a nobler man in Rome than Antony.' Brutus' greatest insult to Cassius is to contrast him with 'noble men'. Once they are reconciled, it is 'Noble, noble Cassius'. And hearing of Cassius' death:

> It is impossible that ever Rome
> Should breed thy fellow.

If the first question in *Julius Caesar* concerns the nature of nobility, the second focuses on reason. Reason is the second and independent value, serving honour. After the assassination, Brutus promises to give Antony the grounds on which they acted. Antony stakes his allegiance to the plotters on his getting these reasons, and on their being plausible. Furthermore, the speeches of Brutus and Antony to the people lay out the opposing arguments. In effect, the people listen to a debate, which they then judge. The first plebeian response to Antony is, 'Methinks there is much reason in his sayings.' Justice requires reasons, a convincing case. Both Brutus and Antony speak cogently, but Antony's argument is the stronger. Again Shakespeare is positing an ideal—of political life founded on honour and justice, served by reason.

Much of this is rhetoric, but brilliant and effective rhetoric at that. This play is a vessel for the English language at one of its peaks, a sustained and intoxicating eloquence of precise meanings and beautiful cadences. What is not rhetoric is the fact that Brutus kills Caesar. Here is the bite of, 'We can become what we will.' The value-creating individual, the great *I*, can, with a good conscience, break the moral code, or so the theory goes. What Brutus does is extreme. He could hardly have chosen a greater violation of what the universal moral code decrees to be good. He kills. Not only does he coolly and deliberately take human life, but his victim is the king, and a good king, a great leader who has done prodigious service for the state. Worse, this king is Brutus' friend, and he trusts him. Caesar's dying words, 'Et tu Brute', are intimate and tragic. Mark Antony insinuates that Caesar really died from a broken heart, at being betrayed by the ungrateful Brutus:

> For Brutus, as you know, was Caesar's angel.
> Judge, O you gods, how dearly Caesar loved him!
> This was the most unkindest cut of all.

Brutus as an honourable man of action attempts by his own will to impose virtue on law and tradition. He breaks the civic law in a manner that makes Antigone's disobedience look like a childish prank. His is the definitive act of regicide in Western culture, all done in the name of his own self-decreed higher law. Brutus embodies a noble reworking of Macbeth. More interestingly, he is the forefather of Dostoevsky's Raskolnikov, who sets out, in the nineteenth century, to prove he is a superior man, a superman, by taking the power over life and death into his own hands—*he* kills merely an old skinflint. What is at issue here is Luther's free-will. Raskolnikov is out to prove that he is free by breaking the central moral injunction against murder. If he can do it with a clean conscience, he is free; he has become who he wills. In fact he fails, for guilt destroys his freedom. Brutus is the same. He attempts the supreme act of free-will:

out of calm, rational choice to kill the most glorious and powerful man in the world, to do it with reason, honourably. Brutus' metaphysical cry to his humanist god is, 'I am free to kill Caesar.' In other words what 'I am free to make values' comes down to, reduced to its essence, is 'I am free to kill the great king'.

It goes without saying that if a man is not free to make his own values, he cannot be free to make himself.

The making of values requires choosing how and when to apply them. Brutus does not invent honour. He chooses it as his god, then he chooses the acts through which to give it form. He gives easily comprehensible, concrete shape to an abstraction. In this he is not an immoralist like Raskolnikov, who obeys no value apart from himself. Brutus obeys a higher code, that of honour—indeed his whole purpose is to enshrine it as the central principle determining human behaviour, in terms of which it is possible to exercise the will. The *I* does not stand completely on its own.

'I am free to kill Caesar' has as its complementary ethical formulation, 'I am free to judge', or, more bluntly, 'I judge'. The simpler axiom of the early Renaissance now gains more flesh, in the figure of Brutus. The new philosophy has it that I, the great individual, am rational and thereby know the moral law and may apply it to the affairs of men, reaching judgment about what they do. Having reason, judgment and will, it is my duty to kill Caesar. I shall do it.

More is at stake than the metaphysical status of the individual. *Julius Caesar* is a political play. Without Brutus, politics would be reduced to an endless series of ruthless and bloody power struggles. Cassius and Mark Antony are the political men, perceptive, calculating, shrewd, practical, and capable of swift and brutal action—Antony, without blinking, has a hundred senators killed. The core of Cassius' great love for Brutus is respect, that he is the better man, a good and honest man, a man of honour. Similarly, Mark Antony's final phrase, 'he was the noblest Roman of them all', is the genuine homage of politics to virtue. Shakespeare rams the point home by painting both Cassius and Mark Antony as the politician at his best, and showing the man they look up to as having poor military judgment and a feeble sense of practical realities.

The case is that there can be no political authority without honour. Machiavelli gave it the broader notion of *virtu*. Without honour, there will be cynicism, deals, corruption—in short, a nihilistic, Hobbesean public life. The gentleman was to become, in the descent from Brutus, the linchpin of humanist politics. The ethic of public duty, of selfless service to the community and the state—*noblesse oblige*—derives from the code of honour. For Brutus, self-preservation and personal happiness are of no account in his political life: they are entirely subordinate to the preservation of his name.

So far, we have considered only the first half of the Brutus story. Whilst Shakespeare aimed to glorify the name of Brutus, the realist in him rebelled. He cast a clear, cool and urbane eye on what he had made. Brutus was not to escape as an ideal. By the time the man of principle dies, he has become a rather tarnished hero.

Like Macbeth and Raskolnikov, Brutus is destroyed by his own guilt. He cannot kill with a clear conscience. He is unhinged by his free act. In an explicit parallel with Macbeth, Brutus' wife, after the assassination, goes mad and commits suicide. Unlike Lady Macbeth, she herself is quite innocent. Brutus is left with not only his grief at her loss, but guilt for having caused it. The most direct manifestation of his rampaging conscience is that it twice conjures up the ghost of dead Caesar. The ghost carries dire warnings, a messenger of impending retribution.

The starkest symptoms of Brutus' deterioration are not, however, visitations by ghosts. They appear in the way he mistreats his devoted friend and fellow general, Cassius. The evidence in the play is unambiguous about the fact that Cassius' strongest passion is his love for Brutus. The most moving thing in the whole drama is the way Brutus tramples on this love, in Act IV, and the despair into which Cassius sinks. Here is the emotional centre of the drama.

The episode starts with an indirect report to Brutus that Cassius has cooled towards him. Brutus starts talking about 'hollow men' and 'deceitful jades'. Cassius, upon their meeting, explains his coolness as due to Brutus having slighted off his letters on behalf of a man taking bribes from the local population in order to pay their joint army. There is a battle to be fought; everything hangs on victory, but first of all the army must be paid. Cassius is obeying political necessity. Virtue's reply is that Cassius has 'an itching palm' for gold. Cassius is rightly outraged at this demeaning and unjust language. After a further exchange, during which Cassius retains his self-control, Brutus loses all composure and shouts, 'Away, slight man!' He then accuses Cassius of rash anger and testy humour (in fact, a projection of his own state of mind), and produces the extravagant insult that from now on Cassius will merely be an object of Brutus' mirth.

Cassius' reply is the pained question, 'Is it come to this?', which the irrepressible Brutus shrugs off with a reference to 'noblemen', in whose company Cassius does not belong. Cassius is conciliatory, but after further taunting he asserts:

> Do not presume too much upon my love.
> I may do that I should be sorry for.

At this, the man of principle boasts in self-righteous anger, 'I am arm'd so strong in honesty', and continues with a pompous speech about his own virtue. Brutus has become an unhinged caricature of himself, his honour reduced to a charade.

Cassius is flattened by this unconscionable behaviour from his friend. His final response is that, now he is 'hated by one he loves', he is weary of life. He asks Brutus to kill him. He reflects that

Brutus loved Caesar more than him. At this, Brutus softens, and they are reconciled. But even after the reconciliation it is Cassius who blames his own rash humour for the dispute. The truth is that Cassius has been the constant and devoted friend throughout, and his temper has been remarkably restrained. Yet even now Brutus judges that the whole episode has been the result of Cassius' faulty self-control.

Retribution follows. The two generals discuss strategy. Cassius' plan is astute, Brutus' foolish. Cassius defers to Brutus out of love. Mark Antony cannot believe the stupidity of their strategy when the opposing armies meet at Philippi. What has really happened is that Cassius, the great soldier, loses his balance when Brutus turns against him and never fully regains it. In the final battle Cassius acts quite out of character, impetuously killing himself because he wrongly believes that Brutus has been defeated. The greatness in his character has been irreparably fractured by the violence with which his untrusting friend has turned against him. The guilt-hounded Brutus has destroyed them both. Ironically, in Shakespeare's other and later Mark Antony story, the Roman soldier will have his own *virtu*, his male, warrior judgment, fatally compromised by love—in his case, for Cleopatra.

Shakespeare's subtext is consistently humanist. Dostoevsky provides an instructive contrast, that of a Christian fatalist for whom murder is a cardinal sin—and that is the end of the matter. Unless the murderer is a monster, he will suffer from an annihilating conscience. Shakespeare's picture is more complex, in a rationalist manner. Events obey a logic. Brutus is unhinged by his guilt not simply because he has killed, but because his reasons were not good enough. Mark Antony wins the debate before the people because he is right. There is not enough evidence that Julius Caesar will become a tyrant. Brutus himself gives away his cause in Act II, Scene 1, referring to Caesar:

He would be crown'd:

How that might change his nature, there's the question.

It is not sure that Caesar will accept the supreme power implied by being crowned. Even if he is crowned, Brutus can do no better than assert that power *might* go to his head. True, there is some evidence later in the play of Caesar's growing arrogance. On the other hand, Mark Antony can remind the people of how generous Caesar has been to them with his spoils of war. The play stresses reasons, and the bald fact is that Brutus' are not nearly good enough for the extremity of the action he takes. He is overwhelmed with guilt in the aftermath. There is nothing obscure about this guilt. There is a plain logic to its source, and to its self-destroying workings, above all Brutus' demented treatment of his friend Cassius.

Shakespeare is no fatalist. Brutus is not an Oedipus, crushed by a harsh and inviolable destiny. Brutus is punished for what he has done: it is the free act of the rational man that starts the chain of events which lead to his defeat and death.

So what remains of 'We can become what we will'? The play has attempted to unify virtue and happiness, the ambition of much of Western ethics since Socrates, by finding a way of life governed by honour that will produce a just and stable politics. It fails, and for a number of reasons. Brutus loses his happiness, destroying his cause and his own life, because he is too narrowly a man of principle, without enough practical sense to see that crafty men are manipulating him, and that his reasons for killing Caesar are weak. As man of honour, his conscience is severe. It undermines him.

Cassius, in contrast, suffers from a failure of will, and because of the most admirable thing in his character, the fact that he loves the man who is better than him. It is the nobility in this not-very-noble man that funds the passion that cripples his strength. We may conclude that the complexity of the human condition—of character, passion, conscience, not to mention the course of external events—rules out any simple humanist utopia.

In *Julius Caesar* the final twist is consummate. Act IV has undermined the principle of honour, by showing up the man who embodies it as a narrow-minded and pompous idealist with little sense of reality. It gives weight to Antony's ironical, 'And Brutus is an honourable man.' In Act V Brutus is punished. In keeping with the psychological laws of guilt, he regains his composure and his dignity on the threshold of his impending death. The enduring goodness of his character resonates at the end in the devotion and love his soldiers show him. He claims, just as he is about to run on his sword:

> I shall have glory by this losing day
> More than Octavius and Mark Antony
> In this vile conquest shall attain to.

The man to benefit in every material sense is the young Octavius, who in the play has done nothing, and stands for nothing. But Brutus is right, and Mark Antony knows it, himself sealing the judgment with the finale, 'he was the noblest Roman of them all' and, even more, 'This was a man!' By the end, both Octavius and Antony are in awe of Brutus. The moral logic has it that once Brutus has suffered enough in retribution—in this case unto death—he is again free to be what he is. Brutus has to lose his happiness in order to regain his virtue. The man of honour is now enshrined as humanism's pivotal ideal.

Honour, will, reason and no illusion were the foundation stones of the Renaissance. In the highest formulation, that of Shakespeare, reason and realism are integrated. Reason does not find its highest authority in the mathematical genius of Newton, nor the later philosophical rationalism of Descartes or Kant. It does so in the immense intelligence of Shakespeare. Reason's presence in *Julius Caesar* is in part in the depiction of the human condition as just— Brutus is punished for murdering Caesar. It is equally, and more enduringly, in the breadth and depth of perception in the play. A simple story of plot, assassination and military retribution is turned into an entire philosophy of life, morals and politics. Shakespeare knew too much for him to be capable of any straightforward lesson. He follows Alberti's injunction to live without illusion, which in his case means to describe what he sees. His intelligence is not abstract. It is concrete, literal and, above all, sceptical. No one understood as much about what Nietzsche would call the human-all-too-human. Indeed, the very term humanism has no more powerful association than with the shrewd and humane intelligence of Shakespeare. In the new secular culture's search for exemplary individuals, Shakespeare himself becomes a hero—a man who could create the very world.

Shakespeare leaves no lucid, readily decipherable code of behaviour. What remains is something like: be honourable, and all that implies, especially being honest and true to friends; be as gentle as possible given the manifold turbulence and constraint of reality, a reality which includes your own character, that of those you encounter, and the good and bad fortune of events into which you are cast. You have some influence over that fortune, as a free, rational and wilful individual. Life calls for action, and for doing the right thing, as opposed to some form of contemplative or religious withdrawal. If you act wrongly, as does Brutus, you will be punished; but in spite of that, what remains of higher significance is your character, and if it is honourable you will leave your mark as a commanding and engaging example of what it is to be human. Shakespeare follows much of classical antiquity in advocating virtue over happiness—he finds that the two are usually at odds. There is wisdom here, of a tender, sceptical, urbane, all-encompassing sort.

It is a humanist wisdom, quite different from that of Homer or of Jesus.

Yet humanism had another mode, oblique to the melancholy stoic realism of Shakespeare. It was earlier and simpler, naive in the way Brutus is naive, but not the less enduring for its narrower path. It was Pico della Mirandola's image of man as the great miracle, set at the world's centre, maker and moulder of himself, constrained by no limits. This is the Gattamelata. Shakespeare had found the limits, but he thereby lost the purity and the force of the founding vision. Brutus is a great miracle; he sets himself at the centre of the world by killing Caesar. He does make himself. But he is transformed by the limits; his call is muted, no longer the clear peal of honour.

Donatello was unencumbered by these complexities, although not because he was naive—his other work makes that plain. His vision was different. He saw the concentrated, essential value, and stripped away the rest. What remains is the grace of pure form. The Gattamelata on a bright noon is an exhilarating tribute to the human individual. Its message is, 'I like him!'

Chapter Three

AMBASSADORS OF DEATH

Holbein and Hamlet

Humanism did not need Luther to point out that its condition was precarious. There were premonitions from within, and from very early on. If a place to stand were not found, what would follow? The conscious mind went blank at this question. But there were signs. Indeed a dismal foreboding pervades the major work of two humanist masters, both northerners. When Hamlet stands, skull in hand, oppressed by mortality, his entire metaphysical universe crushed, and cries out 'Alas, poor Yorick', he is at his wits' end. 'Alas, poor Yorick' is humanism's 'My God, my God, why hast thou forsaken me?'

Holbein had the same vision—eighty years earlier—when he painted his *Corpse of Christ in the Tomb*. This was the work hanging in Basel that would, centuries later, haunt Dostoevsky, who described it as the most horrible thing he had ever seen. Holbein's vision took another eleven years to mature, when in 1533 he painted his huge masterpiece *The Ambassadors* (see front cover), which now hangs in the National Gallery in London.

The Ambassadors is a double portrait, of Jean de Dinteville and his friend Georges de Selve—both life-size. De Dinteville, the 29-year-old Sieur de Polisy, was the French envoy in London. De Selve, Bishop of Lavaur, was visiting his friend, but also undertaking an official yet secret mission on behalf of the French king. De Selve was a learned scholar, and de Dinteville a patron of scholarship, especially in relation to translations of the Bible into French.

Holbein paints the two men as massive, their physical bulk taking up almost entirely the left and right thirds, respectively, of the painting. The remaining section of the work, between the ambassadors, is occupied by a two-level table, on which is placed an array of instruments and books. On the bottom level, or shelf, is a terrestrial globe, a book of arithmetic, an open hymnbook, a case of flutes, and a lute. On the upper shelf is a celestial globe, two sundials, two quadrants, an instrument for determining the position of the stars, and a book. There are assorted other tools of geometry.

In fact, what we have here are two exemplars of the Renaissance. They are men of great eminence in the secular and clerical worlds—with wealth, power, and high office, by birth and appointment. They have the trust of their king, François I. They are also men of learning, with all the symbols of humanist culture at their disposal. Their dress, relaxed stance, and sober gaze, straight out of the painting, speak of authority. They are masters of their world. More than ambassadors of France, they are emissaries of humanism.

They are heirs of the Gattamelata, the noble gentleman on whose shoulders the success of the new culture rests.

All is not well, however. Holbein has magnified the two figures to cramp them within the seven-foot-square frame, in order to show, not their size, but the fact that they are trapped. The painting has no background, no third dimension behind the ambassadors. They are closed off to the rear by a comprehensive green curtain. Furthermore, there is little space between de Dinteville and the left border, and de Selve and the right one. There is no exit to either side, and no depth at all. Beneath their feet is an ornate, tiled floor, leading forward. The painting has an eerie two-dimensionality, with the exception of the one permitted movement out of the static vertical plane of the figures, forward from them and down.

The claustrophobia is intensified by the immobility of the two men. It is as if they are frozen in their pose. Their expressionless faces, deadpan and pale, without emotion, lips straight and closed, gaze straight out of the work—blankly. Holbein confirms the mood in the block symmetry of his design, which is only fractionally offset by the larger bulk of de Dinteville and the displacement of the table slightly right of centre, both counter-balanced by the diagonal form of the object in the foreground, echoed in the lute. Even the arrangement of objects on the table has minimal perspective; it is a clutter, with no relationship to the two men.

The one way out is forward and down, a tipping motion from the line of the eyes to the front lower border, as if the vertical plane containing de Dinteville and de Selve were a cardboard sheet rotating forward on an axis through their feet. They would then meet head-on the distorted spherical object that hovers above the floor alone in the foreground of the painting, the object that commands the work, the focal point of Holbein's masterpiece.

The two gentlemen may look straight ahead, avoiding the forward incline, but their eyes are dead, without inward depth or outward penetration. Those eyes relinquish their direction of the scene to the stance of the two men, oriented towards the front centre, and to the positioning of their hands, which in both cases creates a line of force from the centre of mass of the bodies moving out and down through the midpoint between the hands and intersecting at the object in the foreground. The effect is strengthened by the cramping of the bodies within the frame of the painting—serving to place the figures higher than they would be normally, putting the viewer lower down, beneath the heads, concentrating at a point somewhere in the midriff, further reducing the importance of the eyes.

The distorted spherical object that dominates the work is, of course, a skull. Using the technique of anamorphosis, Holbein painted the skull so that its true form can only be made out from standing to either side of the painting, as close to its plane as possible, and looking directly up or down the elongation. From front on, viewed as the ambassadors themselves do, it is a confusing blur.

The two men are under its sway. Pale in their unconscious fear, they recognise they have been turned to stone, with their cultural toys powerless to help—unable even to distract them any more. They can sense from where the debilitating force is streaming at them, and yet they cannot make out its form. Indeed, they do not want to know—their eyes are averted, staring blankly straight ahead, over the skull.

Death is master, and there is no other. These eminences of the Renaissance have failed to find a place on which to stand. Their inner eye stares into the face of their Medusa, into nothingness, and they are stricken, blind, rooted to the spot.

Other signs mark the painting. De Dinteville has a miniature silver skull set on a gold badge on his cap. The lute has a broken string:

> … or ever the silver cord be loosened, or the golden bowl be broken,
> then shall the dust return to the earth as it was.

But death in *The Ambassadors* has none of the succouring gravity of Ecclesiastes. It is white terror.

These men are—like Hamlet—high courtiers, learned, perceptive, and adept in all the arts and sciences. Perhaps they are even wise. Yet for them life has lost all sense. Without God, without a transcendental law, there is only death. Culture is necessary to stop humans in their tracks, enforcing the 'Nos' that limit their desires. For the ambassadors, the single No that remains is death, the limit of limits—as Philip Rieff would call it. It is the one thing that may check them, constrain their freedom. The problem is that, when culture is reduced to the skull, death takes over. It becomes all that is. So Holbein, who was foolish enough to ask the decisive metaphysical question, 'Will humanism have enough gravity to stay on its feet?', answered in the negative. No, there is little gravity. No, a place on which to stand does not exist. Holbein becomes the first truly modern theorist, having got himself to the brink of the nihilist cliff. He paints life, to anticipate Nietzsche's formula, as either horrible or absurd. For his ambassadors, it is both.

Holbein's grim mockery of the bright humanist dawn does not stop here. His gentleman heroes, his masters of civilisation, are standing stock-still. They have their place to stand, but cannot move. Their position is fixed out of terror, not security. Moreover, the skull hovers; it is mobile; it is free. That which roots them to the spot may move at will. Worse, the skull is the one thing in the entire painting with strength, with vitality. Life and death, under the humanist constellation, have exchanged places. The humanist aspirant must, through an immense act of concentrated will, forge his *I*. When he opens his eyes again he finds that he has turned into Jean de Dinteville and Georges de Selve. Such is Holbein's reading.

Further elaborations are mechanical. The pursuit of knowledge is futile. What is the point if it provides no defence against the skull? Plotting the motion of the stars will not help to provide direction in life. Playing the lute will not soothe raw nerves once the whiff of a corpse has penetrated the nostrils, not unless the music intimates a greater frame, one within which the human individual can stand. The greatest of all humanist institutions, the university, is a mausoleum of dead ideas, a rattling of dry bones. Its teaching is incapable of reaching out to hold the hand through the darkness. Holbein has put it with brutal simplicity: there is no humanist solution. The most learned men have no answer to death. Once faith is gone, fate is reduced to necessity—and the ultimate necessity is death.

The ambassadors are not only learned, they are free. They enjoy free-will. They move about the civilised world using their power to organise the possibilities of men. The fate of kingdoms is in their hands. They carry, in a strictly hierarchical age, the responsibilities for the aristocracy and the church—for the elite. Through their science they know the time accurately; they can chart the seas and cross them more safely than their ancestors did; they can map the heavens; in short, they have access to the secrets of nature. This is not a small achievement. They are the forefathers of the steam engine and of penicillin. Reason and free-will are powerful tools, and humanity has benefited prodigiously from their exercise by these ambassadors and their progeny. As long as de Dinteville and de Selve are absorbed in their science, as long as they keep on the move in their diplomacy, all is well. These are two fine-looking young men in their prime. No one was more eligible. But we have been shown that there is nothing behind them, under them or over them. There is neither anchor below nor light above. There is neither past nor future. There is no exit.

Holbein, callous and pitiless German that he was, has caught them in a moment when they have stopped, and looked up from their work and their lives. He has caught them exposed. He has shown them, and us, that it is precisely because they have free-will that they are rooted to the spot.

Almost certainly, the men themselves did not understand Holbein's truth—in this, too, they would represent the next three centuries of surface humanist confidence. Jean de Dinteville commissioned *The Ambassadors*. Perhaps he placed it on a landing in his family mansion in Polisy, so that he could entertain guests climbing the stairs. As they approached the painting from below he could teach them to look up along the diagonal and view the skull undistorted—from here, the painted men were themselves difficult to identify. Continuing on to the landing, the amused guests would find their host in front of them, with his clerical friend, brilliantly rendered in life-size realism, but death retreating into a mysterious haze. Onwards and upwards, pausing to look back, the skull reappears in focus while the men recede into a blur. And so, while clever tricks may entertain, they conceal dark truths.

Holbein had been a mere 25-year-old when, in 1522, he painted his *Corpse of Christ in the Tomb*. On that occasion he had himself stood in humanist shoes and, with brilliant intuition, saw the new culture's necessary first step if it were to establish itself. It had to kill Christ. What an unerring sense of first principles! Holbein has not left much work behind him, most of it portraits, but in the masterpieces of 1522 and 1533 his assault on the old, Christian culture is done from so close to the bone that it ends up as a challenge to humanism itself.

Holbein kills Christ by demolishing the crucifixion. His Jesus is no more than a dead body. It lies, life-size, within the tomb. We look in from the side. The flesh is black-green with decay around the wounds in the visible foot, hand, and side. Dried-out hair and beard is a jutting, brittle black. A skeletal right hand, the hand of authority, is stiff with *rigor mortis*, the middle finger elongated and pressing down on the stone slab like a hideous dead twig. The light is even along the whole body, without highlight or direction, a signal itself of meaninglessness. The expression on the Jesus face is one of horror, the mouth open, the white of the visible eye enlarged. This man died a gruelling death, and in his last moments there was no peace or radiance—just sheer terror at the nothing beyond. In negation of a serene smile of redemption, what we see is rot and shrinkage, no different from a dead fish washed up on some beach. *Resurrection* is merely a consoling illusion, for this man did not rise from the grave. Flesh is flesh, which means festering wounds, stiffening joints, and the stench of decomposition. Death is death.

The *Corpse of Christ* has uncanny force—which is difficult to understand, for Holbein has merely painted a dead man and titled it 'Jesus of Nazareth, King of the Jews'. To be sure, there is mockery in the title, but most people have seen a dead body. So why is this one—not even real, just a painted image—so shocking? Dostoevsky was not alone in reeling away from it and exclaiming that it was enough to make one lose one's faith. Nor is the challenge restricted to Christians like Dostoevsky. Holbein hit the central nerve of humanist thought, and with it every member of the modern West. No one can escape the elongated, bony middle finger of Holbein's Christ as it collapses downwards onto the stone slab—the new world is empty of authority. Mortality rules. Humans are no more than dead fish stranded on the beach. That they are endowed with consciousness just brings suffering: the fish that lives by instinct does not foresee its own end. Humans, by virtue of consciousness, see the ugly and senseless death of Christ, and are trapped already years ahead of their time.

In 1522 Holbein plotted humanism's first step, to destroy the authority of Christianity, and thereby to clear the cultural decks. Over the next three hundred years the destruction would work its fill. In 1533 he asked the second question: with what shall we replace Christ crucified? The answer was already plain: free-will and reason. However, Holbein was no utopian. His dark vision of 1522 had taught him the singular importance of the Archimedean challenge. The answer he painted is that, once there is free-will, reason becomes an indifferent plaything, and will collapses. He lost faith in the humanist solution.

And yet Erasmus had been a friend. Holbein painted the portrait of the great humanist many times—indeed, it is the one repeating theme in his surviving work. Holbein is best known in most quarters for his portraits of Erasmus; reciprocally, Erasmus is best known as painted by Holbein—the calm, gentle-faced scholar at his desk, putting his thoughts on paper, the paradigm of the intellectual life. It was in the year or two following the *Corpse of Christ* that most of these portraits were painted. Is there not here, then, some unconscious identification of reason with death? The Holbein undertow is that the philosophy of Erasmus is founded on nothing, the metaphysics of a dead fish endowed with consciousness.

In all of this there remains an untied knot. Holbein did not consider Brutus' example—the possibility of an ethic based on honour. Brutus had no fear of death: he was content to die, and his end came without agony. If Holbein is right, free-will excludes honour. Alternatively, if the Shakespeare of *Julius Caesar* has found the right truth then it has to be concluded that, while the pursuit of knowledge will not save humanism, the code of honour of the gentleman may.

The Ambassadors brings one last curse. The eyes of de Dinteville and de Selve may be blank, yet viewers—as they walk around looking at the painting, as they move from left to centre to right, as they move from up close to far back—will find that the eyes follow them. Once inside the room in the National Gallery in London, it is impossible to escape the dead stare of the two ambassadors. The next thing one realises is that through this stare I, the viewer, am locked into the skull which, because of its distortion, I cannot see. The indirection of the skull is that it commands through the hands and then the eyes of the ambassadors, who also do not make it out. Moreover, the volume of the anamorphic form reduces, when viewed indirectly and without distortion, to exactly the dimension of the ambassadors' own heads. Given that they are painted life-size, I find that I am looking at a portrait, to scale, of myself—after death.

The deeper representation of these two humanists is therefore not on behalf of François I of France to Henry VIII of England, but from the skull to us. They are, ultimately, emissaries of death. The highest representatives of humanism deliver their message to whom they look at—you and *me*. We thereby come under the thrall of the skull. In other words, more than a century before Velázquez was more explicitly to bring the viewer into the picture in his *Las*

Meninas, Holbein had done the same, but with a singular propensity to menace his audience.

***

Once the blood began to slow in the humanist veins, as it did precipitately from the early nineteenth century, and darker imagery emerged from the shadows, it would not be Holbein installed as principal teacher. That role went to Shakespeare's *Hamlet*. The fascination that this late Renaissance 'tragedy' has held for modernity is easy to document. Apart from the Bible, it is the most written-about work of Western culture. It is the most performed play. Indeed, in English it has been, from its first appearance, the most regularly performed work in the literature. Modern critical consensus holds that *Hamlet* is the hub of Shakespeare's whole work, the centre from which the other plays reach out as spokes.

Up until 1770 Hamlet himself had been taken as a brave, heroic man—a sentimental hero. After 1770 the focus on his character began, stressing his madness, his weakness, his intellectuality. The 'Hamlet problem' commenced. For the next century, '*Hamlet* fever' took hold in Germany. After 1820, throughout northern Europe, *Hamlet* scholarship turned into a deluge. As one instance, A.A. Raven's bibliography of *Hamlet* literature published between 1877 and 1935 lists more than two thousand items.

There are a number of reasons why *Hamlet* has touched the nerve of modern culture as has no other work. Hamlet is a typical modern individual of the hypersensitive, introspective, and lonely type, suffering from a paralysing inner torment without an obvious source. He is exceptionally gifted in intelligence, perceptivity, and articulacy. As Freud pointed out, the play brings to the surface deeply buried, yet universal, family tensions. The play discourses at length on the problem of the meaning of life in a non-religious world. It contrasts simple and gregarious men of action with their modern opposite.

Hamlet himself fits the model of the humanist hero. He is a gentleman, gracious and honourable, the Prince of Denmark beloved by his people. He is a man of reason, educated in a German university. He is a realist, under no illusions about the ways of the world: one of his strengths is that he sees into the motives of others instantly. He paces the stage bathed in the charisma of thoughtfulness, emanating from a monumental *I* in fear of no man.

Free-will is again pivotal. In the case of Hamlet, however, it is a negative freedom. Hamlet is free *not* to kill Claudius—it is a brilliant inversion by Shakespeare of the metaphysics of Brutus. Freedom is freedom not to do what you have to do, freedom from morality. Hamlet is the individual as hero, the modern individualist unconstrained by the laws of kin or state—which all point in one direction, vengeance. The conflict is not between two different ethics. There is no suggestion in the text that Thou Shalt Not Kill is of interest to Hamlet. He is not in the least concerned about the blood-guilt that might arise from his murdering the new king, Claudius. Morality is focused quite simply on his duty to avenge his father's murder by killing his uncle. He is free not to do his duty. It is this freedom that destroys him, and in the process all of the main characters in the drama. The consequence of Hamlet's dithering is that, in the ensuing chaos, almost everyone gets killed.

Being free to choose against duty leaves Hamlet bogged down in his own depression. This is a man sunk in profound melancholy. His first oration opens with the lament:

> How weary, stale, flat, and unprofitable
> Seem to me all the uses of this world.

He refers to the earth as a 'sterile promontory' and man as 'this quintessence of dust'. The examples multiply. His thoughts return again and again to suicide, an alternative preferable to having to 'grunt and sweat under a weary life'. From beginning to end, Hamlet is lethargic, bitter, morose, introverted, restless yet tired, and at times dementedly rash. The substance of the play is, in fact, his own long monologue of complaint about life, interrupted here and there by drama.

The problem of Hamlet, as countless thousands of critics have noted, is simple: why cannot he do what he knows, and what everybody knows, he should do—avenge his father by killing Claudius? There are three reasons in ascending order of significance. There is the psychological inhibition in Hamlet, as interpreted by Freud and elaborated by Ernest Jones in his book *Hamlet and Oedipus* (1950). Hamlet's incestuous attachment to his mother is pathologically strong, and the thought of killing his uncle arouses parricidal guilt, paralysing his ability to act—that uncle, in murdering his father, has carried out Hamlet's own unconscious wish, so killing the uncle would, in part, be killing himself.

Secondly, Hamlet undergoes a moral crisis. The person to whom he is closest in the world is his mother, whom he loves and admires. A month after the death of her husband, a fine man, she marries his brother, a low character whom Hamlet rightly despises. This act is incomprehensible to him. His first response to the account of Claudius' infamy is, surprisingly, not rage against his uncle, but 'O most pernicious woman'. From then on there is a litany of abuse of women. His mother has destroyed Hamlet's sense of moral order. The person whom he loved above all others has destroyed trust. If there is no trust, how can there be any law? If the most intimate ethical bonds are fickle, how can anything be relied upon? At this level, Hamlet is flattened by his mother's behaviour, and loses interest in everything else.

Hamlet's contempt for Claudius, who is not a worthy adversary, may also be significant. There is a dimension of pride in the

Renaissance prince that finds it demeaning to kill such a low specimen of humanity.

The third and predominant reason for Hamlet's inability to act is that he has met Death. Death opens the play. It is midnight, and sentinels discuss a ghost. It appears. By the end of Act I, Hamlet himself is talking to the ghost of his murdered father, whose parting words are, 'Adieu, adieu Hamlet: remember me.' How can Hamlet forget? Indeed, as he staggers away from this scene, his entire speech apart from his outburst against his mother, 'O most pernicious woman', and his uncle, 'Oh villain, villain, smiling damned villain!', is that from now on his life is under the command of his father's ghost. He identifies with the parting words of death, and swears allegiance to him. He will never again manage to return to the land of the living. The critic Wilson Knight went so far as to title an essay on *Hamlet*, 'The Embassy of Death' (*The Wheel of Fire*, 1930).

Hamlet's talk has two recurring themes. The first is why he cannot do what everything commands him to do. He compares himself with men of action such as Alexander the Great and Caesar, with young Fortinbras going to war for a useless piece of ground, and with actors who can work up a great passion over an imaginary cause—he has a great cause but no passion. He calls himself a coward; he likens himself to a whore, whose heart is hollow. In short, he is sickened by his own paralysis, ashamed of it. In part, he blames consciousness: he thinks too much. Here is the link with the other recurring theme, that of death.

When Hamlet utters his famous phrase that action is 'sicklied o'er with the pale cast of thought' he has a specific thought in mind—death, and its aftermath. The line comes at the end of the most famous speech in the play, the 'To be or not to be' monologue, which is a single-minded meditation on suicide. All the sympathy is on the side of death, that 'consummation Devoutly to be wished'.

The speech catalogues the 'slings and arrows' that are life, a list of reasons against it. The one argument for life is negative, fear of the unknown, the 'dread of something after death'.

In an early 'mad' speech to Polonius, Hamlet's raving is drawn to thoughts of the grave and how willingly he would give up his life. Later, after killing Polonius, instead of showing remorse for this gratuitous murder, Hamlet jokes about mortality. When asked where he has hidden the corpse, he replies that it is at supper, being eaten by maggots. In Act V, when he comes upon Ophelia's funeral, he jumps into her open grave and asks to be buried with her. At the end, his dying words pleading with Horatio not to kill himself include the telling phrase, 'Absent thee from felicity awhile.' The play itself ends with a funeral procession, the body of Hamlet borne off with martial rites.

These are, however, merely flashes as the light touches the silver thread through the work, the spirit of *Hamlet*. That thread has its source in the first meeting with death, Hamlet and the ghost in Act I, in which the 30-year-old prince takes his oath of loyalty, the oath he will not break. It terminates in the third and last meeting with death, early in Act V, as the now pale and enervated prince holds the skull in his hand, and addresses it, 'Alas, poor Yorick.' This, the gravediggers' scene, is the climax to the play.

As much as the shattering of Hamlet's character is determined by his first meeting with the ghost, that formative early scene has its completion, the end-point of its logic, in 'Alas, poor Yorick', the meditation on death stimulated by memories of his father's court jester. Any audience having sat through the gruelling first four acts of long-winded discourse, unrelieved by much action or change of tone, immediately lifts as Act V opens and earthy gravediggers clown through their scene. The play comes alive, the morose fog lifts for a moment, and there is lightness as two yokels crack skulls with their shovels and pun through their philosophy of life. Hamlet, too, for a moment, is a different man. The words he speaks to Yorick's skull are the only ones of real attachment and affection he utters in the entire play:

> Alas! poor Yorick. I knew him, Horatio; a fellow of infinite jest, of most excellent fancy; he hath borne me on his back a thousand times; and now, how abhorred in my imagination it is! my gorge rises at it. Here hung those lips, that I have kiss'd I know not how oft.

Hamlet switches from this quiet, moving reminiscence into further musings on death, on the noble dust of Alexander the Great now a bung stopping a beer-barrel. He is then confronted by Ophelia's funeral. His response is to jump into her grave with her brother, having announced himself with pathetic bombast, 'This is I, Hamlet the Dane', and then boasting beyond all sense that he loved Ophelia more than could forty thousand brothers. Innocence is dead, driven out of her mind by the events and words for which Hamlet is largely responsible, and this is his response. Rather be Yorick! Hamlet has quickly lost his poise, once again. From this point on, the play works through predictable routines until trumpets or bugle bring down the curtain.

Yes, the gravediggers contribute the only cheer in the long dirge that is *Hamlet*. The last of the gods is death; the one abiding and true love is Yorick, twenty-three years gone, his skull stinking. Metaphysics, in the form of the great ontological question 'to be or not to be'—what is the essence of being—is reduced to the profane issue of suicide. Hamlet is as indifferent to whether he kills himself or not as Beckett's tramps in *Waiting for Godot* (although, by comparison, their nihilism is full of zest). Productions of the play have usually sensed all this, in that Hamlet is almost always dressed in black, with a wan complexion and long bohemian hair, and he is shown as obliteratingly alone.

Hamlet in black, emissary of death, takes us back to Holbein's ambassadors. He is paralysed, as were they, by the skull. The difference is that Shakespeare elaborates the consequences. Were he properly alive, Hamlet would kill Claudius, order would be restored in Denmark, and the kingdom would prosper. As it is, his stone-like being, his free choice of not to do what he has to do, his individualist refusal to obey the laws of his tribe result in almost everyone being killed, guilty and innocent alike. After 'Alas poor Yorick' Shakespeare fills the stage with corpses. Free-will means no place to stand, means being frozen to the spot, means havoc. That everything is rotten in the state of Denmark is the legacy of humanism.

Hamlet has been classified as tragedy. It is, rather, melodrama. Shakespeare demonstrates that there can be no humanist tragedy. For tragedy—as Homer, Aeschylus, and Sophocles sang it—there has to be a greater order of things, which is violated by the suprahuman forces of destiny, with or without human help. In the chaos resulting from the violation, mortals do what they can to restore order. *Hamlet* belongs to a different cultural universe. There are no higher laws. Hamlet himself is it: the well-being of the world depends on his *I*. His failure is the single reason for moral and political chaos. Hamlet, by failing to restore order, is the major contributor to greater disorder—Claudius was, in fact, a competent king.

Tragedy, by contrast, ends in the triumph over death: Achilles carrying out funeral rites as his reparation before he is killed, Oedipus accepting what he understands, blinding and banishing himself to meditate alone on his cursed fate. For Hamlet, for humanism, there is nothing above or beyond death.

Hamlet is a last, vain attempt at Western tragedy, signalling the end of the genre for the rest of the humanist epoch. Where is the cleansing metaphysical exhilaration at the end, the exhausted audience rising out of the ashes with the inspired feeling that, in spite of all, life is fresh and good? That it is out of the suffering, the humiliation—yes, even the death—that the life-force triumphs? That out of the tragic wreck the annihilated individual transcends the bounds of his or her own self and is united with the grander order of things? The tragic experience teaches that death is not the limit of limits—the ultimate No. In *Hamlet* it is, and the audience is left stranded on a melancholy beach.

Here is the humanist negative to *Julius Caesar* as positive, written a mere two or three years later. The dramatic forms tell the story. *Julius Caesar* had a strict, classical structure, beautifully orchestrated, precise, and without superfluous elements. It was Roman itself, as if the ethic of honour in place secured the dramatic limits. In *Hamlet* the erratic ebb and flow of the moods of the central character takes over the form, and hitches it to its own self-centred anarchy. There are many sudden digressions in the plot, a number of doubtful relevance. It is as if all limit has gone. Apart from the two anchoring points, the first meeting with death and the gravediggers, the play is unruly, meandering.

It is, however, a little glib to separate the humanist positive and negative so readily. Hamlet is close to Brutus. Shakespeare makes this explicit when Polonius remarks that in his youth he played Julius Caesar, 'Brutus killed me.' In reality, it is Hamlet who kills him. Hamlet is a bleak reworking of Brutus, the change of circumstances being that the skull has appeared. Honour is not enough to neutralise it, or so runs Shakespeare's later reading. In the light of how seriously we must take this change of vision by the greatest of all humanists, we should also note that, viewed up close, the Gattamelata has an awfully melancholy expression on his face.

By 'Remember me!' the ghost had meant 'Avenge me!'—a call to honour. But Hamlet is incapable of the active side. In his case, the decline of honour is proportional to the rise of reason. As honour is to Brutus, so reason is to Hamlet—but reason as curse, no more than the endless chattering rationalisation of why he cannot do what he should. It is excusing reason: under its influence Hamlet becomes the feeblest of men. He has the eloquence and wit of a god, but what is that worth if its practical consequence is to reinforce in him what is ignoble, meriting only scorn, making him a millstone around the neck of the human spirit? In the phrase echoing through Western culture in which he finds the cause of his immobility, 'the pale cast of thought', we are told much. Reason, that pale and therefore spectral force, is deadly. It is not just that the divine eloquence of Hamlet cannot talk itself out of the arms of the Medusa; that talk is itself an engine of mortality. Talk cannot create a rock on which to stand; worse, talk is very bad for sureness of step. The Prince of Reason is at one and the same time the Prince of Death.

Hamlet has come to love the last of the gods. Not just succumbing to its paralysing authority, he has embraced it. 'Absent thee from felicity awhile' speaks of his deep longing, the pitiable last dream of a man tormented to his wits' end, uttered with a heart-rending sigh, the dream of peace and happiness, which he sees only in death. Thus, at the end of the road, the key question about *Hamlet*—the play that late humanism was to take to as the work of works, the one that held the secret truth, the central creation of Europe's greatest literary figure—the question of what it is essentially about produces a most strange answer: death worship.

***

Holbein and Shakespeare stopped humanism in its tracks—and in its prime. It was to recover in a sort of fashion, and flourish for another couple of centuries before its irreversible decline set in. Its recovery was largely due, as we shall see, to it connecting itself to another source of strength, one tapped by Luther and Calvin. However, it also found some inspiration from within, from a figure born out of its own late-Renaissance crisis. As much as Hamlet is Brutus a few years on, he has a brother, his opposite in character, but clearly of the same genealogical stock. That is Don Quixote. Cervantes died in the same month of the same year, 1616, as Shakespeare. The first part of his masterpiece appeared two or three years after *Hamlet*. His heroic knight is an explicit attempt to find a principle of action for a man who can move in the humanist universe.

In 1860, the Russian writer Ivan Turgenev wrote an essay on 'Hamlet and Don Quixote'. Turgenev interpreted Don Quixote as the perfect gentleman: a man who, with no thought of self, dedicates himself to chivalrous causes. He has faith in his ideal and therefore can act. The introspective, self-obsessed, sceptical Hamlet is his opposite.

Don Quixote is not an ordinary knight errant, nor a simple parody of one. He has a capacity for action, for noble action, that all others lack. It is based on his chaste, single-minded devotion to his ideal of the knight—the man of honour. Don Quixote is Brutus as a man of honour, without any other traits or complexities. He is Brutus stripped to the bare bones. His ideal is so strong that he is blind to reality: governed by the ideal he does not see the real, except through the radically distorting lens of his vision. He sees thirty windmills as thirty monstrous giants, attacks, gets tangled in one of the sails, and is flattened. Such are his adventures, leaving him battered and bruised, and the world no better off. Usually, he gets no thanks: even convicts whom he frees beat him half to death.

Cervantes, too, was taking up the Archimedean challenge. He saw that, in order to live, humans must act. To be able to act they need a place to stand. Where is such a place in a godless universe? The only possibility is Don Quixote's faith in honour. Indeed, Quixote is the one thing that moves in the thousand-page Spanish epic. His companion, Sancho Panza—the down-to-earth peasant who puts wine, food, and sleep before everything else—loves his master and sacrifices all comforts to follow him. Half the time, Sancho believes in the Don; for the rest, he suspects he is a deluded madman.

In the second part of the story we follow courts across Spain as they lionise the now-famous knight, and set up adventures for their own entertainment. They trick and deceive him, and in his simplicity he usually makes a fool of himself. But the joke turns back on the audience, partly because the naive honesty of his mission leaves him untouched by humiliation, but more because the courtiers have grown dependent on him. He brings life to the aimless and half-hearted pastimes of the court. Without Don Quixote before them, these courtiers would turn into Jean de Dinteville and Georges de Selve.

Sancho himself learns from his master. When another court jest makes him governor of an island, he applies himself to his job with complete seriousness, makes wise decisions, and transcends the tricks and deceits practised upon him. In short, he, too, has a period in which, as a convert to his master's faith, he can stand and indeed move the earth as a man of will.

The message is extreme: to be able to act you must be under an illusion, to the point of madness. This is what Nietzsche, a great admirer of Don Quixote, was to call 'redemptive illusion', the consoling dream that keeps our eyes from the truth of the horror and absurdity of modern existence.

Cervantes goes further. There is no difference between fantasy and reality, or between being asleep and awake. It is the sleepwalking Don Quixote who slashes wineskins to pieces, believing them to be giants, but he would act no differently were he awake. After entering Montesinos Cave, he falls asleep and dreams his adventure. It is exactly the same as if he had actually had it, and only the witnesses from ordinary life are concerned about whether it physically happened—the irrelevant concern of those who themselves cannot move, the equivalent to the futile thinking of Hamlet. But wait a minute. The alternative to Hamlet is now a conception of action in which the heroism of the warrior is identical with the hallucinations of a certifiable lunatic!

Don Quixote pits his 'I believe, therefore I am' against Hamlet's, 'I think, therefore I am turned to stone.' The *I* can act even in its sleep, whereas the ultra-conscious Hamlet might as well be sleep-walking. Cervantes had recognised Shakespeare's Brutus/Hamlet problem, and that everything depended upon its solution. His answer was to produce a knight errant, and a story that is so full of life it remains pure joy to read. The vitality signals Cervantes' success.

This, however, is honour's last stand, for it has become ridiculous. The courageous knight's acts of chivalry are all dedicated to his lady, the fantasised Dulcinea del Toboso. The fantasy is based at best on an unreliable memory of a peasant girl who, when met in the flesh, turns out to be gross and vulgar, an unpalatable fact that is explained away by the knight of faith as a cruel enchantment. Moreover, at the end of the long tale the illusion/reality inversions suddenly stop, and a now sober and worldly Don Quixote repents 'my former madness', and dies. Reality has returned, a bleak and profane order ruled by necessity.

There is an urbane, humanist reading of *Don Quixote*—what we might call a Shakespearean reading. This story is a parable of life. The good life depends upon a sizeable dose of unreal fantasy to keep it going, ideally mixed with some of Sancho's peasant earthiness. The shape of its events is absurd when looked at dispassionately, not so different from tilting at windmills. The fortunate individual sees profane windmills as sacred giants, acts accordingly and, with a bit of luck, is not too bruised in the event. While existence is horrible or absurd, it is possible to achieve a quixotic, heroic absurd in life which may neutralise the horror. It is only the dying

Don Quixote who recants, knowing the illusion is over or, as Joseph Conrad will put it, 'the glamour's off'.

Well, maybe! Even granting this sceptical line, the question remains: in this universe, is there a firm-enough place to stand? Cervantes seems to have followed Holbein in saying, 'No', although he fought tooth and nail to prove the opposite, and out of the struggle produced the most extravagant and likeable of humanist heroes.

What of Shakespeare? For him, the story has not progressed beyond the enormous question mark that is Brutus. Shakespeare took a look into the hollow sockets of the skull and wrote *Hamlet*. Finding himself in the shoes of de Dinteville, he saw what Holbein had seen, and his anguish was to reverberate through the next four hundred years of humanist culture, shaking it to the foundations. Hamlet, Hamlet, and Hamlet again—the West would come to know it by heart. Shakespeare himself stumbled on, and could still manage the closest he would get to a true tragedy in *King Lear*, a partial and inferior reworking of the Brutus theme in *Coriolanus*, and his beautiful, late, escapist fantasy, *The Tempest*.

Chapter Four

THE PROTESTANT REFORMATION

Luther and Calvin

The story of the rise and fall of humanism is woven from four threads. We have located two of them already: the generative ideal cast by the Renaissance, and the sceptical questioning from within, humanism's own self-doubt. It is to the third that we now turn. That is the Protestant counter, launched explicitly against Catholicism and Rome, but at its philosophical heart a life-or-death attack on humanism. Luther's most important work, *On the Enslaved Will*, the theological cornerstone of the Reformation, was written not against the Pope, but against Erasmus. At the end of the day, what Luther and Calvin established was a counter-ideal to that of the Renaissance, an alternative metaphysics. To sense the enormity of the difference we need only consider Luther's formulation, 'the darkness of faith where neither law nor reason shines.'

The decisive battle was fought in 1524 and 1525, between Erasmus and Luther. Erasmus was a reluctant combatant; but, urged on by authorities as diverse as Henry VIII and the Pope, he wrote his *Discourse on Free-Will* which, as he put it himself, was pitched against Luther's assertion that free-will is an empty term. It appeared on 1 September 1524, printed in Basel, where he was living at the time. Luther replied a year later with his *On the Enslaved Will* (*De Servo Arbitrio*). The angry and intimidated humanist called it a huge book—triple the length of Erasmus' *Discourse*. Luther himself was later to judge it his best book. Certainly, it was his most important.

Erasmus was a reasonable man. He was comfortable in the world, moderate, conciliatory, gentle, and eloquent. More concerned that the Church be at peace than with doctrinal controversy, he identified Christianity with the goodness of humanity in everyday life; if it worked in practice, fierce examinations of faith were a bit beside the point. As a result, Erasmus' *Discourse* is somewhat half-hearted. Nevertheless, its aim was true, as Luther acknowledged in his reply:

> You alone, in contrast with all the others, have attacked the real thing, that is, the essential issue. You have not wearied me with all those extraneous issues about the Papacy, purgatory, indulgences and such like—trifles, rather than issues—in respect of which almost all to date have sought my blood (though without success); you, and you alone, have seen the hinge on which all turns, and aimed for the vital spot.

That vital spot was free-will.

Erasmus' argument is that of a reasonable man. He accepts that God determines most things, but leaves humans some freedom. 'God indeed preserves the ship, but the sailor steers it into harbour.' He argues for a small degree of free-will. His reason was offended by Luther's doctrine of *sola fide* (by faith alone), for he saw the logical implication that humans were slaves with no incentive for moral behaviour. If faith alone can save them, and they have no free-will, why should the wicked try to reform? Necessity, even when it is God's necessity, eliminates moral responsibility. There is no point in trying to be a better person if I have no will of my own, if whether I behave badly or well is determined by God, outside of my control. My only rational response is to resign myself to what is given. *Sola fide* is incompatible with morality. As Erasmus put it, there is no point exhorting those who have no power of their own. 'It is like saying to someone in chains: Move over here!' Furthermore, justice becomes absurd: 'How is condemnation just, when it is the judge who compels evil doing?'

The argument is persuasive. It is reason's reply to the contradictions inherent in *sola fide*. It is an appeal, in effect, for a moderate version, allowing humans some freedom. This would let good deeds in. If individuals have free-will, it is partly their own choice when they do good works. Thus they merit reward. We are back with the Catholic doctrine of works: that living a good life is taken into account by God, and increases the individual's chance of salvation. Again, this is the reasonable view, for any common-sense notion of justice demands that virtue be rewarded. If the gods are just, surely one of their tasks is to judge mortals, which means punishing vice and rewarding virtue. Erasmus is articulating a standard theology, common to most human religions.

Luther understood the argument. Indeed he pulled out its strongest parts and quoted them in his *Enslaved Will*. This was his 'you alone have aimed for the vital spot'. In demonstrating that reason and faith were incompatible, Erasmus showed him the full picture of what he was up against. Once human beings start to reason, as does Erasmus, they have to have free-will. But what starts out with a bit of free-will ends with the death of God. The picture Erasmus painted showed Luther, in addition, that morality, too, has nothing to do with faith. Faith belongs with the night demons, out of the securing light of the human order, down where the torch of human reason cannot penetrate. It is either the darkness of faith or nothing. *Sola fide* had been the easy half of Luther's Reformation: he now moved into harsh terrain where, against all reason, the will is nothing. Everything hinged on this. If Erasmus won, Christ was done for. The history of the next five hundred years would prove Luther right.

The absence of free-will is the crux of the Reformation. Luther's entire work centres on proving it. He is not just pitted against Erasmus and humanism, but also the mainstream of Christian theology. Etienne Gilson wrote, in his *The Spirit of Medieval Philosophy* (1940), that 'all Christian ethics of the Middle Ages, like those of the Fathers that inspired them, have their necessary basis in the doctrine of an indestructible free will'.

Luther's first argument is that God's own will is 'immutable, eternal and infallible'. By that will he foresees and directs all things. Luther's own faith, explicated through the Scriptures, tells him this. Given the foundation of God's infallibility, there is no place for human freedom. The human individual is small, ignorant, and powerless. The immediate consequence of this argument is *sola fide*, by faith alone, granted by God alone. God chooses whom he saves. Humans have no role in this choice. It happens or it does not happen. They cannot buy salvation with good works: what a presumption! It is the free act of the all-powerful divinity that grants grace. Moreover, ignorant mortals can have no idea of God's will.

The second argument is pitched against reason. 'If you regard and follow the judgment of human reason, you are forced to say, either that there is no God, or that God is unjust.' On earth, the wicked prosper and the good suffer—just look around, reason makes this obvious to us all. God's earth is not a just place. Once reason becomes an active force, it applies its logic to human experience and comes to the conclusion that all is not well with the divine plan. Reason gains airs 'in her knowing and talkative way'. In her presumption she seeks to measure God, thus reducing his authority. She turns God into a passive actor, entrusting more and more to humans. She seeks to make excuses for God, 'not reverencing the secrets of His majesty, but peering and probing into them'.

Once reason is given the authority to investigate the ways of God, the battle is over. Its authority is already equal to that of God.

But there can only be one ultimate authority. In this progression God will lose. In the end, reason proudly condemns God. The Renaissance *I* has forced Luther on to the other peak of the metaphysical either-or, 'I am nothing'. Once reason is given an inch, the questioning begins, and there is no way to stop it. This is why Luther calls 'Mistress Reason' the 'Devil's whore'. She is seductive, deceiving, offering a moment of pleasure in order to seize the whole soul. It is the same with free-will: grant it an inch and you turn the universe upside down, with humans on top.

Luther's third argument concerns guilt. 'No free-will' has two sides. One is that God chooses whom he chooses. The other is that we humans are enchained in sin. All are damned in the sight of God. Original sin is the premise of the human condition. 'The whole world is guilty before God.' As a result, the goodness of some particular individual is ultimately irrelevant. Here is the reason the law does not shine in the darkness where faith dwells. As Paul put it, 'By the deeds of the law shall no flesh be justified in his sight.' Luther amplifies Paul: the best of humans, obeying the law, using their highest faculties—will and reason—are all condemned as sinners. This is the fact. It follows that there is no free-will. What also follows is the even harsher Protestant doctrine that morality has no relationship to faith.

Luther clarifies his view of the law by distinguishing between two worlds, that of earth and that of heaven. The fuller exposition is in his *Commentary on the Epistle to the Galatians* (1531). On earth there is law, and works are significant. The Ten Commandments apply. The law bridles the wicked and makes them conscious of sin—those are its functions. However, in revealing sin it does not reveal God. It has no relationship to grace. The most it does is to lead to what Luther calls an 'active righteousness', a worldly righteousness. The Bible is the source of the knowledge that makes possible the consciousness of sin. The goal of philosophy is the knowledge of sin.

Heaven is an entirely separate domain where God, not the law, rules. Grace has a different righteousness, a passive sort with its source in Christ. As Moses delivered the law, Christ is the path to grace. In other words, good works do not make a good person, but a good person does good works. While it is necessary to follow the law, it will not bring faith.

We are now squarely in the Protestant contradiction, which Erasmus had seen, and which Calvin will intensify, making it the crux of his theology. Humans have no freedom, yet they are responsible. At this point, Luther changes direction. Unlike Calvin, he selects reason as his main target. Reason, in its presumption, installs its own law, contrary to the law of God—that is, the law of non-contradiction. Those who worship at the temple of reason will not stomach contradictions. Erasmus is the living example. In the darkness of faith, where the light of reason does not shine, there are bewildering contradictions.

Luther, the master combatant, chooses the contradiction with which to flay reason. In his *Commentary on Galatians* he goes beyond the formulation 'No free-will but obey the law', expounded in *On the Enslaved Will*. He was to hit precisely the nerve that was to stop Holbein and Hamlet in their humanist tracks, 'Death killeth death: but this killing death is life itself.' Thus he breaks out of humanist nihilism and at the same time strikes reason.

'These are marvellous words, and unknown kinds of speech, which man's reason can no wise understand.' Reason teaches that if you will live unto God you must keep the law. Paul declares the opposite, that we cannot live with God unless we are dead to the law. Dead to the law means it has no power over us. Moses or Christ! If the law of Moses accuses and condemns me, I have another law, which is grace and liberty. As Luther puts it, 'This law accuseth the accusing law and condemneth the condemning law.'

Luther then moves directly into his 'death killeth death'. He does not make his argument more concrete. He lets the paradox stand. Indeed, it will not be until Rembrandt and later Kierkegaard that the full ramifications of this paradox at the heart of the Protestant Reformation will be pursued, and then with the anxiety of men who fear that it is on the edge of tearing their lives apart. For them, the first death has become problematical: they are in danger of turning into ambassadors, left with death alone. In Luther's paradox, too, is the seed of the argument put by Dostoevsky's Kirilov, that the only proof of free-will is to kill yourself—Kirilov is the mad, nineteenth-century heir of Erasmus.

Luther does not elaborate on the death that killeth death. 'This killing death is life itself.' The death of Christ, which signals the transcendence of death, enshrines the authority through which faith is possible. This overrides the authority of the law. On earth we still have to obey the lower authority, which is no authority. But there can be only one altar, and that altar is the crucifixion. Our own will, which is no will, being determined, may drive us to obey the law. That does not help our relationship to the crucifixion, before which the best we can do is know our sin, that we are guilty before God, and hope for passive righteousness, which means being open to grace. The Biblical image of the Annunciation is illustrative—in which the passively meditative Mary makes herself, in her whole concentrated being, receptive to news brought by an angel.

The deeper purpose of Luther's *Enslaved Will* is not to debate with Erasmus. It is to create the authority with which to counter humanism, to annihilate it in its infancy. Luther, too, has to find his place to stand. With his *sola fide* and 'no free-will' he sets about forming the new Christians and subjecting them to fate. His message is: I shall so bury you under your own guilt, your own pitiable weakness, your total dependency on the Lord God, that I shall have you living on your knees in prayer. You are nothing. You are nobody. I shall fling you back into the spiritual dungeon where your thinking faculty has no chance of creating the illusion in you that you have some control over your own destiny. It is down there in the dark, where the light of neither reason nor law shines, where only God can help you, that you may find grace. All is determined. Your fate is set. Subjected as you are to this overbearing condition, I shall give you gravity and depth, without which you will not endure. I shall open the way to faith, to becoming a rock.

Let us not forget Holbein. Luther and Erasmus fought it out in 1524 and 1525. Erasmus, a friend of Holbein, had written his *Discourse* in Basel, a year after most of the portraits, two years after the *Corpse of Christ*. Luther writes his *Galatians* in 1531. Holbein paints *The Ambassadors* in 1533. The open hymnbook on the bottom shelf of the table displays Luther's renderings—of the first verse of his version of the *Veni Sancte Spiritus* on the left page, and on the right the beginning of his *Ten Commandments*. At the top left-hand corner of the painting, the green curtain is slightly open, partly revealing a crucifix. What can this mean? The ambassadors themselves have no relationship to the crucifix, and the table and its objects are dead to them. Theirs is the darkness where faith does not dwell. Might this not be Holbein's way of saying that he was with Christ and Luther, the Christ of Luther's Reformation, and not with his own ambassadors?

Holbein was not the only one to make something prodigious from Luther's influence. William Tyndale, a fanatical Lutheran, produced the translation on which the greatest work in the English language is based—the King James' Bible. Tyndale's New Testament appeared in 1526. He had met Luther personally in 1524 in Wittenberg—incidentally, where Hamlet would go to university. So, in the very years of the Luther–Erasmus controversy on free-will, the translation was being made that would exert a formative influence over English Elizabethan culture, by a man whom history would most unjustly neglect in favour of the humanist hero

Shakespeare. Such has been the charisma of the light of reason in the West, and its repression of the darkness of faith.

***

As Luther was the cheerful, companionable, earthy half of the Reformation, Calvin was its sternly thoughtful and inwardly tormented self. To compare their portraits shows the latter as the Protestant of Protestants, the archetypal Puritan. Calvin's *Institutes of the Christian Religion* is, in its massive two volumes, clear, tense, systematic, and comprehensive. Its first edition was printed in Basel in 1536; its final edition, five times longer, was published in Geneva in 1559. Calvin is the father of inwardness. Against Brutus and the ideal of the gentleman, he establishes the psychological and metaphysical basis for the self-rigorous, spiritually concentrated, yet this-worldly pilgrim.

Calvin takes up the Protestant contradiction and makes it the centre of his theology—the irritant in the soul giving Calvinism its generative energy. God determined the human fall; yet all mortals are guilty. It is as if humanity's very weakness makes it the more damned, the more removed from God—the more wretched its state, the more guilt-ridden. Because the human condition is preordained, individuals are responsible. In Calvin, the contradiction is capitalised. Calvin could already have asserted Kierkegaard's view that faith is rooted in paradox. Paradox and contradiction are now active agents.

Calvinism gains a distinctive character from three principal areas of difference from Luther. The first is Calvin's heavy underlining of predestination. The question of election becomes central—of whether I am among those chosen by God, in advance of my birth, for salvation. 'No free-will' is primary, with God choosing whom he chooses in the beginning. All is set, fixed, immutable—determined.

The human individual is merely acting out predetermined routines. There are no grounds for concern here, for what is important is salvation: am I among the elect? Thus *sola fide* becomes more focused, slanting in on lonely individuals who scrutinise their everyday lives in vigilant search for signs that they are chosen.

For Calvin, the free-will argument is over. Luther has won, so the issue no longer concerns him. Likewise, he is less concerned about reason. He does criticise Plato for the view that it is ignorance that produces sin; he does stress that individuals see at best 'through a glass darkly' and that human intelligence is far too miserable to comprehend the ways of God. However, none of this is problematic. Calvin, one generation later, inherits Luther's successes, as well as the responsibility for the continuation of the Reformation. The sites of battle have moved, and the style of fighting has changed. He calls Erasmus an atheist then passes on, leaving the sharp aside—to the rationalist complaint about how can it be just when the judge compels the evil-doing—that when a corpse stinks who blames the sun.

Having focused on predestination and election, Calvin tightens the contradiction, and thereby the spiritual pressure on individuals, by giving them a greater eminence. There are two dimensions. The first is conscience. Humans may be fallen—damned and wretched sinners—but they all contain within themselves a fragment of divinity. It is inborn. It is the divine intermediary, the inner voice given to speak God's instruction. Humanity's highest duty is to learn to hear the voice of conscience. Calvin's definition of conscience is the truest in Western culture, and it plays the vital role in his work that *sola fide* and 'no free-will' did in Luther's. Conscience is 'that which does not allow man to suppress within himself what he knows'.

In other words, true knowledge is given, a knowledge that has nothing to do with reason. It is conscience, not intellect, which has access to this knowledge. Moreover, Calvin takes Paul and Luther further: merely superficial conscience delivers knowledge of the law—guided by parents, teachers, and elders. The Thou Shalt Nots are embedded only in the plane of conscience under social construction: 'The human law does not bind conscience.' The important conscience is deeper, and is innate, planted by God. What it knows is eternal. Calvin puts it that the knowledge of God is a question more of disposition rather than understanding. John Milton was to call this conscience 'God's representative in man'. Jane Austen was to refer to 'the better guide in ourselves than any other person can be'. Austen, like Milton, was one of Calvin's greatest heirs.

Calvin's second means for giving humans greater distinction is *vocation*. Luther had stressed the importance of a calling, but in the traditional sense of religious mission. It is Calvin who starts the Protestant transformation of everyday activity in the world into the central form of religious devotion. He takes worship out of the churches and into secular life. It is through Calvinism, and in particular English neo-Calvinism, as Max Weber pointed out, that *work* becomes holy. The traditional attitude to work—that it is profane drudgery to be avoided by all those not under the yoke of economic necessity—is turned on its head. The Protestant form of prayer becomes individuals at their work, head bowed, concentrating, hour after hour, day after day, year after year, to produce something of quality, done to the best of their abilities. Vermeer would, a century later, catch this meditative ideal of vocation beautifully in his studies of Lacemaker, Geographer, and Astronomer.

All men and women are given predetermined vocations—to each their own type of systematic activity in the world that it is their task to discover, and then execute. The contradiction, however, remains: carrying out a chosen vocation with complete devotion will not bring grace. At the most, it may signal that the devotee belongs among the elect. What is more assured is that those idlers without vocations are not destined for redemption.

Calvin lists reasons for vocation. A vocation is a means of learning God's will, and a discipline that helps tame the passions and reduce restlessness. It is a sentry post, a fixed point—back to Archimedes. A vocation helps secure the human individual. Thus Calvinism provides an outlet for the controlled release of some of the enormous psychic pressure built up by the punitive theology of faith alone, no free-will, predestination, and total responsibility. This theology had eliminated the traditional forms of release—confession, good works, veneration of the saints, and most of the other consolations of Catholic community. The vitality of Calvinism, its extraordinary capacity to seize the psychic-spiritual jugular, was in large part due to the manner in which it built up its intolerable theological contradiction and then exploited it. In the founder's own words:

> when a man has been taught that no good thing remains in his power, and that he is hedged in on all sides by the most miserable necessity, in spite of this he should nevertheless be instructed to aspire to a good of which he is empty, to a freedom of which he has been deprived.

The third significant way in which Calvin diverged from Luther was in his religious doubt. Calvinism is pervaded by uncertainty: am I among the elect, will I be saved, can I be sure? Such qualms are inherent in the theology. Humans, in their ignorance, can never really know. Calvin, throughout his *Institutes*, is himself nagged by such doubts, twisting and turning in an attempt to find an answer. On the one hand, doubt is Satan's most dangerous temptation, for the elect know in their heart of hearts that they are saved, and the damned that they are damned—this, after all, is what conscience is for. There is assurance, and those who truly believe cannot fall away. On the other hand, you can never really be sure, and confidence itself may be a sign of pride—the chief vice. Faith is never perfect, at best 'through a glass darkly'. 'Let him who stands well, take heed lest he fall, for God can cut you off again.'

Calvin must have been beset by doubt. There is no other expla-nation for his endless to-ing and fro-ing. Severe anxiety stalks—full assurance may never be found. You cannot relax, and if you do beware, for you are at your most vulnerable. Even Calvin's discus-sion of the church centres on uncertainty, his principal distinction being between visible and invisible churches. The former is com-posed of those who attend, who can be seen and counted, the earthly church. The latter, however, is the only one that matters: the church of the elect. Only God knows who belongs to his invisible church.

The ever-present brooding atmosphere of doubt is darkened further by what Calvin calls 'right fear'. The right relationship to God is one of fear. It is a fear of provoking divine wrath, having seen all around the disasters that strike the ungodly. Believers fear offending God; unbelievers fear punishment. There is also fear in recognition of the paltriness of humanity, its total dependence on God. 'I will worship in fear', quotes Calvin. Faith, and fear and trem-bling, go hand in hand. It is another matter when fear is too strong and disheartens conscience. False fear is anxiety, and it undermines faith.

In short, the individual who is always afraid in his or her own heart is blessed. What an extraordinary basis for religion! The Old Testament has its fill of 'Fear the Lord', but as one part of a much larger picture. In Calvinism, fear has taken over. All is trembling; all is doubt. The one antidote to the intolerable, constant psychic anguish that results is work—work with such intensity and rigour and wholehearted concentration that it is as if it were the work of the Lord. But it is not. There is no comfort there, either.

The leading sign of the success of Calvinism was the Protestant work ethic, and how rapidly it took hold in the West. Northern

European, middle-class dispositions were receptive to the Protestant contradiction. Calvin touched the dispositional core with his perplexing cycle of faith alone, no free-will, predestination, yet total human guilt and responsibility, and therefore the necessity of vocation. Reason cannot provide a way to understand why anyone should believe this; but they did and, in doing so, changed the direction of the West. Furthermore, Calvin's version of the darkness of faith—doubt—articulated a real human experience, that the religious path is overgrown, its end invisible, its truths obscure and paradoxical.

While Luther had staked out the territory, Calvin had extended his assault on the Renaissance—'the darkness of faith where neither law nor reason shines'. Calvin then turned more insistently to the individual walking that stark terrain, and to inwardness. He preached severity over self, a colossal self-discipline. A vision of the littleness of the human, in contrast with the harsh magnificence of God, is pitted against the humanist projection of the grandeur of *I*. But those meek powerless humans of Calvin have formidable inner strength, once they come to hear the still, small voice of conscience. This strength is asserted through vocation. The new hero is not Brutus the gentleman, but Cromwell the Puritan warrior—remorseless, ungentle, unlikeable, and mercilessly severe.

Calvinism could only establish itself through the Cromwells, and all those Puritan fathers and mothers who wielded the rod over their children, who demanded unwavering obedience. It was harsh, but necessary. Without it, the West might already have sunk back into medieval squalor. It is consistent that, in the nineteenth-century humanist twilight, the two most insightful late heirs of Protestantism, Kierkegaard and Nietzsche, should both have singled out comfort as the decadent heart of their time, the last god that is no god. Luther and Calvin had preached darkness and suffering against the reasonable and the comfortable.

The Puritan in politics failed. The messianic Protestantism of Oliver Cromwell, in England, proved unsuited to running the state. However, in the ordinary, everyday life of society—of men and women at work and forming their families—its influence was profound, and beyond what any of its pioneers could have imagined. There is no better summary of why this happened than Milton's tribute to Cromwell, which might equally apply to any descendants who have managed to find their vocations:

> he was a soldier well-versed in self-knowledge and whatever enemy lay within—vain hopes, fears, desires—he had either previously destroyed or long since reduced to subjection. A commander first over himself, the conqueror of himself, it was over himself he had learnt most to triumph. Hence he went to encounter the external enemy as a veteran accomplished in all military duties.

This is a man who has found his place to stand, on the Puritan rock.

From Machiavelli to Shakespeare, the Renaissance had taken over Roman notions of *fortuna* and *virtu*. Humans have no control over their fortune, which is given—good and bad. This is fate, and it is female. Brutus suffered from bad fortune. At the same time, humans can make something of *fortuna*, shape it, through their own power or will—their virtue. Luther and Calvin tore these notions apart and refashioned them. *Fortuna* becomes divine will, and as predestination it is total. *Virtu* becomes conscience, which has no influence over fate—it cannot will. But it is responsible, and has the channel of vocation through which to act. Fate and faith are fused together in the anti-humanist crucible. The only fate of significance is election; all else is smoke. What comes out of the crucible is not the man of *virtu*, the gentleman, but the Puritan.

After the Renaissance, as the dynamic centre of European culture shifted to the north, it became clear that Calvin had won, and Brutus lost. The cause was *guilt*. There appeared, in northern Europe from the period of the late Middle Ages, a rapid development within the dispositions of individuals, and from expanding social strata, new levels of inner control—of what later would come to be called repression. Renaissance culture had little affinity with the new type of self-disciplined, guilt-hounded individual. It had nothing to say to him or her, just as, for even more obvious reasons, the imagery of medieval Catholicism had become culturally obsolete.

It was precisely here, at the dispositional turning point of the modern West, that Luther, and even more, Calvin, took the pulse of the time. It was northerners, especially Germans, Dutch, Scandinavians, Scots, and English, who, experiencing the fear and trembling erupting without reason from within, took to the Reformation—because it gave form, and therefore sense, to what they were feeling. The Protestant contradiction, as irrational as it was, gave expression to some fundamental psychic knot. It is not my task here to follow the story of how this happened. Let it suffice to note that the decisive historical force behind the Reformation was the rise of an inward condition of dispositional guilt.

Whilst Calvinism may have won in the short term, it would not endure. Guilt and doubt formed an explosive combination that would, in the end, kill God far more effectively than the rational gentleman could ever manage. Protestantism's problem was aggravated by the demise of community. The Puritan's constitutional inability to relax in the world combined with reliance on individual conscience to undermine the role of both priest and church. Protestantism became, in essence, under Calvin's huge shadow, a conglomerate of one-person sects loosely held together by a common metaphysics.

Its achievement was to create another powerful individualism with which to counter humanist individualism. One of its costs was the decline of community. Once there is *sola fide* and Calvin's conscience, the vital unifying role of family, village, and town has been eclipsed. The Reformation threw out the incense and holy water, the chanting, the bleeding Madonnas, and most of the sacraments. It burnt the relics and smashed the statues; it banned the dancing. It found, however, that the church it occupied had cold floors and bare walls. The communal warmth that had been native to age-old tribal culture had gone.

Luther and Calvin *contra* humanism was, in its first principles, a replay of the cultural battle at the downturn of classical Greece. The Greek sequence, however, had been reversed. Socrates, and later Aristotle—against the quite different metaphysics of Homer, Aeschylus, and Sophocles—had staked out the humanist position, championing will and reason. Socrates, like Brutus, was a man of honour, deciding to die for his beliefs rather than escape into exile. Against will and reason, the Protestant Reformation restored the earlier Greek view of the world, the tragic view. It restored the metaphysics of Greek tragedy.

For the early Greeks, everything had been predetermined—by the gods. There was no free-will. Oedipus is archetype, a Calvinist hero before the fact, a reasonably good man cursed to break the law, breaking it because he does not understand what he is doing, breaking it simply because such is his fate. Oedipus is innocent before the human law—what he did was unwitting. But the only law that matters, the eternal one that abides in the darkness, damns him. Oedipus, the man of knowledge who could shine the light of reason where other men could not see, found his knowledge to be useless. Worse than useless, it gave him a false sense of power—of *I*.

In Aeschylus' great work, *Agamemnon*, human reason strives valiantly, desperately, to plumb the meaning of things. It fails, remaining perplexed by the course of events, and especially by the logic of why humans must suffer. What remains after the relentless, crushing violence is for pitiful humans to pray, and to wonder, and, if they cannot help it, to curse.

In the greatest tragedy of them all—*The Iliad*—predetermined fate also rules. Men play allotted parts, getting carried away by their all-too-human passions, and then what is left is expiation, expiation, expiation—before the necessary death. By the last chapter of Homer's masterpiece we are very close to the death of death, which is life, very close to Mark's Life of Jesus, and to Luther. The darkness of faith means a return to Greek tragedy. When Luther calls Aristotle the 'stinking philosopher' he does so with a precise historical sense.

The Protestant Reformation was founded on first principles. Both Luther and Calvin had the philosophic virtue of going to the central issue and stating it simply, often overstating it to ram the point home. By contrast, the strength of Renaissance culture was in its literature and art; its philosophers were of the second, even third rank. We shall return in the next chapter to Donatello when we consider the reply from the south, the alternative Reformation. The Gattamelata was for him merely an opening gambit.

Shakespeare, as a northern humanist, was profoundly divided, arriving at death, but unable to follow Luther in his revival of Greek metaphysics. Shakespeare's own final answer to 'Alas, poor Yorick' was the escapist fantasy of *The Tempest*, a delightful pastime but not very helpful with the central issue. The darkness of faith was not for him. Holbein, another profoundly divided northern humanist, also arrived at death, and stopped with his ambassadors, perhaps sensing that Luther had found the answer, but unable himself to do more than gesture to a half-concealed crucifix and an open text.

Chapter Five

THE ALTERNATIVE REFORMATION

Poussin, Donatello, Raphael, and Caravaggio

There was another way. We turn now to the fourth and final constitutive thread in the story of the rise and fall of humanism. It makes sense that the serious intellectual reaction against the Reformation, in defence of Catholicism, should not have come from the south of Europe but from the middle, from France. We can exclude the reactionary dogmatism of the Spanish Counter-Reformation, with its barbaric Inquisition, which offered no way forward. Luther and Calvin are not rejected outright; instead what is best in their work is extracted, and resown. Jansenism, Pascal, and Racine are examples. However, it is in the life work of the painter Nicolas Poussin (1594–1665) that the fullest and greatest Counter-Reformation vision is to be found. A complete theological philosophy was projected in visual images.

Although Poussin was born in France, studied in Paris, and found many of his patrons amongst the higher French bourgeoisie, from the age of thirty he lived almost without break in Rome. Establishing himself unambiguously in a Catholic milieu was his homage to the south. Rome also had its classical antiquity and its reworking in Italian Renaissance art, exerting a strong additional attraction on Poussin.

It is deeply perplexing that the commanding visual representations of *sola fide*, of saving grace, should not have come from a great Protestant artist, a Rembrandt or Vermeer, but from a Catholic. Luther's rallying cry finds its concrete form in Poussin. Here is a sign already that the gap between the two Western branches of Christianity is less than the institutional, visible churches have ever allowed.

'Faith alone' is embodied in a fuller conception of being, in a notion of the 'I am' counter to the humanist ego, one that draws on Mark's and John's accounts of the life of Jesus. Vocation remains central. And a third and new theme enters, that of finding a redemptive path through tragedy different to the classical Greek model. It centres on fallen worldliness followed by metamorphosis, and finds its articulation through the story of Mary Magdalene.

While Poussin has a close affinity with Reformation doctrine, he pits himself against the cultural logic of both humanism and Protestantism. He does so at the most fundamental level—of what culture is, and how it works. He returns to the classical Greek equation of culture with story. In the beginning was *mythos*, the body of timeless, archetypal narratives that carry the eternal truths. These are the big stories on which every culture is founded, ones that are then told and retold to each coming generation, often in modified guises that speak to the new times. The task of the artist is to retell those stories, and thereby to engage with the ancient currents of shape and form that move in the unconscious dreamtime of the people. Theology and philosophy are too abstract to be of much use in this central task.

If Luther seeks the darkness where the light of neither law nor reason shines, then so too does Poussin. Yet this is now a darkness in which it is possible to move, drawn along by the thread of the archetypal story, which the painter retells in his greatest works. Viewers are invited into the story and, once captured by imaginative identification with the central characters, are themselves taken down into the dark, into the thick of the action, and there subjected to the pathos. With the help of art, each individual's story, however ephemeral and petty it may seem on the surface, is conjoined with timeless mythic forms.

As with Luther, this is a darkness in which the realm of higher truth supersedes the moral law. At the same time, however, there is a radically different divinity, replacing the all-knowing, benevolent Lord God of church Christianity, Catholic or Protestant. The new higher force is the sacred breath, or *pneuma*, moving through the *mythos*.

Poussin was not born *ex nihilo*—out of nothing. His work draws heavily on three great Italian predecessors—Donatello, Raphael, and Caravaggio. In fact, he was the culmination point, the full flowering of a metaphysical rethinking within Roman Christianity, represented at its deepest by those three. This was a Reformation all of its own, moving beyond Catholic orthodoxy and bursting out from its medieval walls. It is more accurately described as an Alternative, rather than Counter-Reformation—itself assaulting the foundations of the Roman Church and its doctrine in comparable ways to the demolition from the north. In this extraordinarily fertile period in the history of Western culture there is a spirit to the age— a *Zeitgeist*. Poussin and his predecessors voice their own truths, in parallel with the Protestant reformers.

***

To understand what was at stake it is necessary to outline Catholic orthodoxy, its medieval world-view. The doctrine of *potestas clavium*—the power of the keys—was the pivot. It relied on Christ's covenant, recounted in the Gospel of Matthew, to Peter (*Petros*), the rock (*petra*) on which his church would be built—in Rome, as it turned out.

The covenant gives the keeper of St Peter's, as God's representative on earth, the authority to forgive sins. This was interpreted as the power of the keys to open the doors to either eternal life or eternal damnation, and thereby to decide which way each human soul would go at death—a power stronger than that over life and death. The coercive bite of the doctrine depended on belief in heaven and hell—and on a holy terror of the latter, which the Church painted in vivid colours.

With breathtaking clarity and simplicity the Church had solved the three great metaphysical questions that confront all humans in all societies: where do I come from, what should I do with my life, and what happens to me at death? It trumpeted to the faithful that all you need concern yourselves with is 'eternal life', and we shall provide you with the means. Every significant theological issue— the nature of salvation, the forgiveness of sins, the good life itself— was condensed into one end, the gaining of 'eternal life'.

'What happens to me at death?' was answered directly. Likewise, 'What should I do with my life?' Two things were required of all mortals during their three-score-years-and-ten: that they conduct their lives virtuously, according to a moral code determined by the Church, and that they actively and devoutly join the Pope's sacred community. The first question, 'Where do I come from?' was answered by the Creation myth, and linked to eternal life by a theologising of the notion of 'original sin', according to which all human beings since Adam have been tainted by the guilt caused by the first man's disobedience of God. Infant baptism is prerequisite to cleanse that depravity, baptism into the Church.

The doctrine of the keys put into the hands of the Church and its priesthood total control over salvation. From this power followed everything else, with almost mathematical precision. The papacy had built itself as the redemptive institution, the unique and vital intermediary between the life on earth of all human individuals and the eternal prospects for their souls. God himself could not alter the decisions of priests appointed by Rome. Half a millennium later, in

1994, a new *Catechism of the Catholic Church* would continue to assert that, 'There is no offence, however serious, that the Church cannot forgive.'

The ordination of the priesthood guaranteed the practical organisation of this power. The sacrament of ordination initiated the novice into the inner sanctum, endowing him with the right to use the gold key and the black key. Humanity was hereby divided into two classes: ordinary people, including all social ranks of society; and a separate elite with the extraordinary power over salvation, with distinctive dress and customs including celibacy, and a privileged knowledge and language—Latin—and participation in rites reserved for itself. The priests were the ground troops of a militant ecclesia who tended the flock and kept it corralled. It was they who heard confession and administered penance, in effect determining the punishment, in number and type of good works and devotional acts, which would allow them to absolve guilt. It was they, too, who delivered Holy Communion, with the magical power to transform the bread and the wine into the body and blood of Christ, enabling the further washing away of the sins of the commoners. If *potestas clavium* was the pivotal doctrine, the Eucharist was the pivotal rite.

Potestas clavium generated a rational religion. It was rational in creating a logical harmony between the separate spheres of the ethical and the religious. Life on earth lived scrupulously—according to the Ten Commandments, the four cardinal virtues, the three theological ones, and further Church teaching on morals—would be rewarded religiously, with access granted to eternal life. In other words God's earth was a just place. Moreover, this rational order was easy to understand.

It valued human intelligence. Humans had been given the power of reason to understand the moral teaching of the Church, with the guidance of the priests, and the power of free-will to obey what their reason and the priests told them. Individuals could not gain salvation without some effort on their part. They must will eternal life, earn it, or God would not respond. This is the 'doctrine of works', according to which good works will be rewarded religiously.

The Catholic method of thought was itself rational in the further sense of developing a systematic, internally consistent, and comprehensive codification of law and belief. St Thomas Aquinas, in the thirteenth century, produced his sixty-volume *Summa Theologiae*, which soon became the doctrinal Bible of the Church—a position it has continued to hold ever since.

Humanism drew much from the Catholic world-view. Leaving aside the vital theological difference, its thinking about morality, reason, and free-will has close affinities with that of the Roman Church—both are rationalist cultures. This kinship is much greater than with Luther, who, from the moment of his first move, with *sola fide*, set himself irrevocably at odds with *potestas clavium*.

***

On fundamental principles, where it comes to the 'vital spot', the alternative Reformation is closer to Luther than to the Roman Church. The formative work is Poussin's *The Plague of Ashdod* (1631: see back cover), now in the Louvre, completed when the artist was a relatively young thirty-six. Rats run about the Old Testament town of Ashdod. The citizens mill in confusion in the square outside their temple, where the statue of their god, Dagon, has shattered in the night. They had defeated the Israelites in battle, taken the Ark of the Covenant—the sacred box of the Jews containing the tablets of the moral law—and placed it in their temple. Now plague has struck. People are dying, and corpses lie everywhere. A baby is being pulled away from its dead mother's breast. Children are being shielded from the contagious bodies of their parents. The architecture of the town is severely rectilinear and claustrophobic. Leading townsmen stand bewildered as their community disintegrates around them.

At front left, a couple, gripped by some sort of inner torsion, is attempting to flee. Near the man's feet is the writhing figure of another man, whose healthily coloured flesh suggests that the torment that has flung him to the ground is more of the spirit than the body. Behind his head is the tipping base of a fallen column. Nature itself is in upheaval. The earth is quaking. Above this prostrate figure a huge rat moves towards the square.

The face of the fleeing man, and the palm of his right hand, are exposed by a cold, unmodulated white light. That hand has lost all strength as the spirit is wrenched out of him. Raised palely in protest, it will not attract healing rays. We are staring at the death of the soul.

Ashdod is a mausoleum, a house of the dead. Dark and sombre, its palaces are turning into charnel houses. Furthermore, once unsuspecting viewers have taken in the range of human and social devastation, they will at some point focus on the large corner edifice on the back right of the square, the central building in the scene, and realise that it is about to collapse. On the balcony above the crowd are three onlookers who believe themselves to be safe from the disaster beneath. In one guise, they represent viewers of the painting looking into the scene, tourists who have not heeded Poussin's implicit warning to pass by. Now that the painter has us, we who have lingered, he challenges: beware that the supports do not crumble under your feet, pitching you into the plague-infested square of Ashdod. Do you know, he questions, on what you stand? Are you so confident about stone palaces?

However, through the chaos there is an overriding order. A triangle of vectors, of invisible lines of force, controls the painting.

Two vertices are inanimate: the top of an obelisk in the background rises up into a brightly coloured sky; and the Ark of the Covenant itself hovering inside the temple, on the top of which are two golden angels, bowed down, wings stretched forward shielding the lid. From each of these vertices long lines run down to the front bottom right of the painting where they meet at the third vertex, the source of order.

It is a young boy. He tiptoes into the scene from off-stage right. He is naked, apart from a loose white shift. His skin is white, and his chubby cheeks are rosy—there is none of the green hue of the plague-stricken. His right hand is in motion, coming up from his side. It has not quite reached the horizontal. The index finger is pointing in the gesture of authority. He gazes with radiant, demonic intensity into the scene. A man covering his own face against infection attempts to keep the boy away, to save him. He need not concern himself, for the one person who will not catch the plague is this boy.

Bare feet and scanty clothing contrast with the ornate garb of most of the citizens and the elaborate architecture. Hollow civilised forms fill with contagion while fire lights up in the eyes of innocence. Yet, in spite of hitching his shirt with his left hand, as if ready for action, he has not completely gathered himself. In each eye there are single tears, glistening like pearls, resting on the bottom lids.

He gazes out across the scene, his vision distant, taking in his own life to be in its totality. He sees the awfulness of the world he has been sent into. He sees the unhinged man opposite, but his tears are not those of compassion. He sees his own fateful burden, and the years to come moving through plague-infested streets, amidst bad character, weak will, foolishness and evil, amongst the defeated and the despairing, guide and teacher, unrecognised and vilified even by those he will help. Is it any wonder that tears have come to his eyes? But there are only two, and they shall not recur. This is his last gulp before emerging centre-stage. His hand is near the horizontal. His focus is narrowing down on the present.

Strands of red hair straggle down his forehead. They prefigure the blood that will drip from the crown of thorns—not that he is Jesus in any literal sense, but representative of the universal truth that to be born human is to suffer unto death. A tear now, blood then. We see the beginnings of strength and power in the eyes, in the deliberate step into the square, and above all in the right hand rising to take command.

That hand rules. The town square of Ashdod is the human condition, stripped of illusions, a vortex of bewilderment, annihilation, and horror. The calm and sure hand of the three-year-old Master, the still centre of this scene, shows up the rest—human flotsam in a swirling gale, the putrid fumes of death thick in the air, statue shattered, pillars fallen, buildings crumbling, the Ark about to crash down. Even golden angels are impotent.

Poussin has painted the call. This is the moment when the boy embraces his vocation, leaving childish things behind. His mission starts here. It could be any town. It could be any time. It just happens to be ancient Ashdod, and plague is a generalisable metaphor for fallen worldliness, for disturbed *being*. The people are without direction, confused, at the mercy of the dark angel of human destiny, like most people lost once taken outside the routines and habits of everyday life. Whether the rats are their own verminous desires, agents of retribution for what they have done, or simply Greek dooms does not really matter. What counts is the redeeming force, and that it has just arrived. It is the only difference, and it is everything.

The *Ashdod* boy has one great ancestor. The baby Jesus in Raphael's *Sistine Madonna* (c. 1513), cradled tenderly in his mother's arms, glares out of the canvas, facing the world straight on. Again the hair is dark-red—curly, unkempt, wild—and the fierce eyes underneath speak of a controlled sacred rage. Indeed, it is hard to call these eyes innocent, there is such a deep knowingness—generations, eternities, of experience crystallised into an intensity of purpose that nothing on earth will divert. Both of these infants have extraordinary presence, and as such they embody a quite different conception of being—of the 'I am'—to the world-conquering humanist ego.

The Plague of Ashdod is a difficult work. Like many of Poussin's dense paintings, it has many layers. It strikes the viewer first as a cluttered mess with overbearing architecture. Once the viewer takes in the boy, however, the work seizes hold with extraordinary force. Yet he is just a boy. A figure of pure grace, he bears within himself the means to revive the town. He is a gift from outside. With his poise of being, mountains may be moved. He is literally the death of death, bringing an end to the death and dying that litters the canvas. The painting could have been titled *Sola Fide*. It is the incarnation of Luther's paradox, and visually coherent. At the same time it is anti-humanist. Reason and will are of no use to the citizens of Ashdod. Possible redemption is wholly with the rosy-cheeked infant tiptoeing barefooted into the scene. The townspeople do not even see him.

To fall into the square is to be plunged into darkness, sombre claustrophobic buildings all around and towering above, a clutching human swirl of panic and confusion, of the dead and dying, stench and putrefaction, a blustery gale, and hordes of bubonic rats purposefully going about their deadly business. Down in the square of Ashdod it is nightmare black. Will this be the darkness of unbelief and *not-being*, exposed by the cold white light on the face of the fleeing man? Or will it be Luther's 'darkness of faith', articulated through the boy to the true light of the heavens beyond?

After the demolition follows the assault, 'Is there anything left on which to stand? Or has the sinking whirlpool got you? In the darkness of the square will you be able to keep your feet? Which of these town citizens are you?'

There is no more powerful image of *life* in Western culture than this *Ashdod* boy. Poussin's gift has been to transform a mere painting into an active agent of sacred force. Once recognised, this boy will not let go. 'Remember me!'

***

The second major contribution by Poussin to the combined *sola fide*/vocation theme is the 1640 painting, *Matthew and the Angel*, now in Berlin. Unlike *Ashdod*, here is a simple image. Matthew is an ordinary-looking man with none of the charisma of the 1631 boy. He sits centre-foreground in an idyllic landscape holding a blank sheet of paper and a pen. There are ruins of a classical temple around him. He is near the bank of a river, which takes up most of the centre of the work, winding through the painting into the distance where there are further ruins, mountains, and a partly cloudy but vivid sky.

A golden-haired angel has appeared next to Matthew. His robe is white, as are his wings. His arms and right shoulder are bare, a lovely pale flesh. His left hand lightly holds the top of Matthew's page; the right points to where the text should begin. He is inspiration, bringing to this common mortal the sacred word. The pen is in Matthew's right hand. He gazes up into the angel's face. The angel looks down joyfully. Matthew is concentrating on his most important act, what he was called to do, finding the appropriate voice to tell the story of Jesus, the man who transformed his life. So far his own dullness has meant that he remains blind; his mind, like the rest of him, blank. But an angel has arrived, and on the instant Matthew is more than his lacklustre, everyday self. The pen races across the page. At long last he can fulfil his vocation.

The scene is an ideal landscape bathed in reverence and peace. Nature itself echoes the mood, a tranquil yet alert clarity. Even the ruins of human creation are a part of the divine harmony, with their double symbol of transcendence through grace of the mundanely human, and of transforming Greek classical culture through Jesus into a higher plane. Here is revelation, but not with lightning and thunder. Poussin's angel is gentle and helpful. The whole work has luminous intensity: this is what it is to be visited by an angel. Grace is everything.

There is no free-will—the angel is a gift from beyond, utterly outside Matthew's power. But the Protestant imagery stops here. The bleakness of the Calvinist fall is absent. There is no torment or strain. The air is Catholic. Vocation is relaxed and humans may move easily through a sublime natural order; if there is grace, there is harmony. In mood, there is little of Luther or Calvin, although they provided the seed. Poussin is producing an integrated vision— neo-Protestant-Catholic and more.

Matthew and the Angel is preceded by its shadow self or twin, Caravaggio's masterpiece on the theme of vocation. *Call of Matthew* (1600: see fig. 2) hangs in the Church of San Luigi dei Francesi in Rome, where Poussin would have known it well. The paired works fulfil the story of Matthew.

This scene is set inside a dingy room, with a swarthy youth sitting at the end of a table collecting taxes. Without refinement of look or manner, he is hunched over, a clumsy mop of dark hair hiding his identity as far down as his lowered eyes. A prosperous-looking middle-aged man is next to him paying over gold pieces, two young dandies sit opposite, and an old man stands behind the tax collector looking on.

A stranger has just entered the room. From the shadows he slowly raises his right arm, light catching a richly coloured burgundy velvet sleeve, and his hand nonchalantly points towards the table, index finger cocked. The assembled five recoil in horror, each in his own different way, as if to protest, 'Please, no! Not me. Go away!' Unconsciously, they all suspect that this is the moment of the call, although the identity of the stranger remains unknown, as is the nature of the vocation, and each fears he is not up to whatever may be demanded. Moreover, it is unsure which of the five is singled out by the vector of elective force spearing at them from those eyes, arm, and finger.

Only Matthew and he know. Little wonder that the tax collector hunches over, head down. He is too young. All he wants to do is drift on through life, enjoying nights at the tavern with the boys, a girl or two, his pleasures funded by his profane job. He is not up to this. In fact, his vocation will only manifest itself decades later, long after the death of this man whom he would join, who would become his master; a death followed by year after year of aimless drifting and prevarication. Matthew was not ready; Matthew was not yet Matthew. Decades later, when he happens to sit down beside a river, and finally attempts to write the story he was chosen to tell, only then, when an angel visits him, will he truly receive that call from so long ago. Only then, on the threshold of his own martyrdom, will he fulfil it, and by fulfilling it lose all fear of his imminent death.

Vocation, as Calvin conceived it, is the way to encounter the divine. The path that once led up to the church doors, and inside, now winds its way through secular domains. It is work that becomes holy, the meditative device to enable an inner state of reverence. Not work that is holy in the sense of the special preserve of a separate caste of priests; but any activity, however secular, that is made sacred by the psychic orientation of the individual who takes it on.

Although Caravaggio and Poussin choose the disciple Matthew, whom the Roman Church later titled a saint, to represent the call to the central life mission, their message is Calvinist. Tax collecting suits the artists' purpose, in that it represents the most mundane of jobs, socially stigmatised and utterly profane. Even it, approached in the right manner, they suggest, may be transformed into a means for retelling the life of Jesus, a retelling that requires the author to get inside it, to live it himself. For that to happen, the ordinary man or woman needs to be receptive to grace, and to be visited by an angel. Matthew is thus the exemplar of vocation, every vocation.

***

Poussin painted the Seven Sacraments twice. In the later series, now in Edinburgh, a third element is added to the alternative Reformation vision. In his *Penance*, or *Confession*, of 1647, Poussin focuses on the representative penitent in the recorded life of Jesus, Mary Magdalene. The scene is Jesus dining at the villa of Simon the Pharisee, a wealthy Galilean Jew. A dozen guests recline around wine and food set on a low triclinium, or U-shaped table, which occupies the centre of the painting, its wings aligned towards the foreground. Simon sits at the front-right wing, a large figure. Jesus, dressed in bright crimson robes, lounges opposite on the left.

Magdalene has just burst into the room and flung herself at Jesus' feet. Golden robes slip off a fleshy shoulder, as thick, long, golden hair loosely bound by a white ribbon cascades down. She is opulent sensuality incarnate, now bent over, weeping, caressing Jesus' foot, wiping it with her hair. She pours precious oil over it, the fragrance filling the room. His right hand is raised over her bowed head, in recognition.

Simon is outraged that Jesus, this reputed holy man and miracle worker, does not realise that Magdalene is a town prostitute. He should send this human filth on its way. Jesus poses a riddle for Simon, which mocks his self-righteousness. As Simon's feet are being washed by a servant, a merely profane cleansing, he is being taught about true virtue and openness to grace. So is the beloved follower, the young John, sitting close behind Jesus, and he will tell the finale of the Magdalene story, years later. Judas sits next to Simon complaining that the expensive oil that is being wasted on dirty feet could be sold, and the proceeds given to the poor.

Mary Magdalene is the great fallen one who, once she sees Jesus, recognises her own degradation—the horror of her past life as she has lived it. She is the commanding figure of worldliness out of balance, followed by transformation. In part, she loses her old self, scorched away in wretched shame. Collapsed at his feet, shedding torrential tears, wiping and kissing, she is obliterated, reduced to *not-being*. Jesus takes her seriously, however, not because she is repentant, which she is, but because, as he puts it to Simon, 'she loves much'. She always has and always will—indeed, her identity is as the woman who loves much. It is her nature that saves her—and, as a result, there is nothing for Jesus to forgive.

Gaining balance, she finds her vocation—as Jesus' leading follower. It is she who is in the Garden to meet him on the Sunday dawn after the crucifixion, outside the empty tomb. It is to her that he addresses the intimate prohibition, 'Touch me not!' She becomes his messenger to the world. Protestant theology was severely impoverished by its neglect of women and, above all, of the two Marys central to the Jesus story as it would be retold and richly filled out in European art in the two centuries between 1440 and 1665. The humanist heroes, too, were all men.

Poussin rehabilitates the sensual. For him the flesh is not essentially evil, or the source of transgression, as in Paul, Augustine, Luther, and Calvin. Poussin's most memorable figure of evil is to be found in the second *Eucharist* (see fig. 3), also from 1647: Judas, a man alone and without grace, is beside himself with bitterness because there is a better man than he—Jesus. His darkness is not due to temptations of the flesh—lust, sadism, greed, gluttony, or drunkenness. It is fitting that Judas hates Magdalene, as Poussin shows, they being the two figures close to Jesus symbolised by kisses—she the redeemed one, he fathomless rancour.

In general, for Poussin, the pleasures of the body are among the gifts of the gods, and should not be denied, although it is true that they harbour forces of potential devastation. He best illustrates this fusion of sensual and spiritual, each force needing the other on the human plane, in his depiction of exemplary women—the two Marys.

Poussin drew heavily on Raphael for his *Ashdod* boy; he does again for Magdalene. 'The divine Raphael' has often so dazzled admirers with his virtuosity of technique that they have overlooked his metaphysical genius. He was born in 1483—the same year as Martin Luther. Moreover, when Luther arrived in Rome in October 1510, an ascetic German monk on pilgrimage, about to be shocked to the point of loathing by the worldly corruption of the papacy, Raphael was working in the Vatican, and at the height of his powers. The huge *Sistine Madonna* would be completed in the next couple of years. The *Deposition* (see fig. 4), now in the Borghese Museum in Rome, had been finished three years earlier. Raphael was wrestling with *sola fide* just as profoundly as would Luther over the next two decades. Young Luther might have learnt something in Rome in 1510 if he had known where, and how, to look!

Raphael's *Deposition* is full on *death of death*. The body of Jesus has just been taken down from the cross. Two stylishly dressed young men stagger under its load. They are powerfully built, yet for them the body is an almost unbearable dead weight. It is as if they carry Holbein's *Dead Christ*. Over to one side, Mary the mother is collapsing in grief—for her, death is no more than death, and this is her beloved son. Lost in herself, like Holbein's ambassadors, the suffering may finish her. Meanwhile, the young follower, John, stands bent over the corpse, looking down at the face of his master, in consternation, questioning whether he can really be dead, even he, and if so then what can this horror mean—how can life possibly have sense?

Magdalene takes centre-stage. Raphael does not choose the usual scene to portray the climax to her story—the 'touch me not' meeting outside the empty tomb at Sunday dawn. This is Crucifixion Friday. She bursts through the crowd and moves straight over to the corpse. She takes a cold, clammy hand tenderly in her own, lifts it and, with her other hand, gently touches the white binding cloth in which he is being carried, as it rises up next to his face before running over the shoulder of the pallbearer and streams away in the wind. She gazes into his face, her mouth falling open with dread and burning compassion; her eyes are warm, direct, their intensity now completely with him, he who brought her back to life, giving her the power to be. Here she draws on all her accumulated strength, which has been made possible by him. Now she can touch him, and does.

Viewers who approach the corpse through her, rather than through the graceless young men, who see it through her eyes, touch it through her hands, will suddenly find it mysteriously transformed. Jesus' face, no longer frozen in a death agony, is concentrated, his eyes closed, gathering a last breath of energy to focus on this moment of serene intimacy with Mary, whom he loves. He eases himself into it. She enables radiant togetherness—pure being. His body seems to be floating, lightly, effortlessly. Her sacred touch kills death. It does so far more persuasively than Luther would ever manage.

***

Poussin and his three predecessors may have breathed in Catholic cultural air; yet they, in effect, waged a war against the central tenets of their own church. They were all deaf to *potestas clavium*. For them, it no longer spoke to the times. It was culturally extinct, and with it the whole doctrinal edifice it supported. The *Ashdod* boy is representative of their alternative view: all that matters on earth is individual being, the grace of the 'I am' expressed through vocation—the sacred work of the person's central life activity. Priests have no special powers; churches themselves have no distinctive role, and are just as likely to be 'whited sepulchres', beautiful on the outside, dead within. To be born human is not to be cursed with 'original sin', but to suffer from fallen worldliness as exemplified by Magdalene. The finding of right being, of balance in the world, depends on grace, a gift from beyond. This perspective is as radically and exclusively individual-centred as both humanism and Protestantism in their different ways.

Poussin was as disdainful of the medieval Catholic vision as had been Luther and Calvin. The Church is not the location for the central metaphysical quest of finding a place to stand: its teachings had become frozen, not allowing the eternal *mythos* to breathe within its walls. The rapid loss of belief in the old man with the long grey beard sitting up above, watching benevolently over his creation, was symptomatic. When, in 1511, Michelangelo painted him onto the Sistine ceiling, touching life into the hand of Adam, he was drawing on the imaginings of a dying culture. Poussin explicitly lampooned this figure, around 1662, in the first of his *Four Seasons*.

The Roman Church was declining from its own internal sclerosis. Thus, for Poussin, as for Luther, the big battle was with the rising culture on the move, humanism, and its own trinity—the seductive combination of ego, reason, and will.

To win that battle would depend on breathing renewed life into the archetypal stories—above all, that of Jesus. The *death of death* was, as always, the key. Poussin failed ever to paint a convincing Crucifixion. He rather displaced his meditation on the meaning of death—tragedy—into five major works. There was his *Eucharist* of 1647; *Landscape with the Ashes of Phocion* (c. 1648); *Lamentation over the Dead Christ* (1657), which reworked Raphael's *Deposition*; *Autumn*, one of his greatest redemptive works, in which the crucifixion is symbolised by a bunch of grotesquely large grapes and a ladder; and the sequel to *Autumn*, his last painting—*Winter* (1664)—which lacks almost any Christian trace.

In the *Eucharist* (see fig. 3) the scene is the Last Supper, as recounted by John. Judas in red is exiting through a door on the left. Jesus presides in a gloomy room, dimly lit by a tri-branch oil-lamp with three small flames hanging over the circle of disciples sprawled around a low table. This is the Lutheran darkness, but not exactly that of faith.

Nor is it the sacred community founded on *potestas clavium*—the orthodox depiction of the Last Supper as celebration by the inner circle, bound together in fellowship sharing bread and wine. Poussin is rethinking the Eucharist, the central rite of the Catholic Church and transforming it beyond recognition. What he paints is holy terror, with any communal bonds shredded by insecurity.

The only ties between humans that will ever survive Poussin's metaphysical wrestling are those within families, especially between mother and son; between grieving widow and husband's remains; between teacher and follower; between friends; and a sort of soulmate union of which the blueprint is Jesus and Magdalene. A mode of Gnostic individualism replaces both the tribalism of Jewish religion and the sacred community of the Pope.

It does so by focusing on a solitary Jesus at his Last Supper with followers who have proved relentlessly incapable of understanding him—who are not up to him. John, the beloved disciple who, in this scene freezes in horror, mouth open, will record decades later the central teaching: All you need to know is that 'I am'. And here He *is*, for the last time. 'To be, or not to be' is indeed the question. In effect, Jesus changes the course of Western metaphysics, wrenching the pivotal question away from God and eternal life, and onto the nature of individual being, here and now on earth. He uses his own tragic story to give flesh to his teaching about the *I*.

Poussin's Jesus is a massive figure, wearing a white tunic covered by a heavy red cloak. He sits erect, with his right hand, the one of command, pointing, it seems, inwards to his own breast. With his other hand he holds up, in front of him, a gold bowl—the cup of fate, about to be fulfilled next morning, with the help, he mutters, of the one of you in this room who is least true to me. The wine in the bowl is his blood—reflecting the red cloak. The bowl itself is numinous, as if hovering weightless, resonating with his presence. It combines with the lamplight above, and Judas over on the far left, to hint at some transfiguration of the wine into charged vapour—*pneuma*—which becomes the essential medium of the scene. A curtain hanging behind Jesus shields the breath of spirit.

In John's account, as painted here, the single disciple to receive bread dipped in wine—the unholy wafer—is Judas. Poussin depicts Judas in deep shadows with his right hand raised, index finger extended close to his lips, as if motioning himself to silence. In his mouth, the wine has not been transmuted into sacred blood. The gesture signals that his own breath has stopped—in shock. The 'I am not' is doubly damned, being without *pneuma*. The remaining eleven disciples sprawl around in their dark circle, agog with incomprehension and dread as simultaneously he who is categorical *not-being* exits the room, shuffling breathlessly out into endless night.

But what is the nature of the Jesus presence—the 'I am'? His form is misty, enigmatically obscure—charismatically dominant yet, at the same time, absent. His eyes no longer penetrate the world, seizing it, taking it on, as did those of the *Ashdod* boy. Abstracted, they are already in transition, distant, gazing beyond. His pointing at himself seems in part to anchor his being in the world for one last moment, as if to warn about not taking outer forms literally, for all that matters is what in-dwells, however fleetingly, shaped in the cup of destiny. All you need to know is that 'I am!'—infused with the sacred breath of *pneuma*.

The alternative Reformation did provide its own explicit crucifixion. It was fifty or a hundred years ahead of its time. Donatello was the master. Appropriately enough, it stands today in the place for which it was sculpted, through the doors behind the Gattamelata, in Padua, in the dark. To see it requires a guard to unlock gigantic iron gates. It is the centrepiece of the High Altar of the Basilica of San Antonio. Just as Donatello anticipated humanism in his equestrian statue, he anticipated Reformation in his altar.

There is nothing medieval about this work, although it was executed around 1450. And it is deeply, vitally unhumanist. Outside Mark's Life of Jesus—written in Greek—it is the masterwork of Christian tragedy, Christianity's reply to the ancient Greeks. Donatello had provided his own counter to the Gattamelata, his explanation for the great warrior's melancholy face.

The bronze Jesus is very high. He looks down from the Cross. His face is harrowed with anguish, with both the pain of slow, torturing death, and recognition of the tragic completion to his mission, 'My God, my God, why hast Thou forsaken me?' It is a wracked, inward face, taut furrows gashing down his forehead, the eyes heavily lowered, the mouth open, grimacing, wheezing, gasping for breath. This is a man, and he is dying a terrible death. The body is in the prime of manhood. Although the ribs show, as the breath is drawn in, his beautiful arms and legs are not tense. However, the open palms have thick steel nails through their soft centres, spiking the sacred source from which the power once streamed. There is no sublime transcendence here, no immediate release to sit in peace beside his heavenly father. This is mortality, kin to Holbein's *Corpse of Christ*.

At the foot of the Cross, directly under Jesus' feet, is Mary. It is not the older Mary of the *Pietà*, the mother cradling the body of her dead son, but the young Madonna. She sits on a throne holding her infant son, and this is no conventional *Madonna and Child*. She sits forward, her face tense, her slight head carrying a heavy crown. She senses what is above her. She knows the fate of the baby she holds. Indeed, she thrusts it forward, in an instinctive maternal attempt to save it from the tragic destiny that looms ahead, a darkness which will shadow her for more than thirty years. But the infant Jesus is himself secure and confident, eager to begin his mission.

The dying Jesus, looking down, sees not only you and me, the viewers. First and foremost he sees his mother, as mother. In his agony, he is not entirely lost in himself. He is with her, grieving for her—and the curse that she should have had him for her son. She, in turn, has accepted her vocation, and what mother would choose to be her? She steels herself, her narrow shoulders there to help carry his burden, as it weighs momentously over her head. Just as she nurtures the infant, she will be there for the grown man. He is not alone.

Here is death unveiled—a horrifying death, the worst imaginable. There is no magical resurrection. It is a man dying. Viewers can as little escape the unnerving look of this Jesus as they can Holbein's corpse. But here it is all right. Jesus, with the help of Mary, says Yes, in spite of all. Mary, too, the most cursed of mothers, not having the consolation of blindness to her son's fate, says: Yes, I can take it, I shall not turn to stone. This is the Mary of Raphael's *Sistine Madonna*; the infant is the *Ashdod* boy.

We have the completion of the human cycle, with the death of the man. Because of her son above, Mary can bear it. Through Mary we, too, participate. She is our guide, our way in. She teaches vocation, terrible vocation. Luther and Calvin have become concrete, real flesh and blood—images that can hold.

Part Two

MIDDLE ACTS

Chapter Six

DISCORD

Velázquez and Rembrandt

The vision of the alternative Reformation from the south was complete by the death of Poussin in 1665. However, it did not take root. No theology or philosophy appeared to map its territory intellectually. At the decisive moment, the great opportunity was lost, and the main current of Western culture took a different turn. What followed in France was the legacy of Descartes and later Rousseau, not a Catholic Luther or Calvin.

It was in Rome itself that the great opportunity had been squandered—by one of the pre-eminent popes, Urban VIII, whose incumbency lasted from 1623 to 1644. Urban, a patron of taste and distinction, had two artists of the first rank resident in his city to choose between—Gian Lorenzo Bernini and Nicolas Poussin. They lived on opposite wings of the same street, with the Piazza di Spagna in between. If each stepped out, not far from their respective front doors, and peered into the distance, they might have daily made out the other's form. Bernini—a rare honest man— would, while visiting Paris in his old age in 1665, be shown Poussin's second series of *Seven Sacraments*. Engrossed in each, one by one, he finally rose from his knees and exclaimed to his host, 'You have filled me with self-disgust today by showing me the work of a man whose great talents make me realise that I know nothing.'

Bernini had, in effect, with this 1665 judgment, struck the death knell over the Catholic Church, for in Rome it had been Poussin who got the papal cold shoulder. Thenceforward he would find his patrons mainly in Paris, to where the West's centre of cultural gravity was shifting. Urban VIII chose to patron Bernini, who went on to create many of the magnificent fountains and piazzas, and some of the churches, with their sculpture, that have bequeathed to Rome its peerless civic beauty. Yet Bernini's Baroque style represented the denial of metaphysics, the turn to decorative culture and gilded vaudeville.

The brilliant Urban VIII had fatefully rejected Luther's 'vital spot', leaving the Catholic Church to stagnate in medieval doctrine and drab stories orbiting around a sanitised, morally nice Jesus. His own superficial passion was rather to turn the interior of St Peter's into a celebration of imperial monumentalism in the tradition of secular, egomaniacal Caesars. Bernini's *Baldacchino* formed the centrepiece, as it still does. Huge, heavy, and ornate, it is an extravaganza of coloured marbles, grotesque in its vulgarity.

In England, the Anglican Church was ideally placed, with its moderate Protestantism and its Catholic tendencies, to provide an institutional basis for an integrated Christianity. In this it failed completely. After Milton, English culture produced no Christian theorist of distinction. In practice, the Anglican Church quickly degenerated into a bastion of upper-class complacency, sheltering within a blurred mental focus and half-hearted beliefs. Radical Protestantism itself headed into a metaphysical blind alley, giving birth to Methodism.

Probably the momentum towards secularisation, led by the glittering humanist ideal, was already too great. The combination of reason and free-will was starting to bear fruit, above all in the successes of science. By the late seventeenth century, a great individual like Newton, using no more than his intelligence, had been able to discover the laws of gravity and plot the motion of heavenly bodies.

So our scene is now set, with the great opposing forces of Renaissance and the two Reformations in place. Humanism's own self-doubt is also there. We can move into the middle acts of the story. Between 1600 and the terminal decline in the nineteenth century, humanism passed through an unfolding drama with a number of major stages. There was an attempt to integrate the Renaissance and the Protestant Reformation by forming a composite-character ideal of gentleman and Puritan. This bourgeois fusion, with its own theory of family, education, and politics, and its own ultimate metaphysics, was to prove the most stable and enduring of the humanist offspring. I shall examine it in the next chapter.

As the bourgeois fusion itself began to disintegrate there was one last attempt to revive humanism, by two polarised schools. One, the Enlightenment, reverted to a narrow, hard-core humanism stipulated on a deified reason; the other, Romanticism, staked its individualism on trying to invest passion with sacred status. I shall consider the Enlightenment and Romance in Chapter 8.

The aftermath of the head-on clash between Luther, Calvin, and humanism was high cultural volatility. Once the dust had settled, notable movements in two quite different directions became visible. First, there was a momentous act of cultural subversion, which, because it had digested the Protestant-humanist debate, was far more broad-ranging in its nihilism than Holbein's *Ambassadors*. It set the scene for what was to come as a flood two hundred years later. Second, there was the first crisis of Protestantism, in which tensions from within began to erode the fortitude necessary to maintain a theology centred on contradiction.

Strangely enough, it was one generation of painters contemporary with Poussin, in a short, forty-year period in the middle of the seventeenth century, which got closest to the heart of these new directions. Two very different men from two different cultures, Velázquez and Rembrandt, from their distant locations in Madrid and

Amsterdam, gave the right form to the immediate post-Reformation trials of humanism. Indeed, in the history of Western art there is only one other generation—that of Donatello and van der Weyden—that both coincides with one of the seminal crises in belief and gives that crisis its most profound expression. Moreover, in considering the period 1630–70 there are other significant figures in art, notably Georges de la Tour and Jan Vermeer. De la Tour stood as an independent French contributor to Poussin's alternative Reformation, while Vermeer would play a modest role in the bourgeois fusion.

***

Still today, *Las Meninas* (see fig. 5) is regarded as the most important painting in Spain. It dominates the Prado Museum. The title is Portuguese for 'Maids of Honour', and was first used in the museum's 1843 catalogue, replacing the more accurate description *The Family of Philip IV*. Velázquez painted it in 1656. It is a humanist masterpiece, and the most subversive work of art in Europe.

Five figures and a dog occupy the foreground. At the centre is the Infanta Margarita, a five-year-old princess. Maids of honour serve on either side of her. To the right, two court dwarfs are positioned, the second with his left foot resting on the sitting mastiff's back. In the right middle-ground stand a female servant and a butler. To the left is Velázquez himself, lounging at a huge canvas (we see its back), holding palette and brush. All these figures are contained within a hall-like room with a high ceiling, walls covered with paintings, and an open door in the back wall. Through that door we see, on stairs leading into the room, the Queen's chamberlain. Next to the open door is a mirror reflecting the figures of the King and Queen.

Velázquez is painting the King and Queen—that is the canvas within the canvas. They are not, however, posing for him. The

Infanta has suddenly been alerted, looking straight out of the painting. She has just seen her mother and father, who must only now have entered the room. The standing maid, Isabel de Velasco, interrupted in the middle of her curtsy, is half turned towards the front, as if the mark of deference to her mistress, the Infanta, is now reoriented towards her ultimate superiors.

The great power of *Las Meninas* is founded on the covert but pervasive authority of King Philip IV, which structures the entire work. His presence is indirect, seen in the mirror, and through his command over the alerted figures in the frame. The Infanta, gorgeously robed, bathed in light, is an image of delicate, innocent obedience to the authority that has just entered. At the same time, she herself has queenly poise, and a force of character reminiscent, in a more worldly way, of the *Ashdod* boy. The kneeling maid, side-on and bowing forward, serves the princess, gazing at her with reverent devotion. She illustrates the inexorable royal hierarchy. So, too, does the curtsying maid. Her reason for being is to show proper obedience. Her service is to the royal chain of power.

The dog, the princess's protector, and the figure most to the fore in the canvas, has head bowed and eyes closed. A leonine symbol of authority, he is at ease—all is in order. Finally, the female dwarf stands to attention, acknowledging her master. The front five figures and the dog welcome the King and Queen. They are the inner circle, led by the Infanta, of the true court.

The large room with its dark walls and high, tenebrous ceiling is oriented forwards. Its gloomy spaces are suggestive of a closed world bounded by a strict order. The light shines where it should. The darkness is finite, under control, resonant with the authority of the King, and this King holds office by divine right. On the back wall, framed in black, the mirror glistens with a blue aura, its figures blurred as if seen through a glass darkly. As sacred icon, it commands the room, its inhabitants, and the viewers.

Two features of the painting compromise the King. The open door at the rear breaks the closed circle of royal command. There is a clear light through the door and it is brighter than the mirror set next to it. Moreover, the chamberlain is outside the door, casual and independent. It is unclear whether he is coming or going, or merely observing. The door is open; there is a way out. This man has been able to step outside the chamber of authority, and as such he embodies free-will. His nonchalant mien shows no sign of deference.

The second compromising feature is the artist himself. At a first view it is fitting that he includes himself in the painting, a member of the second circle of the court. He is at work. However, that is as far as it goes. His stance shows him recoiling slightly, but not out of fear of the King. Proud and self-assertive, he looks straight at his monarch, head cocked to one side and slightly backwards—aloof, brazen, almost condescending. There is a sinister cast to his closed, thick, sensual lips. His charged defiance contrasts with the sensitive respect shown by the Infanta for her parents.

The painter's right hand holds a brush, the left his palette, with a similar studied independence—indeed the tools of his trade are suggestive of sword and shield, in keeping with the large red cross on his jet-black doublet. Velázquez is the modern Crusader. The artist stands to one side, his canvas larger than the actual canvas; he is outside the hierarchy. His head is higher than that of anyone else in the painting.

Here is the first direct representation in Western culture of the artist as great man, the free, world-conquering individual. It is a development of Pico's, 'I can become what I will.' By contrast, when Michelangelo had included himself in his *Last Judgment* (1536–41) and Caravaggio in his *David and Goliath* (c. 1605) both did so as acts of penance, showing themselves in lurid horror as belonging among the damned.

The humanist crusader has one further devastating stratagem to complement his self-aggrandisement at the expense of the King. He places the King and Queen in the same spot as the viewer. The Infanta and her circle look straight at you and me; as does the painter. You and I have equal status to the King and Queen of Spain. Here is the ultimate disrespect, and it is a simple and logical extension of the humanist credo—*I am everything.*

Velázquez is a democrat. We are all equal. The authority that orders *Las Meninas* doubles as the authority of each individual. Every passing tourist with his or her thirty-second gawk at the great work is equal to King Philip IV. No wonder the work is popular, making everybody the royal source of order and meaning in the world. And it is the Infanta who is the first to catch your eye, with her intense, quizzical stare, straight at you, respectful and welcoming. The last is Velázquez himself, scrutinising you from head to foot, inviting you into his magic circle. Now you are an intimate part of the painting. But do you know in whose shoes you stand? Indeed, are you up to where your culture, care of the great artist, has placed you?

None of this was necessary. Velázquez could still have kept the King and Queen out of the frame, standing them to one side, skewing the room to face them, and then reflecting them in the mirror. Poussin would have done it that way, but then he would never have dared include himself in such a painting. He had little humanist ambition for personal grandeur.

That mockery was the motive backing *Las Meninas* was clear to Spain's other great painter, Goya. In 1800 he reworked the greatest of his nation's works of art as *The Family of Charles IV*. Here, the entire royal family, including the King and Queen, are in the foreground in the light. Following Velázquez, the painter places himself and his huge easel on the left, receded into the shadows behind the group. Superficially, this is a standard royal portrait. However, the family is staged as an assembly of stiff cardboard figures. The painter, in positioning himself to the rear, signals that he is peeking behind the pompous, mannered façade. What he reveals is their true empty selves, and with merciless contempt. The difference from *Las Meninas* is that by 1800 the King has shed all authority, and the triumphant painter is restricted to a grim psychological analysis of failed monarchy.

Las Meninas stands on the cultural brink. Here is the secret to its power. The old order retains immense authority. This is shown magnificently, from the presence of the captivating girl princess—painted with love—to the reverence of her two maids, the dwarf at attention, the slumbering solidity of the mastiff, to the glistening mirror image of their majesties. Within this closed order the King rules. The artist, although working alone by himself, still serves. In fact, Philip IV valued this painting highly—legend has it that the King himself painted the red cross on Velázquez' doublet, to represent the Order of Santiago, which he bestowed on the painter in 1659. Indeed, as a private portrait, to be viewed by the King and Queen alone, *Las Meninas* is possible. The royal presence, doubling in the mirror, keeps both chamberlain and artist in check.

However, once a courtier stands in front of *Las Meninas*, not to mention a commoner, the sedition begins. Two immensely powerful figures confront each other, in a fateful cultural war that only one can win. The man of the future, the scornful, crusading artist, already has the measure of his monarch. The King and Queen are halfway to becoming models, at the mercy of the creative individual and the image he will make of them. The first faint, rank whiff from the rubbish tip of history wafts in through the open door at the rear, and across the room towards the old European order.

Culture must serve right authority, and unequivocally. The moment it wavers, as here, it becomes subversive. Velázquez had the genius to be honest, while at the same time deceiving his monarch, who admired his masterpiece—mind, the painting is of such technical virtuosity that it is easy to be carried away. Once the self-important *I* strides on stage, God is dead. Without God, there is no King. Velázquez has taken this next inevitable humanist step. Each *I* becomes God and King in one. Each individual becomes dependent on his or her own charisma—here Velázquez himself, decked in his glorious crusader tunic, is exemplar. He makes his universe as he will. He is the most powerful man in the world. He is, as Nietzsche will call him, a value-creator. The Reformation freed humans from the law; now high humanism frees them from faith, leaving nothing but *I*. That *I*, believing only in itself, creates its law, including its own political order.

I, the viewer, take in the painting not only from the front. The chamberlain, the observer from the rear, who drops in to see what is happening, or drops out, also represents me. The actual chamberlain's name was Velázquez, perhaps a relative, certainly a link between the two subversive foci. The chamberlain has the free choice of joining or leaving. But does he? Once there is that free choice—call it free-will—then there is no choice, for once anyone lounges on the back stairs they are outside, and cannot get back in. They are stranded in a cultural no-man's land, a wasteland which humanism in its death throes will call *nihilism*. Outside the rear door, the magic circle of faith is broken, and free-will cannot reconnect it. The court official, and with him the viewer, has become a tourist.

Without God, there is no above and beyond. The only beyond in *Las Meninas* is through the open door. All that is there, however, is a profane staircase, going nowhere, and the viewer—you and me. The deception is that next to the door is the mirror, leading forward out of the painting. It should be the beyond, and indeed it is at first viewing, but it loses that power once the subversive forces come into play.

Today, *Las Meninas* is revered as one of the marvels of the Western world. And it is. At one time it had its own room in the Prado in Madrid, dark like a crypt focused on its priceless relic. Lit by a single spotlight, much of the subtlety of the paintwork and its multiple planes was lost to view—to the disgust of art historians and the man who directed its modern restoration. But the lighting, that of the bordello, seductively exaggerated the subtle features of its degenerate beauty, and suited the moral tone of the work.

Finally, Velázquez introduces a new element that will come to plague humanism as it develops—rancour. *Las Meninas* is so awesome that the rancour against royal authority is diffused, the needling away at the King heavily concealed. The more common face of rancour appears in the painter's many studies of dwarfs, buffoons, and cripples. They are painted with a sympathy which suggests genuine compassion. But a strain of perversity colours these works, a fascination with deformity as such. That Velázquez is not sound is clearest in his portrait of revellers, who stare out of his painting with gleaming, diabolically sinister eyes. His self-portrait in *Las Meninas* should have been enough of a warning. Shakespeare, who was sound, felt driven to compromise his own humanist hero, Brutus, as did Holbein his ambassadors. Velázquez is of the new breed. They do not blush. He is the man of the future, a pioneer of the rancorous glorification of self.

***

Rembrandt was not rancorous. His problem was rather that of the Protestant who had great difficulty carrying the burden of his tribe, the honest Puritan who, following his vocation, saw too much, and became paralysed. This is a long story, one of tireless, lifelong wrestling with the angel, an illustrious chapter of the northern Reformation—carried out in Calvinist Amsterdam. In the ways that matter, however, Rembrandt did not succeed. Let us examine why. The message is that humanism's one viable alternative with cultural momentum, the place that Luther and Calvin had found to stand, had as its own greatest threat not the external enemy, but its own internal ordeal.

The key work is *The Sacrifice of Isaac* (see fig. 6). The first version, painted in 1635, is now in the Hermitage in St Petersburg. The second, from a year later, now in Munich, offers a more complete vision. Rembrandt chooses the climax to the story. Abraham is under instruction from God to prove his faith by sacrificing his only legitimate son, Isaac. Abraham has faith—Kierkegaard will title him the father of faith. He agrees to journey with his son to Mt Moriah, without telling his wife, Sarah, the reason. They travel for three days with an ass and two servants. Isaac is himself a miracle given to Abraham and Sarah in old age. We can assume that mother and father dote on their only child, whom Abraham is now ordered to kill.

Rembrandt recognises that this story—which Calvin himself singled out as an exemplary trial of faith—is the most demanding test of *sola fide*. He uses it to probe Luther's doctrine. He paints the moment of the killing. Isaac lies on wood built up for the sacrificial fire, naked apart from a loincloth, his arms bound behind his back. Abraham clamps a huge left hand brutally down over the boy's face, forcing the head back while covering his eyes. He kneels in the shadows over what in a few seconds will be his son's corpse. His right hand holds a dagger, poised high to swing down and cut the boy's throat. An angel has just hurtled down from the sky—in the Genesis account there is merely a call from heaven. Rembrandt has him violently seizing Abraham's right wrist, forcing the knife out of the old man's grasp. The angel's left hand is raised, about to strike Abraham. His look is angry. Beyond the bare bones of the story, this version has little to do with the Old Testament, Hebrew Bible. It is all to do with Reformation.

Rembrandt's concern is not with faith itself. This Abraham obeys God's command without hesitation—his faith is absolute. Calvin's doubt is not the issue. The painting's focus is rather on the demands faith puts upon mortal humans. Under examination is Luther's 'darkness of faith where neither law nor reason shine'.

The angel points the way. This one is not the usual sensitive ethereality, smiling sweetly, but tough and powerful—a harsh Protestant divinity. But even so, why is he enraged? He is about to strike the father of faith. The cause is the old man's blank stare, the fact that his eyes are mad. Abraham has had to so steel himself to carry out this act—horrible beyond imagining—that he has turned himself into a machine, hostile even to the angel's interruption of its motion. In the 1636 painting, Abraham's mouth is open, agog, not just at the violent angel, but at the horror. He has seen his own Medusa. The act demanded of Abraham by God has driven him out of his mind.

This is only human. God has required Abraham to ruin his life. The boy is the father's pride and joy. How will he live on, day after day, night after night, haunted by one nightmare image, of his own right hand slitting that adored son's throat? How will he live on with Sarah, who will not understand—how could anybody? Every day his wife will stare at him with uncomprehending hatred whenever he enters the room.

Abraham is not only asked to destroy his happiness, but to break almost every important moral law. Thou shalt not kill. Thou shalt protect the innocent, especially your own children. The trusting Isaac calls out, 'Papa, what are you doing?' Abraham is also transgressing his political duty as head of family and tribe to continue the bloodline.

God has not set Abraham any old test; he demands what is most difficult, what may well prove humanly impossible. He demands that his chosen representative on earth, the best of all men, violate the human law and destroy his own happiness. God demands that Abraham annihilate his own life. This is what *sola fide* requires. It is a lofty and austere doctrine, offering the sublime breath of divinity; as such, it comes at the highest cost, requiring a superhuman test. The faith holds, but the human character does not. Abraham goes mad. Rembrandt portrays a man whose soul has withered under the ordeal.

The angel is fiery-dark with rage. This man who represents humanity has failed his divine mission. He is not up to it. You cannot separate faith and law—as Jesus and Luther required—and expect the human animal to survive. Faith asks too much. Weak humanity must obey the law in order to keep its sanity. The *death of death* is not life; it is madness.

Yet the 1636 angel's face shows more than anger. There is also tenderness and grief. He is sorry for Abraham. Here is the pitying recognition that the fragment of divinity in humans is only a fragment: they are not godlike, at best they glimpse it, darkly and momentarily. Not too much should be asked of them. Angels are powerful; humans are weak.

There are parallels with Brutus. Rembrandt reworks Shakespeare's theme, in relation to faith rather than honour. Just as Shakespeare had a rigidity of character that was almost demented in the archetypal man of honour, so Rembrandt imagines the same in the man of faith. However, Brutus recovers whereas Abraham does not—he is just a broken old man. Any hope is concentrated in the lithe, spotlit body of young Isaac.

Two conclusions may be drawn. The first is that Protestantism is impossible: it asks too much of lowly humanity. Luther's darkness of faith is too intimidating and even the greatest of men, the father of faith, could not bear up. The alternative conclusion is that Rembrandt himself cracked. Born into the Protestant fold, and in his genius seeing more clearly than anyone else between Calvin and

Kierkegaard what was required, he could not carry it. Let us examine this second possibility, for it is of great moment for our story.

Rembrandt was keen on powerful angels. They reappear again and again. The finest of all dominates his version of the *Resurrection*, also in Munich, painted a few years after *Isaac*. This is a dark work, set in deep shadow apart from a brilliant burst of light in the centre, radiating out from a huge angel. Wings open with a vast eagle span, the angel is wrenching the lid off a coffin, sending soldiers who guard it flying. The human world is a murky tumble of confusion and fear, weapons and armour useless against the messenger of the Lord. Rembrandt projects a richly Protestant rendition of faith alone, no free-will and, above all, right fear. Yet he destroys the grave Calvinist mood by including a comic Jesus, also in light, sitting up dazed in the open coffin, a nightcap on his head, seeming to wonder why he has been disturbed.

So the great Dutch painter in again achieving a compelling image of sacred force, close to the Protestant heart, undercut it, leaving the human world without direction. He turns the Resurrection into a circus. Faith is too demanding. Somewhere, Rembrandt did not believe. Unable to take it all seriously enough, he was unconsciously driven to wreck his greatest potential achievements, both close to a *death of death*. The Protestant nerve was failing.

Recognising that his attempt at assault has stalled, Rembrandt tries to turn retreat into a sort of compromise victory. There is a favourite solution that recurs from his early to his late work. That is soulful resignation. The individual withdraws into introspection, giving up the pilgrim ideal as superhuman. Rembrandt settles down with his characteristic portrait of the individual soul gazing out helplessly from under the burden of its defeat, its inability to make anything of the world.

The more dynamic side of this is the quixotic Puritan, images like the *Polish Rider* (1655) in which the external world is a detached stage—with all its pomp, costumes, finery, swords, and sturdy horses no more than a charade. Only the inner is real. Here is Calvinist inwardness in visual form. The Gattamelata is rejected as a sham, worldly show. The outcome, however, is passive, as epitomised in the consummate Rembrandt solution—his many self-portraits. The artist throughout his adult life returns endlessly to look into his own eyes for signs of the fragment of divinity, for signs of grace. Again, this is vintage Calvinism, the only question being 'Am I saved?' The only journey worth taking is that of self-discovery— for signs of election in one's own soul, communicated by conscience. No one, before or after Rembrandt, has asked the question so intently of his own face.

Yet the self-portraits are a further sign of faltering. They give away a disconnected inwardness. Calvin knew that vocation is essential—action in the world. Conscience needs the *I* to act if it is to set its bearings. In what a man or woman *does*, signs may be seen. There is both impudence and hopelessness in an obsession with self. On the one hand, Rembrandt overrates his own importance; on the other, he finds the world contracted to no more than his own meagre self. Also, there is something adolescent about a fixation on one's own mirror-image. Protestantism in decline becomes detached from the world, and bogged down in lonely subjectivity.

Certainly, the soul stays vividly alive in Rembrandt's world. It is only in his Abraham that we see the dead eyes of the Ambassadors, and for a different reason. But it is a soul trapped in the body, bewildered and melancholy, unable to make anything out of its earthly mission. An old philosopher, plunged in meditation, housed in the Louvre, has no way out. The one window in his room is closed; he has lost contact with the outside light; the door down into a cellar is locked; and a lovely spiral staircase winding upwards is not for him. The only life to be witnessed here is in a fire tended by his simple wife, but she is apart, also alone.

Rembrandt left a vast body of work. It was in his late years that we see a number of attempted ways out of the metaphysical paralysis into which he had found himself cast. Around 1665, at the age of sixty, with only three or so years left to live, he paints his *Jewish Bride*. It is a tender idealisation of marriage. The introversion of both husband and wife has an external focus, the other person. Here is more than disconnected inwardness. The painting presents a poignant image of companionship, in which each is devoted to the other, trusts and is trusted, and shares an intimacy with the whole fidelity of their being. It is marriage as a type of vocation, with the Puritan inwardness of each (there is no evidence that they were Jewish) giving a peculiar intensity to the union. It is the visual representation of the greater emphasis both Dutch and English Protestants placed on the conjugal bond.

This is one way out for Rembrandt, but the solution is partial. The problem is not necessarily with choosing the institution of marriage as the earthly domain for the experience of reverence—such was important to the bourgeois ideal. It is rather that the bridal couple, with their companionate friendship, can be no more than one element in either the social or the metaphysical hierarchy. They are not the whole world. To ask too much of them will crush them in the end. And indeed, closer inspection of the *Jewish Bride* reveals a guilty calculation in the husband's expression, and discontented reverie in the wife's.

A second resolution attempted by Rembrandt is to portray a Christianity of compassion and forgiveness. Twenty years after *The Sacrifice of Isaac*, he reworked the same theme in an etching. This time Abraham is distraught, and very old, but he is not mad. A compliant Isaac kneels, bending over his father's knee—there is no tension in his body, which this time is clothed. The greatest difference is in the angel, who is close up behind Abraham in the middle of the etching. His wings are vast, spanning the work. This angel is tender, virtually embracing the old man, whispering to him over his right shoulder, his own right hand merging with Abraham's, covering the boy's eyes. It does not command or judge. It has come to succour and forgive, its wings protective—of the humiliated man. It expects little.

Rembrandt was never tempted by humanism. It is true, however, that in some self-portraits painted during an affluent period in his thirties he dressed himself as a cavalier or a wealthy burgher. These portraits display a naive and awkward vanity. In the same years, when he celebrated his wife, Saskia, by casting her as Flora, the most striking effect is a comic disjunction between the ordinariness of the person and the loftiness of the role and its grand robes. Rembrandt's instinctive orientation is Calvinist, mocking visible forms, especially ostentatious worldly ones, while seeking the invisible truth.

There is no hint of the value-creating individual. Rembrandt's focus is not on the active person deciding events, but on the helpless soul hurt by harsh fate. His wholeheartedly Protestant interest is in fallen humanity, in its impotence and its guilt. It is telling that the great theorist of the Renaissance, Jacob Burckhardt, should have dismissed Rembrandt's forms as ugly.

In the later work the problem is whether any room is left for action, for movement—that is, outside the companionate marriage. The 1655 etching is titled *Abraham's Sacrifice*. The reversed title is suggestive of the new metaphysics. Abraham has given up his heroic mission as the father of faith, in abject defeat. As failure he is worthy of compassion. It is the worthless, incompetent human individual, Abraham, who is sacrificed, in order to be embraced by the angel. Isaac is incidental. But what comes after the weeping? This is another old and broken man. When there is only the weeping, can the human individual survive it, for what else is there? Is this right fear or false fear?

Rembrandt's penitential imagery is problematic, at least in the Western tradition, because it does not follow a day in the field of battle: it is not Achilles with gore on his hands carrying out acts of penance for the outrageous impiety of his murdering without limit. There is no normal story here of temptation, transgression, remorse, and punishment. There is just inwardness and more inwardness: the Protestant pearl may be blighted.

Rembrandt's third and last way is to be predicted, given the logic of the other two. It is tragedy. The work is *David and Uriah*, hanging today in the Hermitage—the date around 1665. The story is from II Samuel 11 and 12. King David sees Bathsheba bathing and, intoxicated by her beauty, he orders her to his bed. When Bathsheba becomes pregnant, her husband Uriah returns from the war but refuses to sleep in his own house. David sends him back to war, and issues a command that he be left stranded in the front line of the fiercest battle so that he will be killed. When this ploy is successful God is angered, and sends Nathan the Prophet to accuse David by means of a parable.

Rembrandt paints the moment of David ordering Uriah back to the fighting. Uriah, dressed in a deep crimson robe, stands, an immense central presence taking up most of the painted surface. Under a bejewelled turban his head is bowed, eyes lowered. His right hand is across his breast, in submissive resignation to the heart-stopping shock. His left hand is clasped in a sash that binds his robe—not a gesture of strength or command, but of tension, of bracing himself for disaster, and of trying to regain composure, that his spirit not be crushed beyond recall. He knows. The King has taken his beautiful wife, and now he sends him to his death. He must obey the King. The King is all-powerful and his lord. Such is fate. It is terrible. All Uriah can do is bow to it. Rembrandt paints a version of tragic recognition.

Behind Uriah, on the right, is King David, a golden crown sitting on top of his own bejewelled turban. He wears an ostentatiously heavy gold chain. His beard is luxuriant; his lips thick and red. He, too, is meditative, with his head tilted away from Uriah, knowing the awfulness of what he does. He retains, however, the complacency of the King. He will not change his mind—pleasure wins out over law. The die is cast. To the left, lower down and further to the rear than David, is an old man. He, presumably, is Nathan, yet to arrive on the scene. His face is gravely troubled and sad. When the time comes, he will speak his judgment.

Rembrandt has returned to a more traditional mode, a story of the strongest human passions, power and lust, combining to drive a man to excess. It is a return to universals, of law and temptation, of punishment and guilt. The central theme, however, is Uriah's tragic fate, and the perspective is Calvinist—under the metaphysical canopy of predestination. David is merely acting out what is in his character and his preordained script, more the agent of what is given than the free, wilful King. Uriah suffers the consequences, without curse or protest—this is how things are. The difference from other works by Rembrandt is that here inwardness is focused, not on an intangible resignation, but on Uriah's own quite explicit life-path. He has been honourable, a Brutus serving his king faithfully, risking his life. In return his wife, who loves him and whom he loves, is stolen, and he, the victim, is sent to his death because his innocence shows up the King's shame, and his presence stands in the way of the King's lust. Fidelity is repaid with betrayal.

The companion work is the *Jewish Bride*, which gestures tentatively towards trust as the highest human value. *David and Uriah* accepts that prescription, then moves on to a higher plane, more explicitly Protestant: its focus is conscience dwelling on fate, the attempt to move through a state of inner dejection, of tragic recognition, into an openness to grace. Rembrandt has followed his mentors Luther and Calvin back to the ancient Greeks, with an image that is almost Homeric.

There is a problem, too, with *David and Uriah*. Tragic works either have it or not, that consuming, sacred force which stops viewers in their tracks, scarring the psyche for life, never to be forgotten. This work does not quite survive such a savage ranking test; so very few do. Metaphysically speaking, Rembrandt's genius, in the end, is one of near-success, and therefore of failure. But what a failure!

There is a final sortie, in perhaps the last work that Rembrandt painted. It is the gigantic Hermitage *Return of the Prodigal Son*—the figures larger than life-size. Rembrandt retreats from tragedy back to the main thread in his life's work, redemption through soulful resignation to suffering and defeat. The prodigal son of the Jesus parable had left his father's house youthful, naive, and rich, optimistically eager to take on the world. He has returned broken by life—a vagabond in rags, filthy, alone, his head shaven, the soles of his sandals worn away. He kneels abjectly, nestling into his standing father. That father, too, has had enough of life, the final burden being grief at the loss of the favourite son who has now come home. Old and weary, he welcomes, in forgiveness and joy. His right hand is planted on the middle of his son's back, drawing him closer in embrace. The left rests on the son's right shoulder, steadying and blessing. These hands centre the work, evoking sighs of gratitude and reconciliation. The old man looks resignedly down, in his relief unable, however, to hide some ambivalence: one eye looks slyly awry, and there is regret, even guilt, tingeing his facial expression.

The son, redeemed by his father's forgiveness, is secondary. The father, crushed by life and self-pitying grief, is being given a last awakening. He is so frail, it is almost as if the shock of joyful solace will kill him. Here is his last act. It is not that of tragic suffering; not the world of Homer or Aeschylus; of King Lear; or even Uriah. There is neither valour nor fortitude; heroism nor grandeur. This man is not the father of faith, nor the noblest Roman of them all. Here is unsavoury character, discontent, and humiliation. It is through the annihilation of all worldly hope, and with it the failing and compromised *I*, that a muted type of redemption becomes possible. We are back to the early Christianity of the meek and humble, the human condition accepted with passive resignation rather than the staunch, fighting resolve of a Luther or Calvin.

The prodigal son is himself still young, but now, having slunk home in defeat, he has nowhere else to go. His life, too, is likely over. On the crumbling rock, the collapsing old man hopes to be showered with divine pity, and grace. But his own furtive inability to relax into the moment of reconciliation indicates that Luther's monster has not been killed.

None of this bodes well for Protestantism. One of its greatest sons, with a prodigious vocation for painting, dedicates his life to the cause. He has brilliant theoretical instincts. He sees clearly, he is sane, and he has an indomitable will. In a lifetime of struggling with the monster without whose killing we cannot live, he produced in the order of five hundred paintings, and two thousand drawings and etchings. Rembrandt never gave up.

In his last years, he tried his most interesting new tactics for killing the monster. On the way, he had found that the faith which transcends both happiness and law, annihilating them, cannot be lived. He retreated into himself, into a soulful inwardness disconnected from the world. He tried to break out. There is the sacred intimacy of husband and wife, but it is not enough. There is the tragic suffering of Uriah, but it is just not intense enough to forge a place to stand—not enough steeped in what Henry James would call 'sacred rage'. Finally, there is the Prodigal Son, the culmination of the artist's lifelong quest in search of divine reconciliation.

Rembrandt cannot manage a death of death. That he evades decisive engagement with Jesus, preferring Abraham, reveals his problem—the Jesus who enigmatically formulated, 'Before Abraham was, I am.' Rembrandt does return repeatedly, in paintings and etchings, to the crucifixion, yet never manages to bring a Donatello-like focus and intensity to the scene. If someone of his instinct and talent cannot take on Jesus, who in the Protestant camp can? Luther and Calvin were abstract men, theologians. Rembrandt stuck to depicting life here and now, in visual images that cannot lie, where fantasy is checked in its comforting distortions. He did so with ruthless honesty. Here was a major empirical test of Reformation doctrine, and it failed to kill the monster. In Rembrandt, Protestantism suffered its first great crisis.

So it was: in the same few decades in the early to middle seventeenth century in which the alternative Reformation found its fulfilment in Poussin, the masterpiece of cultural subversion appeared, and Rembrandt wrestled through a long, attempted Protestant revision, and failed.

Chapter Seven

THE BOURGEOIS FUSION

Vermeer and Bach

Concurrently, a new cultural form was emerging that would predominate for the rest of the humanist epoch, establishing its own practical way of life. That was the bourgeois form. In essence, it was the product of the fusion of secularised Protestantism with humanism. Home and family are the hub of the bourgeois ideal, to which all other elements connect as spokes. The home is the sacred site of the culture. It is the domain principally of the mother, her spaces, the world within which she nurtures and instructs her children, and is companion and wife to her husband. The father is the head of the household and the principal agent of discipline, yet much of his time is spent away from home, at his work, which is a vocation. In the full high bourgeois—that is, upper-middle-class—ideal, work should take the form of a profession. The cardinal virtues are honesty, sobriety, reliability, industriousness, and duty. Education and culture are valued.

These are the bare bones. To get a fuller picture we need to separate the constituent elements. Let us consider the Protestant contribution first. In some places there was a Puritan bourgeoisie without significant humanist influence. Max Weber described as much in his study of the Protestant Ethic. There is no clearer picture of this social type than in Vermeer's work, idealising the seventeenth-century Dutch middle class.

Vermeer paints the home as sacred. His middle-class interiors are a world unto themselves, complete. The light filters in through lead-lighted windows from the outside, but the outside world is unimportant, unnecessary. Within the rooms it is women who impose a tranquillity and reverence, whether they hold a water-jug, work at lace, model, or play musical instruments. The women themselves are exemplars of vocation, as in the 1665 painting of the lace-maker, her head bowed over her work, her whole being concentrated on her hands, in the physical work which doubles as a spiritual discipline. In this Puritan domain the state of grace of the individual within her sanctuary—the home not the church is the sacred ground—invests everything she touches with her higher conscience. The profane water-jug becomes a holy chalice. Moreover, for Vermeer, in true Calvinist spirit, there is no social hierarchy. His kitchen-maid has a rough complexion and a stocky figure, like the earthenware she uses, but she, too, in her humble vocation, has found a state of grace which the painter conveys by bathing the objects around her in a luminous, earthy intensity. The bread feels realistic enough to pick off the canvas and eat.

Vermeer is so rigorous in his emphasis on home as sanctuary that he depicts his representatives of male vocation—astronomer, geographer, and artist—as working in middle-class lounge-rooms or studies. The ethos is strictly Protestant, whatever Vermeer's own religion. The *Astronomer* and the *Geographer* (see fig. 7) embody the Puritan ideal of vocation. Both men use their work to meditate on the secrets of heaven and earth, to wonder at the glory of creation. This work involves them entirely, body and soul, a means of integrating the unconscious passions from below with the light from above. The right hand in one case holds a pair of dividers; in the other, it acts as dividers itself. Here is the point of union of physical and spiritual, of inner and outer, taking the measure of things, seeking their balance and thereby establishing it. For both men work is prayer, a state of concentrated meditative openness to grace. The Puritan bourgeois ideal thus focuses on revelation and salvation, but in the ordinary, private, everyday world.

The things usually taken as significant in life—romance, adventure, and crisis—are not specially important. Neither are such distinguished locations as palaces and cathedrals. The events that occur, great or small, are taken by the individual as fate, predestined, to be digested in the same manner as geographer or lacemaker work through their simple piety. Inwardness is all, but it requires both a sanctuary and a vocation.

The place that bourgeois culture found to stand was thus Puritan, a derivative of the Reformation or, in the French case, the Counter-Reformation. As Vermeer showed so brilliantly, it was a secure place as long as the intensity of the Puritan core remained. Critics of the bourgeois have usually typified it as materialistic, obsessively attached to profane routines in work and family life, driven by fear and greed, and a need for status. Their caricature is, in essence, false. Bourgeois culture got its strength from precisely the opposite: it managed to find a sacred core in the daily practices of home and work. A man's armchair and a woman's favourite fruit-bowl became emblems of the divine presence, objects of deep and lasting attachment.

The middle-class Puritan ideal was too one-sided to succeed on its own. There was too much in both human nature and social life neglected by it. We saw these limitations with the *Jewish Bride*. Vermeer himself saw another flaw in the vision, that the heavily meditative image of vocation could combine with the conviction that events are predestined to produce an inhibitingly passive or resigned response to fate. In his *Man and Woman Drinking Wine*, he shows a woman slumped in shame because she has tacitly agreed to a seduction by a black-hatted stranger which she knows is wrong, and the signs are that she does not even desire. It is as if the man is fate, which she must accept, with resignation. Afterwards, she will devote her spiritual energies to accommodating what she has done, trying to turn guilt into penance and to restore the balance. Her philosophy seems to have undermined her capacity to say, 'No'. In a number of works, Vermeer paints the vulnerability of his closeted middle-class women to temptation. He prefigures the fascination of nineteenth-century bourgeois literature with adultery.

Moreover, Vermeer only paints individuals. The home is sanctuary, but there is no family, no sacred community. Rembrandt was closer to the 'home' part of the ideal, especially in his various holy families—he used very ordinary men and women as models for Joseph and Mary, thus implying that every family should contain some of the formative sacred community. Vermeer had already intuited the loneliness of the Protestant, and later bourgeois, reality.

In bourgeois culture these Puritan individuals, bent on the solely religious goal of salvation, concerned about their soul and not their ego, fused with a worldly conception of the individual whose concern was rather with *I*. The ego's goals were the age-old ones of wealth, status, and power; its pleasures were derived from mastery over others and the material world, and prestige in the eyes of others, being looked up to as somebody, having social eminence. Bourgeois culture could not admit that the ego's goals were what they were, and introduced a brand of vulgar Calvinism to justify them as having a higher spiritual end. The argument went that worldly success was a sign of God's approval. God showed the elect that he had chosen them by predestining their success in business and society. Conversely, the poor were poor for a reason, as a sign of spiritual damnation. Here was the source of that hypocrisy for which bourgeois culture soon became notorious, the moralistic self-satisfaction in which confidence of chosenness, stripped of humility, combined with brash egoism.

It was at this point that humanist metaphysics entered the fray.

The ego was active in its pursuit of its worldly goals. For material success, the *I* had to flex its muscles. In bourgeois neo-Calvinism we are back with Erasmus: God decides events but he leaves the ego of the chosen individual to will its own glory. The bourgeoisie took pride in their position in society, for they had achieved it—it was not merely predestined. 'Self-help' was a part of the ethos or, as the adage put it, 'God helps those who help themselves.'

The second humanist fortifier followed. The willing ego, using its supreme faculty, its reason, working hard at its vocation, could create a world in which the individual was better and happier. The bourgeois social world's own view of itself was that it *was* better than any other, past or present. Within it the individual was happier, and more virtuous. Thus followed another humanist axiom, the belief in progress. At its height, this cultural form did fulfil in its members a secure satisfaction about their condition. This is well caught by Georg Lukács in his 1909 essay on 'The Bourgeois Way of Life', taking a German focus, and finding the beauty of this world exemplified in Theodor Storm's short stories, in 'a lyrical description of a quiet, warm, simple life-mood'. There is contentment in simple things. Vermeer's contemporary, Pieter De Hooch, had painted a similar tranquillity in lower-middle-class Dutch domestic interiors. However, on this as other fronts, there was an uneasy alliance between the gregarious humanist optimism of the self-made man and the pious Puritan fatalism that Vermeer had revealed. In the case of the lower middle class, barriers to material advancement tended to reinforce a more fatalistic orientation, as exemplified in the Methodist movement in England.

In the dynamic high-bourgeois mode, the value-creating *I* would typically devote itself to building not just a home, but also a place in society. The self-made man would use his fortune to establish himself in a part of town or country suitable to his means, and then attempt to buy the accompanying style of life, manners, and education for himself and his family. He would build solidly, to last. It was a central but unacknowledged part of the bourgeois reality that its members came from nowhere, socially speaking; but once they had arrived they worked relentlessly to consolidate their legitimacy, their right to belong. They were particularly keen to give the impression that they were part of a tradition. Thus, in its public dimension, the bourgeois family aped the aristocratic mode, with the difference that the lack of name and blood was compensated for by a greater emphasis on good breeding. Out of social insecurity, it attached itself with anxious devotion to a cultural creation—proper behaviour—and became far keener on manners than anyone with genuine breeding.

The new social hierarchy was not aristocratic. Blood and name could not be bought. The 'gentleman' was therefore redefined in a less aristocratic manner. His breeding was learned rather than inherited. A greater emphasis was placed on cultivation. Education becomes the key to creating a privileged caste, when blue blood was missing. Children sent to the right schools, and then university, could be taught to look and behave like aristocrats. As a result, the humanist ideal of education, of using knowledge to make people better and happier, was fused with a snobbish ambition to employ education and culture as a means of distinguishing those of superior class. Culture becomes a marker of bourgeois prestige.

The bourgeois enthusiasm for education and culture was not, however, at its core a social affectation. It had a deeper drive, and again its source and its rationale was hybrid humanist-Puritan. On the one hand, humanism placed central emphasis on education as the means for exercising and training the highest and defining human faculty—intelligence. The improvement of the world depended on trained intellect. Protestantism was no less keen on education, but on the separate grounds that everybody should be literate in order to understand the Bible. Conscience, the mediator

Figure 1   Donatello, *The Gattamelata, c.* 1447

Figure 2   Caravaggio, *Call of Matthew,* 1600

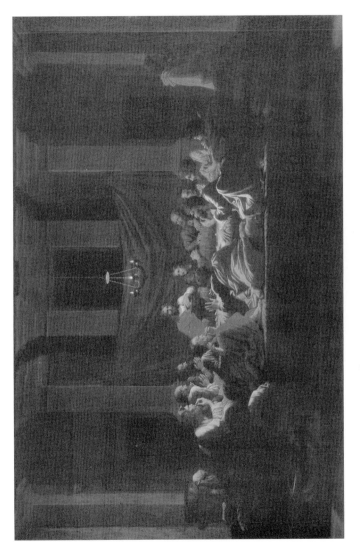

Figure 3   Poussin, *Eucharist*, 1647

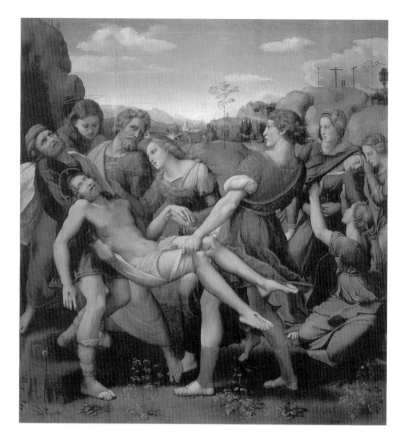

Figure 4   Raphael, *Deposition*, 1507

Figure 5   Velázquez, *Las Meninas*, 1656

Figure 6   Rembrandt, *The Sacrifice of Isaac*, 1636

Figure 7   Vermeer, *The Geographer,* 1668–9

Figure 8   Munch, *Madonna*, 1895 / 1902

between God and individual, could not evaluate daily conduct unless it knew the laws by which humans should live on earth. They were to be found in the Holy Scriptures. Even in predominantly Catholic France, it was Protestant schools in the seventeenth century that led the way in educational reform.

Once bourgeois education developed, its ultimate goal, if usually unstated, became the pursuit of 'truth'. This vaguely mystical grail beckoning to the prosaic material world was itself a humanist–Puritan hybrid, combining the rationalist faith that clarity of mental insight brings virtue and happiness with the Protestant focus on revelation, the journey after spiritual knowledge. These quite distinct, worldly utilitarian and religious strains have nothing in common; but as 'truth' was not examined too closely, it survived as the siren song of bourgeois culture.

Bourgeois education was pioneered in France. Well before the Revolution of 1789, humanist ideals had come to dominate educational practice. The ultimate goal was 'general culture', with special emphasis on teaching children to think logically and to write graceful prose. The curriculum concentrated on the Greco-Roman and French classics. Under the influence of the Enlightenment, there was already a sprinkling of more utilitarian subjects such as science, history and geography. The *Collège de France*, founded in 1530 by François I to promote humanism, had seven of its nineteen chairs by 1770 devoted to science and mathematics. The Revolution itself merely underlined this humanist practice, with the guiding ideals of reason and progress as its official doctrine. Napoleon then completed the model by building a strict hierarchy of institutions under central bureaucratic control. Apart from reforms in the 1850s, which further increased the status of science, the system remained basically unchanged until 1960, by which time something resembling its structure could be found in all Western countries.

The picture is complicated in an intriguing way by the English case. In England, the middle class developed earlier and expanded more rapidly and extensively than anywhere else. After Cromwell, it became integrated into, and increasingly contributed to, the evolution of a political and social order of unique stability. Yet English education, dominated by Oxford and Cambridge, and the public schools, remained essentially aristocratic until well into the twentieth century. For instance, it was not until the 1930s that the humanist value of 'culture' made any headway in the English public schools.

A key difference in England was the enduring vitality of a social hierarchy led by a confident upper class, one that was open to the middle class with money. Entry was through sending sons, and eventually daughters, to public school. Those elite schools had the aim of developing 'character', which they did mainly through an emphasis on sport and a Spartan disciplinary regimen that had special effect because they were boarding institutions with total control of their pupils. They were not greatly interested in their students learning much—the curriculum until well into the twentieth century was devoted to the rote learning of the ancient classics. The main nineteenth-century reform, pioneered in Thomas Arnold's Rugby, was the addition of a severe evangelical Protestantism, infusing the character ideal with piety: the school's task was now to turn out more godly, morally superior gentlemen with a strong sense of civic duty.

The public schools retained their aristocratic goal of reinforcing the class hierarchy. Character was not simply a question of piety and goodness: it was also about 'tone'. There was an inviolable code of how to speak and behave, what views to hold, and with whom to associate. Here was the crucible for the intensely coercive formation of the small, exclusive caste that dominated English society and occupied almost all of its important offices. In this system there was no need for the humanist ideal of culture. The thrall of the aristocracy was enough, and it was invigorated from the 1820s by a radical Protestant zeal, and with it an image of virtue that had nothing to do with reason. There was thus a divide between French education, soon followed in Germany, which in effect devoted itself to developing a humanist elite centred on culture, stressing talent and merit, and English education that retained an aristocratic aloofness to ideals of cultivated learning.

The humanist university, while in its early stages a creation of Renaissance Italy, was consolidated in France from the eighteenth century, and followed the same principles as the schools. It centred on the humanities, its guiding ethos being to transmit a general culture and develop mental excellence. As its full bourgeois form developed during the nineteenth century, the professional schools—notably, law, medicine, and engineering—gained in importance. Napoleon himself had already established the training of engineers, for his own military purposes. The quintessence of a bourgeois education became to balance a general familiarity with the humanities with practical training in a profession. In the American system, the latter often followed the former at a separate institution. The public pillar of bourgeois society was to be the cultivated doctor, lawyer, or engineer, regular in church attendance, and devoting a significant part of his leisure to honorary work for the community.

Another bulwark of the bourgeois achievement was its politics. The form was parliamentary democracy, and here England led the way. Its evolution took most of the humanist epoch; it was largely complete by 1867, when Walter Bagehot published his enduringly insightful analysis of its workings, *The English Constitution*. Parliamentary democracy is bourgeois in form, although not in the manner in which it came into being. The middle class played but a minor role in its formation. The steady development from the absolutism of King Henry VIII to the constitutional monarchy of Queen

Victoria was largely due to the success with which the aristocracy steadily wrestled power from the monarch, and then consolidated that power in parliament. A parliament is quite unlike the typical aristocratic model of governing, the oligarchy or federation of powerful nobles. Its executive and legislative decisions are made by a committee, the cabinet, under the charge of a powerful chair, the prime minister, who is elected by the collegiate of the majority party in the parliament. An independent bureaucracy serves the cabinet.

The democratic part came with citizens' right to elect their representatives, and having the further check on those in power by means of a free press, public opinion, and free associations or pressure groups—features stressed by Alexis de Tocqueville in his classic two-volume study of aristocratic and democratic political forms, *Democracy in America* (1835; 1840). The election of representatives was a humanist derivative, in giving special power to each *I* among the citizenry. It depends on 'liberal' assumptions about the capacity of all adults to reason, to think intelligently about how they are ruled, and about them being free to will what they think right. The Protestant stress on the pre-eminence of the individual's conscience also played its part, especially in the turbulent seventeenth century. A further humanist derivative, the belief in merit, was also important, leading to ability rather than social background—or personal patronage—being the factor deciding who should occupy public office.

An ethic was still required in politics, and this was Protestant. A just politics depends on conscience, individuals acting honestly for a good higher than that of their own egos—that of the nation. It depends on vocational commitment. The heroic figure of Abraham Lincoln in American political imagery illustrates the point. Moreover, the Protestant ethic became the more necessary as the traditional aristocratic honour code of *noblesse oblige* receded, with its obligation that nobles devote some of their time to politics in an honorary capacity, serving those less privileged. Without either ethic, politics degenerates into a chaos of competing pressure groups, deals, buyings off and, before long, corruption and greed. Bourgeois politics was in essence neither corrupt nor Machiavellian; it was honest and just.

Parliamentary democracy depended for its success on one further factor: a respect for tradition, and its practical manifestation in an independent judiciary. This created a legal system free from the political one, with its own history and tradition, and its own collective conscience. In the crises of English political history, it was usually reliance on a long-established constitution, and its legal forms, that thwarted any tyrannical moves by the monarch. This factor is neither Protestant nor humanist. Indeed, it is at odds with humanism, as Edmund Burke pointed out in his polemic against the French Revolution. By the end of the eighteenth century the wisdom inherent in the English political system had little to do with reason, or ideals about progress and the 'rights of man', or the arrogance of the humanist *I*. It had rather to do with good civic instincts and healthy prejudices, a respect for what generations of fathers, and their fathers, had slowly and sometimes painfully built. In other words, bourgeois politics depended in good part for its stability on an anti-humanist scepticism about the power of human reason, a conservative warmth and attachment to the irrationality of custom and tradition.

The European aristocracies had a genuine culture, with authority and weight. It was founded on ancestors, their blood in the veins, their portraits on the walls, the swords and decorations from wars, and the stories of generations of valour. This was clan culture consolidated in property, the ancestral home, a horde of dependents, and the status of the family title, all engraved in a fixed social hierarchy with a king above and commoners beneath.

The Protestant Reformation created its own quite different culture. Humanism, however, never succeeded in its own right. It never managed to transcend 'Alas poor Yorick!' and Holbein's ambassadors. While it had its own unique and trenchant ideals, it failed to grow roots. It was a parasitic form that, to survive, had to feed off strengths external to it. There had been Christian humanism, still tied to the Catholic umbilical cord. There was aristocratic humanism—in fact, the case of Brutus, whose code of honour was inherited from the nobility. The ideal of the gentleman consisted of humanist notions integrated into an aristocratic core. The Renaissance created the glittering humanist fantasy, but once it lost its Christian root the ethic on which it sought to ground itself was not its own.

The third and last parasitic form was Puritan humanism, the case of the bourgeoisie. Bourgeois culture had a tendency to swing backwards and forwards between Protestant and aristocratic poles, especially in England where the class organisation of society survived longest. In the nineteenth century, sons from hard-working middle-class entrepreneurial families would often, on entering Oxford or Cambridge, soon distance themselves from their Puritan home backgrounds and take to aristocratic habits, under the influence of the poise, confidence, and style of the upper-class gentlemen. Their fathers usually approved—for them the harsh Calvinist God was now little more than a distant ancestral ghost. By this time, in France and Germany the aristocratic presence was weaker, and the bourgeoisie compensated by making culture a much stronger ideal. As a result, humanism was more central and vigorous there, the university more culturally significant, and indeed the bourgeois ideal itself more creative and independent. It was, however, less stable.

When bourgeois culture moved away from its Reformation root, it did not necessarily move in an aristocratic direction—that aristocracy being itself in decline from at least the eighteenth century. It was inevitable that worldly success would, as always, tend to undermine piety, weakening the need for devout religion. It became a standard pattern in bourgeois families for an early Puritan asceticism to give way, over time, to a self-satisfied materialism. Here, too, however, the humanist *I* proved to lack the internal strength to move into the cultural vacuum and impose its own form. As a result, once members of the bourgeois class lost their Puritan souls, they found the solid order they had so laboriously built to be hollow, comfortable rooms echoing coldly with a brittle, routine snobbery, and a wooden and weary self-importance. Often as not, psychopathology of one type or another took over, Vermeer's *Woman with the Water-Jug* turning into the neurotic housewife obsessed with cleanliness. In the place of Oliver Cromwell, or Abraham Lincoln, appeared secular entrepreneurs accumulating wealth for its own senseless sake, or bureaucrats dedicated to their own absurdly hermetic rules—experts in process, blind to culture.

My argument here is that, in the Western tradition since the Middle Ages, there have been four distinct domains of real culture—Catholic, aristocratic, Protestant, and the alternative Reformation of the artists. Humanism attempted to replace both Catholic and aristocratic, and failed—that is, as a separate culture with its own roots. Almost immediately, it found itself confronted by a new cultural force, Protestantism, with which it ended up going into alliance.

There is one complication to this argument: to know a culture means to know the sacred site on which it was founded. In the case of Catholicism, there is the crucifixion, the pre-Passion stories of Jesus and, above all, their institutional consolidation—*potestas clavium* anchoring the papal church in Rome. In the case of Protestantism, there is the crucifixion, reoriented by the metaphysics of Homeric Troy and Greek tragedy, as articulated by

Luther and Calvin. The aristocratic case is more difficult to read, with its origins in warrior clans.

Cultures divide according to which are tribal and which individual-centred. The most enduring of tribal cultures subjected to the vicissitudes of history—Jewish—centres on family and especially the mother, and their responsibility for continuing the ethnic bloodlines. The tribe's mission is stipulated in a holy text that hinges on a covenant struck by God himself with his 'chosen people', sealed in fire on the sacred mountain with the tribal first among equals, Moses. It is the people and their history that counts.

By contrast, Western culture is, from the mythic outset, individualist. At one pole, Homer shifted the locus of meaning away from the tribe and on to the individual—Achilles is a tragic hero caught up in his own wrestling with his life-path, not much interested in his people, whether local Myrmidons or national Greeks. Homer's *Iliad* became the Bible to fifth-century classical Athens. At the other pole, Jesus stressed that the 'I am' is all that matters—thereby installing a metaphysics which is radically individual-centred. Family is irrelevant, as is ethnic band or nation. Salvation belongs to the individual, not the group.

Aristocratic culture was a mix of individualist and tribal strands. Its defining code of honour drew its *mythos* from Homer's Achilles—and as such was individualistic. Yet the context was name, ancestors, family, and property—a tribal ensemble. As a further complication, the exemplary aristocratic figure became, in the Middle Ages, the Christian knight, and the exemplary war the crusade against infidels. Aristocratic culture in the Western tradition became integrated with the Roman Catholic one, if temporarily.

Jane Austen, in *Mansfield Park* (1814), painted a forensic picture of an aristocratic family in decline. The argument works just as well for the bourgeois family. In the novel, it is a timid, physically frail girl from the middle class, Fanny Price, who restores order. She has an indomitable Calvinist conscience, and her judgment is always right. However, it is a special Puritan mood that is the secret of her influence. That is intensity. It is Fanny's intent resoluteness in what she knows, the backbone of her extraordinary fortitude of character, that wins through. It is the same intensity that saves the bourgeois family from the aimless monotony of the prosaic everyday life that its critics have emphasised.

Intensity versus pleasure. Fanny's intensity is linked with her shyness. Jane Austen was herself to remark, 'What has become of all the shyness in the world?' Without the shyness and the intensity we are back with the ambassadors, in whom learning is deadness—they are the antithesis of Vermeer's geographer. Without the shyness and the intensity, the sacred turns to the profane and the women began to feel trapped in their lounge-rooms, restless and bored, the chain on their instincts losing its sense. The bourgeois family in decline has its untethered passions bolting into fantasies of adultery, its own pious culture subverted by Romanticism.

Where there was the intensity, faith and fate still ruled. As with Vermeer's women, as with Fanny Price, the individual soul was inviolable. Life was under the thumb-screw. Men went about with severe, rigid faces, stiff of movement, their characteristic dress the high starched collar with tie, the black suit and black top hat. Their women were tightly laced, and intent in their interior domestic spaces, lost once they relaxed. While all this presided, humanism was saved from the skull. In turn, humanism saved the bourgeois from a demented fanaticism, or a disconnected inwardness. It softened the sense of iron predestination. But here was the problem that in the end would tip the equilibrium. The inviolable Soul needed an implacable and inexorable Fate, the two great polar forces living off each other. Tame one, and the other would wither, in the end. Luther had seen this. An intense bourgeois culture had created comfort as an incidental. Once, however, the intensity dimmed, the

surface habits and rituals of that comfort—the plush rooms—
became the last hope of a sinking culture, while increasingly anxious passengers clung to the broken spars of the wrecked ship.

Or, bourgeois culture sank into disconnected inwardness. This is
the world of the Rembrandt self-portraits. Thomas Mann will chart
the end of the high-bourgeois German family in his 1902 sociological novel, *Buddenbrooks*. That family has no future when its last son
is a hopelessly unworldly, sickly, and hypersensitive artist.

Puritan intensity had its own internal problems. Apart from
Luther—and his greatest follower, Johann Sebastian Bach—it lacked
an active engagement with the demonic, and especially with death.
We saw this in the case of Rembrandt. The problem became aggravated in the bourgeois adaptation, in that humanism led in quite the
opposite direction, itself being completely at odds with the metaphysics of Greek tragedy. Its worldliness was not that of Poussin.
Indeed, from a bourgeois perspective his desolate, weeping
Magdalene is immoral, even disgusting—she deserves to be stoned.
In Vermeer, to take one of the highest Puritan examples, there is no
terrible angel. Nor is there any tragedy. Consequently, a certain
coldness pervades the exquisitely painted work.

In high cultural terms, the great Protestant creations were in
philosophy, opening with Luther and Calvin, ending with
Kierkegaard and Nietzsche; in the English novel, notably Jane
Austen and Henry James; and in German music, its zenith the work
of Bach. It was Bach who gave the Protestant cultural form its best
chance of achieving a death of death, and in a bourgeois context.

From 1723, when the 38-year-old Bach took up his position in
the small provincial city of Leipzig, until his death in 1750, he acted
in effect as musical director for the town. This included composing,
providing choirs and musicians, many of whom he taught, and
planning the entire musical year. He had all four main churches
under his jurisdiction. It has been estimated that in some years he

was responsible for the performance of 250 pieces.

In his early period, he wrote a cantata every Monday, copied for instrumentalists and singers to learn by Friday, when he rehearsed them, ready for a single dress rehearsal on the Saturday. He then conducted it on the Sunday—sometimes from memory because he hadn't had time to write a score for himself—in his own church, the *Thomaskirche*. The result was music for every sacred day in the Christian calendar—and many other special pieces, including the *Oratorio* and *Magnificat* for Christmas, the *St Matthew Passion*, the *St John Passion*, and at least one other Passion—subsequently lost—to be performed every Easter, as well as music for weddings and funerals. Bach's working life was more like that of a conscientious tradesman, an uncompromisingly perfectionist one.

It would be a mistake to glamorise Bach's devoutly Lutheran town as a cosy, close-knit, harmonious bourgeois ideal. It was more likely riven by all the usual human small-mindedness, hostility to neighbours, troubled family life, and arduous work underpinned by a vicious moralism and shallow piety. Then each Sunday all gathered together at church, for up to four-hour services. It was the done thing in their social world—there would be social comment, perhaps exclusion, if they did not.

What was different was that the parishioners of the *Thomaskirche* and the other three Leipzig churches, once inside, were in the hands of a genius. Many would have remained deaf to the fact. Yet some, perhaps a significant minority, perhaps even more, would have found themselves transported out of the bleak cares of the everyday and given an explanation and a sacred connection. Bach redeems the bourgeois soul.

Bach integrated high-culture virtuosity into a popular frame. He was at the technical forefront of his time—sometimes ahead of it—writing music of an intellectual and practical complexity that remains, still today, the hardest to play. But there is simultaneously the recurring pulse of dance, and of a peasant folk exuberance—the conductor, John Eliot Gardiner, redirected a Luther image to joke that Bach stole the devil's best tunes. Bach may be the cleverest of composers—he is also the most bacchanalian. It is as if his entire work is the sublimation of a sustained explosion of unfathomable volcanic passion—yet always kept under rigorous control.

This is notable in the *St Matthew Passion* (c. 1727–44). At the centre of the work, Bach represents the crowd of common humanity by two choruses, chanting violently for its choice of whom to release from death, 'Barabbas', followed by a repeated, sadistically sensual, screaming at Jesus, 'Crucify him!' The choruses are positioned overbearingly on either side of voices singing plaintively, hopelessly of Jesus' selfless love. A crescendo of mob evil drowns all in its environs, including the weak protest of Pilate, which had been anticipated at the start of this central dramatic sequence by Peter's denial. The *Passion* has descended into the underworld of human rancour, from which point it will slowly work its way back to a musical rebirth.

Of the three hundred or so Cantatas written by Bach, two hundred survive. The great ones project the wounded pain of existence. Nothing is to be taken casually or frivolously in what humans are given. Moreover, any inclination to protest or lament indicates discord. Many of these Cantatas focus on how individuals ought to orient themselves to their own death, and in a way that underscores the responsibility they bear for the entire cast of their earthly span. Bach takes up Luther's challenge, and answers with a play of musical force within which the *I* can release and lose itself, dissolving into the grander ocean of existence beyond the boundaries of the self. A haunting chant rises, steeped in cosmic pity, as the soul cries out, struggling in its melancholy to contain a life in its entirety, express it, bring it to a fitting completion. The spirit, now grave with finality, seeks a way to embrace the whole.

This music is only possible within the shaping form of the Jesus narratives. The typical Cantata opens with a statement of a life problem, laced with a general sense of the low state of humanity. Then an answer or solution from the Gospel is provided. The music enables a conjunction of one person's woe with the higher order opened by the archetypal story. This serves to place each life, with its seeming pettiness and futility, in a grander scheme of things. Finally, the music lifts up in a surge of infectious vitality, even a trumpeting joy.

The Cantata BWV 21, *Ich hatte viel Bekümmernis*, is illustrative. It provides one of Bach's strategies. There is a duet between the gloomy soul of the individual, soon to depart, and the spirit of Jesus. The soul presents its catalogue of fears: mortal, it is sunk in a pit of misery, wounded, about to be destroyed, lost to sorrow, and worst of all, Jesus hates it. Each time, Jesus counters: No, the soul shall live, lifted out of its woe, the hour of sweet restoration nigh, and, as your true friend, 'I love you!' Bach is summing up a human life in terms of the impact on the soul of what has ruled—the accumulating defeats and anxieties of the bourgeois ego. That life is now saved from a hopeless darkness of eternal suffering. The soul's state of grace is expressed in its love duet with Jesus.

Bach's music is a triumph of balance—the bringing into equilibrium of the most extreme forces to which human life is subject. In spite of the worst that fate can dish out, it thereby calms, instilling a spirit of the rightness of things. Everything is as it should be. Everything is in its proper place. Supreme order envelops the human condition—and, care of this music, it prevails.

Bach creates the final great *midrash* of the Jesus story—that is, potent retelling in a way that engages and compels the new times. A century on from Poussin's own Jesus *midrash*, this will prove the last staking out of new cultural ground during the humanist epoch. It does not suffer from the abstraction of the theologians—with music having a more direct impact on the rhythms of the human spirit than the written, or even the visual story. As a result, it seems to matter little that the Biblical German drawn on by Bach borders on the wooden, the doctrinaire Lutheranism practised in his Leipzig already, in its own time, dated.

The music is written and performed for ordinary people absorbed in daily town life—not for heroes, saints or the specially gifted. Without Bach, they would have little to avert their attention from a self-centred materialism casting its flimsy veil of illusion across Holbein's skull. The music's high, uncompromising intensity is focused on wrestling bourgeois consciousness away from the profanely worldly, and onto the journey of the suffering, but immortal soul. Its goal is the death of death. Bach himself invites Aristotle's category of he who is great of soul—*megalopsuchos*.

Chapter Eight

ENLIGHTENMENT AND ROMANCE

Descartes, Mozart, and Kant

Humanism did finally make the attempt to go it alone. The time was the eighteenth century, the place France, and the movement the Enlightenment. At last the ties to Christianity—Catholic or Protestant—were cut, and indeed the leading figures turned with vehemence against all religion, denouncing it as superstition, a barbarian shackle on the triumph of rational humanity. Moreover, the attempt to graft humanism onto an aristocratic morality was also ditched. Reason was enough, able to create its utopia on earth out of nothing, with no more to lean on as an ethic than Voltaire's advice to the individual, 'Remember your dignity as a man.' The very term Enlightenment said it all: the bright midday sun of the Renaissance was now a complete and perfect reality. Where truth illuminated the way there was no need for religion. Nor was there need for morality. This was to be culture without shadows.

The Enlightenment was the fulfilment of humanism. It was the purest and most single-minded embodiment of its ideals, the most energetic, optimistic and successful of its children. The eighteenth century was the Age of Reason. Its hero was Sir Isaac Newton, Voltaire merely setting the tone by eulogising him as 'the greatest man who ever lived'. Its method was 'critical intelligence'. It formed and developed the major sciences of physics, chemistry and biology.

It did the same with the new sciences of man—psychology, sociology, history and economics. Intellectual progress was the presiding ideal, and it proved brilliantly successful in practice. For the first time the scientific method was abstracted from non-rational interests: the study of facts, as Hume urged, was separated off from values, theology, aesthetics and metaphysics. Mind was applied to the analysis of all things. The aim was no longer to explain the ways of God to men, but to understand the nature of humanity and its world.

Alexander Pope put it that the proper study of mankind is man. No one disagreed, and Diderot went further, arguing that it is only the presence of humans which gives the world meaning. Human individuals were unambiguously at the centre, and they were on their own there. Furthermore, from Locke onwards, the doctrine of original sin was rejected: humanity is freed from its past, from transcendental determinations. Bacon had already asserted that science can free humanity from the Fall. In tandem, the belief in free-will was radically generalised into the ideal of 'freedom'. Kant in his 1784 essay, *What Is Enlightenment?*, wrote of man's final coming of age, his maturity as a free and rational being, under the motto *sapere aude*—dare to know.

In fact, what happened was as Luther had predicted. Reason and free-will were on the other side of the scales from faith. Emphasise them long enough and the scales would tip, as they now did. Luther's outraged cry against Erasmus, 'You are not devout!', came to fulfilment with the Enlightenment. This was in part necessary, for the root of Christian faith was fast withering, leaving humanism either to graft itself onto another culture or go it alone. For the moment it went alone, and took the other cultures with it. In France, a high proportion of the more literate of both aristocracy and clergy had Enlightenment books in their libraries, and Enlightenment ideas in their heads. What Luther had not foreseen was that reason and free-will, in practice, would produce the steam-engine and penicillin, and that material abundance and the conquest of disease would weigh the scales for a very long time against the darkness of faith.

While the men of the Enlightenment themselves looked to Newton, it was another post-Renaissance figure who pioneered the metaphysical way—Descartes. Descartes, the father of modern philosophy, enshrined reason as the presiding god of secular Western culture. The utopian simplicity of his pure rationalism established the new authority that made the Enlightenment possible. At this level, Newton had merely refined Descartes' method and then executed it with superhuman effect. The key work is *The Discourse on Method*, published in 1637. Descartes was an exact contemporary of Poussin, but whereas the great French painter exiled himself to Rome in the south, the philosopher and mathematician moved north, to Holland.

For Descartes, reason is all. The world can be recreated anew, by mind. Descartes provided the philosophy for Bacon's assertion that knowledge is power. He himself embodied the life of heroic reason. In his *Discourse* he makes much of the story of how he came to his method, spending an intense day of thought alone in a heated room. He states as his aim to spend all his life cultivating his reason. The essence of the human individual, and especially of Descartes himself, is to be conscious. The method that follows is radical, starting with a clearing of the decks of inherited beliefs, all of them. The task of reason begins on *terra nullius*, to create the world again from the ground up. The building blocks themselves must also be created out of nothing, by the single power of mind. Unless reason has demonstrated it to me incontrovertibly, I shall not believe it. Descartes' own portentous criterion is 'clear and distinct', without doubt. The palace of reason will be constructed only from propositions that are clear and distinct. The rest is waste.

The most important application that Descartes made of his method was to himself. The question he put was: What am I? What is the nature of being? How do I even know that I exist? The answer, stated as the first principle of the method, was that the one thing I know clearly and distinctly is that I myself am conscious. The incontrovertible manifestation of my being conscious is that I doubt, understand, will, imagine and sense. The first principle of philosophy follows, 'I think, therefore I am.' The literal translation from the original French is 'I am thinking, therefore I exist.' The defining feature of human individuals, what distinguishes them from the beasts, is that they think. Here is the new Archimedean rock. I am, not because God made me, but because of my own innate capacity to reason.

The third and final stage in Western culture's fundamental readings of the nature of being is reached. First, there had been the Hebrew God's, 'I am that I am.' Then Jesus had followed, recasting the central life question in terms of 'I am'—as revealed through his own tragic story. Now, Descartes hitches being to consciousness. He does so without any inhibiting trace of Hamlet's shadow metaphysics, 'I think, therefore I am dead—therefore I do not exist.'

The Cartesian method is deductive. There is no barrier between geometry and physics. An uninterrupted chain of deduction leads from the mathematical origin to revealing the entire natural world. It was at this point that Newton, in his *Rules of Philosophising*, reversed the method, to start with the facts and then move to the theory, the method of induction. According to Newton, the laws of nature are not given—*a priori*—but are in things themselves. In this the Enlightenment, and subsequently most of modern science, followed Newton rather than Descartes, but nearly as much for another reason, the dazzling pre-eminence of the man himself. In his laws of gravitation, Newton had shown for the first time that there are general cosmic laws, not just particular ones as with the orbits of the planets. If there are general laws, accessible to the human mind, then humans can understand everything. Thus the 'I am' through the 'I think' could gain power over the universe. Descartes himself had been boundlessly confident about the results of practical science, and especially medicine—that it would, in time, make humans 'the masters and possessors of nature'.

It is in Descartes' twin formulation, the 'I think' and the 'clear and distinct', that the humanist antipode to Luther's darkness of faith and absence of free-will is finally established. Erasmus' feeble defence of free-will is no longer necessary. Descartes himself simply posits unbounded free-will, the one thing the human individual has infinitely. It is the instrument of reason, 'I can do whatever the intellect presents.' As a result it is impossible for me to do wrong.

The unshackling of reason was the palpable result, and like a young stallion, after being locked up in stables during a long winter, it galloped free with wild and virile exuberance. The main shackle to be cast off was religion. Although Descartes himself had retained a rather formal deism, the eighteenth-century men of reason turned with venom against Christianity. Hume and Diderot mocked the Resurrection as mere illusion; Voltaire made his war cry, *écrasez l'infame*, crush vile superstition. Then, out of this eruption of the 'I think', the decisive blow against religion was struck by history, which now replaced myth. It overthrew the traditional way humans had viewed and valued their past, as a repository of magical stories about ancestors, the formation of the world, the defeat of monsters, and the heroic foundations of peoples. It thereby undermined the traditional Christian orientation which had accepted the Biblical chronology from Genesis to Christ as gospel, and devoted its scholarship to the venerable inspection of the sacred texts in order to illuminate the holy law and its saintly bearers. Rational, critical methods came in, and before long the authority of the Bible began to diminish.

Once there was history then, as Hume demonstrated in his *History of England*, the facts became supreme. Bayle wrote of his ideal historian, 'Truth is my queen; to her alone have I sworn the oath of obedience.' The Bible suffered from internal contradictions. It also suffered at the hands of the new sciences, discoveries in biology and geology being at odds with Old Testament chronology. Once the past was rational history, subject to the methods of the clear and distinct, then Christian culture had lost one of its main supports. God was in process of being reduced to a god of the gaps in understanding, gaps which would be steadily closed. The way was prepared for the progressive view of evolution, that the history of humankind and its cosmos was one of continuous progress, reaching its high-point in the eighteenth century with the emergence of the free, rational individual. Of course, this was just another myth, the liberal one, which reality in the next two centuries would tarnish, but at the time of the Enlightenment it seemed another glorious jewel in the crown of the 'I think, therefore I am.' As we shall see later in our story, the cultural consequences of the replacement of myth by history were to be profound.

In its exhilarated rampage, reason trampled religion into the ground. Morality suffered a similar fate. Here the story is more complicated, with a number of threads weaving together to produce a vision of a human world beyond good and evil. The first thread was the ancient Socratic one, that it is ignorance that generates evil. In the utopia of rational adults humans will be too enlightened to do wrong. Descartes put it that if he saw everything clearly it would not be possible for him to sin. This was extended in the economic liberalism of Adam Smith with the notion of the 'invisible hand', a principle in the free market that is assumed will automatically correct imbalances, and injustices. A conception of the moral law survives here, but it is in the process of being demoted to servant caste in the kingdom of reason.

The next stage is utilitarianism, and the view that free individuals pursue their pleasure, and this pleasure is their virtue. Morality is thus dissolved into the category of happiness. This thread ended with Bentham's 1776 formulation that the measure of right and wrong in a society is 'the greatest happiness of the greatest number'. In effect, morality has been eviscerated into a technical computation of units of pleasure. It has been rendered rational. Ethics, if it is anything, is a derivative of reason and pleasure. The one theory of punishment celebrated by the Enlightenment, that of Beccaria, was wholly utilitarian, only interested in deterrence, with no notion of retribution—that a crime sets up a moral debt that must be paid off.

Another thread in the Enlightenment 'beyond good and evil' was material determinism. Reason rampant, following Newton, was discovering laws of nature in every nook and cranny. The inevitable result was that the free play of critical intelligence destroyed the newly won freedom. The life of plants is determined by natural laws, just as the orbit of planets is determined; the nature of animals is determined, so too must be the nature of humans. La Mettrie provided the metaphor, in the title of his book, *Man the Machine*. Holbach saw everything in nature determined by its essence. The direct conclusion was that there is only determined being, and therefore no morality, only necessity. The human individual is a tool of the laws of nature. Diderot put it that all a man can say is that he was born fortunate—call that virtue; or unfortunate—call that vice. Nothing is 'against nature', so there is no point moralising against the facts. The facts are simply facts; accept them. Sadistic pleasure is a fact; psychopathic violence is a fact; incest is a fact.

Actually Spinoza, already in 1674, had anticipated the argument. He put it that a stone endowed with consciousness would imagine that it was rolling downhill of its own free-will.

In this manner, the Enlightenment watered the seeds of its own destruction. Unbounded reason is restless, it fidgets, it cannot sit still. Remove the traditional limits, and it will pry into every drawer. Exploring every logical possibility, it becomes perverse, perhaps out of boredom with itself, and finds its greatest pleasure in contradiction—this is the masochism of reason. From Descartes' arcadian palace, it soon bolted head first into the wall of material determinism. From that impenetrable barrier it rushed straight into another, the sceptical one championed by Hume. Hume's scepticism was built on the thought that, if we can trust only the senses and the method of induction, then we cannot be sure about anything. That the sun will rise tomorrow is merely a supposition based upon past experience. We cannot be certain. There is no clear and distinct knowledge except in the remote and exclusive world of mathematics. Not only is the moral code a convenient fiction, but even the so-called laws of nature are provisional. Starting with the 'I think', and being ruthlessly consistent, leads to the 'I doubt'.

In the wake of the Enlightenment, science continued to prosper. The Cartesian ideal survived, and its authority held through the demonstrable success of practical science, although it would never again throw off the shadows of either determinism or scepticism. The consequences of rampaging reason for morality were, however, more grave. A hint of things to come was provided by the most dizzily acrobatic of all eighteenth-century minds, that of Diderot. Here was chatterbox reason incarnate. Diderot's reduction of virtue to fortune, and his biological determinism, that nature gives us our character and there is nothing to be done about that, leads him into a primitive utilitarianism—if it brings pleasure, do it. It also impels him to advocate new titillations for playful human individuals. Why should not the devotees of reason, for whom scientific experiment is a pleasure, try out cross-breeding? Would it not be fascinating, for instance, to create a man-goat? What fun!

Diderot was entirely naive, without any idea of the monstrous world with which he was flirting. It would not be long, however, before another Enlightenment disciple of 'I think, therefore I am', the Marquis de Sade, was taking this line of thought one further stage, that of deliberate depravity.

Reason also moved into politics, creating the form that would dominate the West for the remainder of the humanist epoch—liberalism. Here the ideal of freedom combined with the *I* to enshrine the autonomous rational individual as the central unit of society. Liberal political theory leaves individuals free to pursue their own happiness. It entrusts power to those elected by autonomous citizens choosing of their own free-will. Socialism, in terms of these first principles, was to prove no more than a subspecies of liberalism. In practice, reason's politics worked in England, where its ideals were gradually integrated into institutions whose stability had, as we have seen, strong aristocratic and Protestant roots. When, however, it tried to go it alone, with a full utopian surge driving to build a liberal system out of nothing, the result was the French Revolution of 1789. Here was reason's greatest test: it had the chance to show what it could do left to itself, what it could create once it had annihilated the prejudice, superstition, intolerance, gross inequality and exploitation of the existing European social order.

The greatest happiness of the greatest number was not the result of 1789. No rationalisation could excuse the Terror, followed by the Napoleonic devastation of the entire continent—the French sacrifice alone through this period being of the order of two million lives. We are back to the fact that humanism on its own is not a culture, and the attempt to make of it more than it was, opened the way for demonic forces that only real cultures can check.

For Descartes, the humanist *I* was not enough. He had to predicate it on the 'I think'. He thereby inaugurated radical rationalist humanism which drove the extraordinary burst of intellectual enthusiasm which was the Enlightenment. Its greatest gift was science, and, above all, medical science. Its greatest immediate curse was to give authority to the childlike utopianism that spawned the French Revolution. The 'I think' had severely limited the 'I am' in spite of all the gushing about freedom. The deification of reason leaves much in human nature in the dark. The Enlightenment was in fact rather narrow-minded, naive about human motivation, about society and about politics, always in danger of barricading itself inside an arid and abstract intellectualism. Moreover, it was from within its own ranks, and early in the day, that it produced the first reaction against itself—Romanticism.

Already in 1750, Rousseau wrote that reason corrupts us, the arts and sciences degrade all that is sacred. His alternative god was to be passion, his own riposte to Descartes: I feel, therefore I am. Rousseau himself set the mood with his personal delight in nature, his rhapsodic description of being alone at night in a boat, on a lake in moonlight. Wordsworth would prefer storms and mountains, as would Byron, adding adventure. Romantic love was the golden path to the experience of full passion, the more turbulent, intense and anguished the better. Actually, love needed to be unrequited to generate the intensity of longing that gave Romantic heroes their aura of poetic sensitivity, of all-absorbed, delirious dedication to their beloved. From one extreme, of deified reason, Western culture jumped to the opposite, deified passion.

Romanticism shared with the Enlightenment a radical individualism, valuing autonomy—and hostile to custom, tradition, and, above all, the bonds of human community. It kept freedom as its pivotal ideal, an unbounded free-will. At the same time, it had no sense for the normal business of society, including politics. Nevertheless, its other-worldliness, absorbed by the personal, the intimate and the private, was complementary to the Enlightenment, starting where the other stopped. Whereas the Enlightenment was reason, light and optimism, Romanticism was emotion, darkness and pessimism. It was heir to a curious cross between Calvin and Hamlet. Its individualist intensity, obsessed with the inner self and its emotions, was a sort of degenerate Protestantism, with salvation displaced into passionate ecstasy, moral conscience into an intoxicated reflection on self and its sensations. Many Romantic artists, poets and philosophers were the sons of Puritan clergymen.

The Hamlet lineage is equally revealing. For the Enlightenment, there was no recognition of death. The brightness of the rationalist noon removed the shadows. Death was simply out of mind. In eighteenth-century France, in general, hell became unpopular, and the devil was turned into a comic figure. However, the repressed returned in force in the Romantic reaction. Byron, Keats, Shelley and Schubert all died young. The formative German Romantic work, Goethe's *Sorrows of Young Werther*, had as its climax the hero taking his own life once he realised his love would be eternally denied him. Death becomes more explicit in late Romanticism, its imagery prevalent in the paintings of Caspar David Friedrich and, differently, the Pre-Raphaelites. The 'love-death' is central to Wagner's *Tristan and Isolde*, and to Tennyson—in *Morte d'Arthur*, *In Memoriam*, and *The Lady of Shalott*.

In the earlier Romanticism of Wordsworth, it is the violent passion of nature that infuses enough vitality into the sensitive anti-social individual, now without God, to keep death quiet. This is short-lived. The next move, once awakened Romanticism has turned to face the skull, is to give a mysterious transcendental quality to death, the corpse of the pale and beautiful Lady of Shalott drifting into Camelot, or the fantasy left with Keats' knight-at-arms, 'alone and palely loitering'. The heartland is melancholia. We are back with Hamlet's 'absent thee from felicity awhile'. And, of course, it was the Romantic movement that enshrined *Hamlet* as the central imaginative work in Western culture, replacing the Bible. Just as the French Revolution replaced the Christian calendar with its own secular one, starting at Year One, so too the alternative messiah had been found. It was not to be Socrates, the more obvious choice. It was Hamlet, and he proved an enduring icon, casting his baleful authority across two further centuries. Thus, we have arrived at the true Romantic ideal, to experience a beautiful death. Moreover, this beautiful death was to be humanism's own last ideal.

Behind the scenes, the eighteenth century was directed by the problem caused by loss of faith. It was the decline of Christianity that led to the schism between reason and romance. Poussin had united spiritual and sensual. Now the spirit floundered without its animating faith, and sought its substitute in enchanted reason. This degradation, aggravated by the neglect of the sensual, immediately produced a counter-solution, that of enchanted romance. Fate and soul still survived, although the former was in danger of the profane transformation into material determinism; and the latter, of either the banalisation into ego, or the madness of being housed in unstable isolated individuals addicted to emotional chaos. Reason and romance were opposites that needed each other, just as the bourgeois needed the bohemian. (The bohemian was, by the way, Romanticism's most stable child.) The schism remained, and in the nineteenth century, when reason was not prospering in natural science it began to inflict its own curse, the rationalisation of the world, just as Romanticism turned increasingly towards the skull, and became nihilistic. In the eighteenth-century prime, we witness both the high-point of humanism and the beginning of its decline, as things fell apart, and into fragments none of which were able to stand alone and command the world.

Romanticism would endure in the West, as one of the dominant presences in its fantasy life, above all articulated through popular culture—from the nineteenth-century romance novel to twentieth-century Hollywood cinema. Perhaps its most influential medium was that of popular music, and in this it drew on its late-eighteenth-century high-culture masterpiece, the operas of Mozart.

Mozart applies reason to romance. What he finds, in his perfectly formed work *Così Fan Tutte* (1790), is that all of his lovers, without exception, are fickle. One moment they swoon of their eternal passion for the other; in the next breath, once put under the slightest pressure, they switch the object of their till-death-us-do-part promises. The truth is that they are in love with being in love, not each other—it is the passion itself that engages, the other person hardly more than an arbitrary triggering device. The intoxicated words are a froth of nonsense. Mozart is echoing the wisdom of the pungent French psychologist, the Duc de la Rochefoucauld, who in his *Maxims* of 1678 wrote, for instance, that, 'Love, like fire, needs constant motion; when it ceases to hope, or to fear, love dies.' Rousseau's 'I feel, therefore I am' is exposed, by the cool eye of reason, to be an excuse for weak character lacking in moral fortitude, and puffed up with self-important promises, whilst hypocritically blind to itself.

Yet Mozart redeems romance. The solos and duets sung by his lovers are put to the most sublime music ever written. Through feeble characters and their silly actions, the soul speaks, and with a breath of such intensity that they are transported into a higher, sacred realm. The crystal fineness and beauty of the music inspires the feeling that it voices the one true love, yet in reality the content is just as likely to be narcissistic remorse over a recent betrayal. To Mozart's view, the narrative does not matter much. As long as the soul sings forth its divine communion, the imperfections of the housing character are trifling—profane distractions. So romance enables both a spirited exuberance about life, and a rising above the none-too-admirable human plane.

***

There was one serious attempt to save the Enlightenment, right at the end. Kant realised that it was not true that reason could survive without a moral foundation. He further realised that the liberal utilitarian reduction of virtue to pleasure merely displayed the shallowness of reason on its own. In *The Groundwork of the Metaphysics of Morals* of 1785, and *The Critique of Practical Reason* of 1788, he developed his response—a rationalist ethics. Kantian ethics is the masterpiece of the Enlightenment, and it gave humanism its one real chance to stand on its own feet. Moreover, with Kant we are back with Brutus. Already in the late 1770s, in his *Lectures on Ethics*, he had stressed that the universal end of humankind is moral perfection, and that in morality honour is pre-eminent. It is not necessary that I should live happily, but it is that I should live honourably. The dishonourable life is not worth living. This time, however, humanist ethics is independent of the aristocratic root. Its main debt is to Socrates, and the view attributed to him at his trial by Plato, that the higher life should be dedicated to knowing goodness, in order to act justly.

Kant's system centres on the moral law. This is distinct from the natural law, the laws of nature which science studies—the domain of pure reason. It is a universal code of morals, given *a priori*, neither dependent on human experience, nor derived from human nature. It holds for all humans at all times who have reason and will. The principal task of human reason is to understand the moral law, which it serves—this is practical reason. The moral law is opposed to self-love; reason is opposed to instinct. In illustration of how seriously reason takes its moral task, Kant notes that the one subject of enduring interest when mixed company gets together in conversation is the moral worth of an action and how this reflects on character. Humans take a keen interest, whether in gossip or serious discussion, in evaluating good and bad behaviour.

The moral law has, in effect, replaced God, centre-stage for Kant. God is an abstraction, not essential to the system, although Kant himself does keep him in the wings. The view that there exists a body of universal moral laws governing the human condition is standard to the Western tradition. It is implicit in Plato and Aristotle's model of the cardinal virtues; it is explicit in Roman Catholic doctrine—indeed, Kant's moral system echoes Stoic philosophy on the one side, and Thomas Aquinas on the other. What is new is welding this system to the humanist conception of the individual.

'The moral law is holy.' Known through reason, it acts through will. Will is autonomous, that is, free. Human individuals as rational beings may act against their impulses. They know what they ought to do, and are free to do it. Freedom is the condition of the moral law; conscience is impossible without free-will. Free-will is thus the sole principle of ethics. It is what makes humans more than animals. It is determined by reason, but reason in turn acts in obedience to the moral law. Finally, the motive for obeying the moral law is not egoism, that is pleasure, but reverence. The moral law is sacred. Its subjective, psychological correlates in the individual are shame and duty, not happiness. Its reward is that it opens up revelation of an intelligible world.

There are two further principles of Kantian ethics. Firstly, there is the *categorical imperative*. It follows from what has already been stipulated. In practice, an individual should always act in the same way he or she would judge it right for every other individual in the same situation to act. In other words, act in obedience to a universal law, irrespective of the consequences of the act—irrespective of personal interest. The act is good in itself. Kant's suggestion is that, in reality, this is precisely what good people do—only listen to everyday conversation about the action of others in ethically difficult situations to understand this.

Kant calls the second principle the practical one. It is independent from what has gone before. Man is an end in himself. He should never be treated wholly as a means. The individual, as a rational being with an autonomous will, is a member of a kingdom of ends. To treat others as a means to an end is to treat them as objects or slaves: it is to deny the key to their humanity. 'Morality is the only condition under which man can be an end in himself.' That is, his dignity is dependent on morality, on him being treated as an end in himself.

Kant well knew the foundations of humanism. He knew Pico's axiom that man can do whatever he wills, that he is free. He knew that an ethics is necessary, that its principle should be honour, and that the *I* must be subordinate to it. Working within the parameters of the Renaissance, but adding his notion of a universal moral law, he developed a system which is coherent, comprehensive and plausible. It both disdains the immoralists of the Enlightenment, like Diderot, and pitches itself directly against utilitarian liberalism—reason is counter to instinct, the moral law counter to pleasure or happiness. In fact, Kant gave liberalism a moral future, by investing the autonomous individual with an ethical dignity, a place to stand as a rational person with free-will respecting the law—'Remember your dignity as a man.' Humanism had at last found an ethics worthy to counter Luther and Calvin, one that was profoundly to influence subsequent Western assumptions. If liberal humanist culture has any gravity of its own, it is in what Kant spelt out. Just one piece of simple, late Kantian anti-utilitarian advice is enough to signify the wholly different calibre of his meditations on ethics, 'emphasise the shamefulness of vice not its harmfulness'.

Here is the foundation for what Durkheim will call, a century later, a 'religion of humanity'. It posits the human person as 'the only idea retained as unalterable and impersonal above the changing torrent of individual opinions'. The attempt is to deepen the humanist *I* by steeping it in moral being, postulating an ethical sense as innate to humanness. That ethical sense is absolute in the Kantian manner. The appeal is to a common humanity, overriding selfish motives. This try at a viable humanist culture will be reviewed in Part Four of this book.

The most enduring and tangible legacy of the Enlightenment, apart from science, was the added strength it injected into the liberal-democratic political form. By the second half of the twentieth century, a belief in universal human rights—that all humans are in essence equal, whatever their differences of culture, race, class, gender, age, or capability—had come to prevail throughout the West. While the origins of this view lie in the teachings of Jesus, it was the Enlightenment's reformulation that slowly came to influence both public opinion and practical politics. Kant's principle that every human being should be treated as an end in himself, or herself, had gained cultural sway, and provided political democracy with a moral basis. Here is one of the major achievements of the modern West.

***

Kant, like his great German predecessor, Luther, knew that free-will was the crux. He went the opposite way. His conscience is at odds with that of Calvin and vintage Protestantism. It depends on a paradox, as Kant himself admitted. Will, being autonomous, is a law unto itself. Yet it obeys laws. Kant assumes that the rational person, knowing the moral law, will obey it. This is the core axiom of any rationalist ethics, to be found originally in Socrates, and later in Descartes. Without it, the Kantian system collapses.

Experience suggests that the axiom is not just naively optimistic, but false. From *The Iliad* on, the greatest of Western literature has regularly portrayed people knowing what reason tells them they should do, not doing it. Achilles knows he should not get carried away in a man-slaughtering rampage; he knows he should respect the corpse of Hector; in the heat of his rage for revenge, he takes no notice of reason's supplication, nor does he later regret his excess. Hamlet knows with unambiguous clarity what he should do—kill Claudius—but his will refuses to obey his mind. Hamlet cannot control his own will. As a result of his lack of free-will, his inability to act, just about everybody gets killed, guilty and innocent alike. The consequences *are* important. Moreover, the fact that modernity should have chosen as its messiah such a strong embodiment of the lack of free-will as Hamlet—and over Socrates—is a sign of how unconvinced, beneath the rational surface, it was by the Kantian line.

In reality, reason does not determine will. We do not need Homer or Shakespeare to tell us this. At the end of the day, the brilliance of Kantian ethics suffers from a superficiality, its failure to take account of the power of the demonic in human nature, the weak, subsidiary and circumscribed role of reason, and above all that, as Luther thundered, faith is only to be encountered in the dark, where the individual is in chains, without freedom. That the moral law is universal, and sacred, is all very well, and true, but to know it, in the vital sense of coming under its thrall, is not within the power of reason. The forces which determine goodness—that is whether humans obey the moral law or not—have little to do with either reason or will. They have to do with faith and its obscure minions.

Kant was deaf to the death of death. Indeed, this admirer of Rousseau, even after he knew about the Terror, continued to defend the French Revolution as the sign of the progressive triumph of reason. He continued to defend the men who had made it, for according to his moral logic their high-minded ideals made them good men, excusing the reality that in the name of freedom they had tortured and murdered on a barbarian, subhuman scale. Indeed, the Enlightenment had abolished the traditional hell of the religious imagination, only to prepare the way for its earthly incarnation. Descartes, the modern founding father of reason, had spent years alone by himself wondering whether anything exists. His greatest son, Immanuel Kant, for all his rectitude and lucidity, could not face the truth about the clear and distinct in political form, and so he too finally retreated inside the floating glass balloon of pure reason.

Part Three

FALL

Chapter Nine

MOCKERY, MOCKERY EVERYWHERE

Marx and Darwin

With the end of the Enlightenment the spell breaks. The clear and distinct light of naive reason is eclipsed. Worse, the eternal quest to achieve a death of death, and gain life, is abandoned. Holbein's corpse rises and begins to haunt the darkening world. Humanism's third movement has started—its descent into oblivion. Reason survives, but without honour, and it turns nasty. In its prophets a new unconscious current surges, driving reason to profane and to mock. All that was fine and beautiful and good in Western culture is turned upon—with malice. Demons awake and grope towards the surface. We have entered the period of the wrecking.

At the concrete historical level, it is the events in France between 1789 and the defeat of Napoleon in 1815 that break the spell. It is ironical that Kant should have completed his ethics on the eve of the French Revolution, the event that was to compromise his system fatally—as, that is, a metaphysics which might stand alone. The period 1789 to 1815 destroyed the cultural ideals of the Enlightenment. The exercise of naive reason was no longer possible, except in the narrowly circumscribed domain of science. In fact, science was forced into a cultural vacuum, sealed off from moral issues, where it was left to its own logic—and there it continued to prosper.

The same period that saw humanism's political ideal shattered in practice, witnessed across the English Channel the industrial revolution, the pioneering phase of technological innovation and factory organisation that would transform the material life of the West. Very soon this economic revolution would begin its own eating away at the foundations of the old cultural traditions, by generating vast quantities of new money, and creating entirely new processes of work and leisure. On its own narrow, liberal-rationalist front it revitalised the Enlightenment, giving it authority through major segments of the middle classes, ones that had lost contact with their roots and were yet unaware of darker developments at the cultural frontier.

In the nineteenth century, in other words, the main span of bourgeois culture continued happily on in a liberal, rational and optimistic manner, flirting with Romanticism. But the illusion had cracked, and where it mattered in the long run—at the cultural frontier—the wreckers were advancing.

The impact of the French and industrial revolutions was possible because the old authorities were already tottering, under threat from within. The main reasons for weakening authority were, as we have seen, that the humanist ideal in its Enlightenment form had gravely loosened both Christian and aristocratic roots, and been unable to establish itself on its own. The only form remaining at the start of the nineteenth century with some vitality was the bourgeois one—a Protestant-humanist hybrid. England was a partial exception, where the aristocracy still retained some of its traditional confidence and presence.

The weakening of cultural authority released two forces. The first was *rancour*. When the gods fail the leading believers—inevitably highly-strung, emotionally wrought, intense characters—turn in rage against them, as did Milton's Satan against his God. Jesus' didactic saying, 'He who is not with me is against me', applies to the intellectuals—the priests of culture. This is son against father. As the old cultures falter, they are turned on viciously, and ground into the dirt. The sons smell blood. First come the beasts of prey, then the vultures. Such are the simple mechanics of rancour, and they are universally to be observed when cultures decline. We have already considered the most subtly brilliant harbinger of modern Western resentment—Velázquez.

The second force was *chaos*—as characterised by the ancient Greeks. In the nineteenth century, it manifested in two forms. One of them was honest: nihilism. The last places to stand, the rocks of Christian salvation and aristocratic honour, had splintered, leaving nothing under the feet. Voltaire's 'your dignity as a man' and Kant's 'dishonourable life is not worth living' were soap-bubble ideals—at least, when required to survive on their own. The new reality was Nietzsche's 'death of God' and Dostoevsky's 'everything is permitted'.

Chaos came too in an alternative form, that of the liberal pretence that it is possible to live according to reason and free-will. Bourgeois culture in decline—as faith in its Protestant God faltered—was redirected along these lines, imagining that the mansion of the clear and distinct, of wealth and status, would allow its denizens to sleep securely and contentedly at night. This illusion would not redeem for long. Under the sunny liberal surface the demons were astir.

The completeness of the nineteenth-century degradation of Western culture is illustrated in a painting with which the century closes—Edvard Munch's *Madonna* (see fig. 8). A woman is naked. Long black hair swirls crazily; a red beret mimics a halo; red lips, black closed eyes; she is caught in a dreamlike vortex of helplessness and anguish. In the face there is a shade of peace, of the end of torment, but it is the peace of a corpse—as Munch himself made clear in an accompanying text. The colours are those of lurid, perverted sensuality—and death. Nothing matters, apart from a peaceful end, Hamlet's felicity. Yet this is no longer Romanticism's beautiful death. She is a profane, soulless animal trapped in an empty world, wanting to escape her torment.

Under attack is one of Western culture's central sacred images—Mary the Madonna, as representative of the vocation of motherhood. Munch is painting against Raphael. Spermatozoa frame his Madonna, including at her bottom left, a hideous embryo: all she can give birth to is death. She cannot even nourish herself. It is hardly two centuries since the high point of Poussin's Magdalene and what we have reached is no culture, culture with one last mission—to disenchant, challenging that this is the true Madonna, life is no better than death, join me in despair. Velázquez, not Poussin, has gained sway. Munch pictures one of the victims of dead culture. Even the mocking is over. It has won, and all there is left to paint by 1900 is, 'I am *not.*'

The story of the nineteenth-century demolition of its inheritance could be told through painting. It could be further focused down, onto the progressive desecration of the female body. Such a narrative would start in the late eighteenth century with Goya's *Maja Nude*, a stiff blank-eyed body stripped of the constraints preserving the sanctity of woman, vital to the classical genre from Titian to Rembrandt. Goya's nude, scandalous to its time, is frigid flesh with a brazen stare.

The story would continue with the exquisitely crafted pornography of Ingres, and in particular his nude *Odalisque* (1814)—she is winking flesh, a seductive object for voyeuristic male indulgence. It would reach its climax with *Olympia*, Manet's deliberately shocking masterpiece of 1865, the naked whore who stares mockingly out of the canvas, goading the viewer. Shameless, she too is an object drained of spirit, in whom the sensual decays into unblinking indifference. In this painting, black cat and African maid are both terrified by their mistress—they see the human beast exposed. Manet, who referred to Velázquez as 'the painter of painters', had made his intentions explicit with his *Picnic on the Grass*, of 1863, and even more with his *Christ Corpse* of 1864, an echo of Holbein's profane messiah. Within this history, the last significant work in the neo-classical mode, articulating higher truth, was painted in 1824—the tragic *Massacre at Chios* by Delacroix.

Such an overview would provide vivid illustration to the attack on the Old Masters, and the comprehensive success of that attack. The result is Munch's *Madonna*, followed by Marcel Duchamp's *Urinal*, a piece of plumbing exhibited in 1917 in New York as a work of art, asserting its own profane self to be of equal value to a Raphael *Madonna*. Duchamp challenges: By what authority can anyone today judge my urinal to be less true, beautiful or good than anything else. There is no such authority. Everything is permitted!

These two works speak for themselves, and for what happens when things fall apart, when culture deliberately destroys itself in order to give birth to chaos. However, painting did not play a leading role in the nineteenth-century fall of European culture. It merely provided one of the ancillary battalions. As a subversive agent, Manet, for instance, produced nothing of the force or calibre of *Las Meninas*, nor of his revolutionary contemporaries—Marx and Darwin.

***

Humanism's third movement, its fall, is to be located squarely in the nineteenth century. By 1900 it is all over, and where twentieth-century culture remained in the humanist mode, as it almost entirely did, it no more than continued to work through a destructive logic already well established. There are three quite distinct phases to the humanist going under. The first stage is active demolition of the old cultures, the period of the mockers. The second stage is recognition of nihilism, one that produces resistance, a fight back—what might be termed dynamic nihilism. The third stage is acceptance of nihilism, as inescapable, and the giving in to it—what might be termed resigned nihilism. It led to withdrawal into the unconscious, surrender to oblivion. These three stages will be dealt with respectively in the next three chapters.

The master wreckers were Marx and Darwin, although the latter was unsuited temperamentally for the unwitting role he played. There were, of course, hundreds of others, in all cultural areas. It was these two who grasped hold of the holy tablets of the Law and smashed them so comprehensively that they could not be pieced together again, at least not in the humanist epoch.

Marx was chief mocker. Three aspects of his character combined to make him ideal for the role: an instinct for where the enemy's strength lay, an intelligence that in its learned incisiveness made him tower over other political radicals, and an unscrupulously violent temperament. He was driven by his own aggressive disposition into apocalyptic imaginings of the total destruction of Western culture. His work is loaded with emotionally charged images of devastation, and a mere handful of pages in the many thousands is devoted to his utopia, the communist Eden that would grow out of the ashes of revolution. When questioned by a journalist late in life about the essence of human existence, Marx answered, 'Struggle'. What he really meant had been anticipated in a poem he wrote when he was eighteen, in which the hero, Oulanem, asserts:

> The world which bulks between me and the abyss
> I will smash to pieces with my enduring curses.

Marx saw that the remaining cultural form with strength was the bourgeois one. So he set out to destroy it. Rancour was his main weapon, attributing mean motives to the object of attack. The key work is *The Communist Manifesto* of 1848, the handbook of revolution, socialism's unholy Bible. It works with a combination of at times brilliant invective and simple theorems. Bourgeois society is based on greed; it is avarice projected as a social principle. It reduces personal relations to self-interest, to the 'callous cash principle'. Its method of operating is 'naked, shameless, direct, brutal exploitation'. Its culture is hypocrisy, with ideals of law, morality and religion merely prejudices cloaking self-interest. It has destroyed all that is honourable in work and soaked it in 'the icy water of egotistical calculation'.

In other words, the bourgeois individual is mean and selfish, with no higher motives than his or her own material gain. The caricature extends, into the inner sanctum of bourgeois culture—the family. It too is based on gain. The wife is merely an instrument of production, a possession, little more than a prostitute. The greatest pleasure of bourgeois men is in seducing each other's wives. Marx, in effect, takes the Romantic contempt for the bourgeois—as a boring and hypocritical mediocrity—several stages further by introducing moral categories. The bourgeois is the force for evil in the modern world.

As the bourgeois is driven by one motive, greed, he has reduced all social life to one dimension, the economic. Here Marx introduces his most important and enduring observation, that in modern times the great revolutionary force is the economy—capitalism itself. The remorseless process of industrial creation and destruction undermines all traditional beliefs and customs. Marx blames the bourgeois for the supremacy of economics. Then, in a curious identification with the enemy, he asserts, as an objective law, that history is dominated by economics, and can only be understood by his method of dialectical materialism.

Thus for Marx, as for his postulated bourgeois, economics becomes god. Two intellectual motives underpin this move. The first is that Marx has convincingly observed that economic change has become the great cultural destroyer. The industrial revolution is doing the dirty work. The second is that economics is impersonal. Marx was profoundly misanthropic and it would not have suited him to find revolutionary heroes amongst his despised humanity. He took special pleasure in using terms like 'scum'. The view that humans are merely pawns of world history, its tools and victims, suited his disposition. The economy is an avenging god, and it is just—the engine of secular apocalypse. Even the political sphere— from the influence of singular leaders to the different forms of the State—is reduced to a plaything of economic forces.

The last axiom in this vision of negativity is that while the present is diabolical, the past was no better. Just as humanity is scum, it has never created a golden age. What came before the bourgeois epoch was oriental despotism, the idiocy of rural life, and various other modes of exploitation usually held together by that opium of the people—religion.

The understanding that human history when scrutinised closely is not an elevating sight is as old as the Greeks. Marx brought some new perspectives, pivoting on the observation that there are different social classes, each with its own interests and consciousness. They play complex interacting roles in forming institutions, and history is in part a struggle between competing classes for power and resources. He gave flesh to this theory through a range of historical studies. He pioneered sociological thinking about the nature of labour, and its relations in one direction to the human essence, in the other to social productivity and wealth-creation. Marx was also the principal and most influential figure in drawing attention to the plight of lower social orders—the impact of history on them.

Marx is tainted humanism. He asserts that 'Religion is only the illusory sun, around which man revolves, until he begins to revolve around himself' and gives pride of place in human activity to science.

While concurrently developing a systematic way of thinking about social processes, he falsely claims the status of natural laws for his theories of economics. The works of Shakespeare were his Bible. He continued the Kantian emphasis on humans as ends in themselves—not to be treated as objects. He believed that once the individual is freed from necessity—alienating labour, class oppression, scarcity—then the I would flourish, in the confident, self-defining humanist manner. His *Economic and Philosophic Manuscripts of 1844*, calling for emancipation from all alienation, is a type of humanist manifesto. His entire work hinges on the assumption that, in the communist future in which there is no scarcity, society will be a dynamic and harmonious assembly of creative Renaissance individuals. The West's experience in the second half of the twentieth century, of what individuals actually do with material abundance, makes it clear that this assumption was false.

On the other hand, Marx is the father of social determinism, according to which humans are feeble pawns in the hands of history, the creation of the society in which they were born. This Marx is profoundly sceptical about humanist free-will, more inclined to the Greek view of domination by necessity. Capitalism, while freeing humans from one type of determinism—that of tradition—has instituted its own equally coercive economic order. Individuality is an illusion; we are social products. Marx argues that a painting by Raphael is merely the result of the material circumstances of the age and place in which the artist lived. This eloquently rancorous example thus reduces one of the sacred objects of Western culture to profane economics. Marx would have admired Duchamp's *Urinal*.

Nietzsche observed that the temper of modern culture, set by the intellectuals, is rancour. He could have found no better case study than Marx. There was not just a sneering vindictiveness. After Marx's public attack on fellow socialist Wilhelm Weitling, Pavel Annenkov noted his proud and faintly contemptuous manner and remarked that his 'sharp, metallic voice was well suited to the radical judgments he was delivering on men and things'. There was also hypocrisy. Marx scrutinised his daughter's suitors with bourgeois strictness and never acknowledged his own bastard son.

That the 'scientific' motive behind his work was entangled with a darkly apocalyptic one is illustrated in his dependence on reports from the factory inspectorate on cruel working conditions. The very existence of that inspectorate in England, and the continuing reform of factory conditions through Acts of Parliament that their reports produced, directly contradicted one of Marx's leading arguments—that under capitalism exploitation of workers must increase. Moreover, the prophet of equality, of the free relations between person and person, was no democrat himself. He scorned elections, and tried to take over and run in a ruthlessly dictatorial way any organisation he had anything to do with.

'Equality', as an ideal, turns rancorous. What it really means, in its modern political mode, is tear down everything superior, starting with Raphael. Marx himself displayed no interest in democracy; 'equality' becomes an ideological whip with which to profane the existing order. The 'dictatorship of the proletariat' is a rationalisation for smashing political order, put into practice in the Russian Revolution, which is symbolised, as was its French predecessor, by the ransacking of the palaces.

The extent of Marx's self-identification with his bourgeois caricature is shown by the hallmark achievement of his ideal society, the communist utopia—material abundance. Goods will be plentiful; there will be no scarcity, no need for private property. Thus, the man who mocks the core of bourgeois culture as a mania for possessions, has as his own dream a world of plentiful commodities. What the dialectic boils down to is that after the West has been turned into rubble and corpses, we will see a miraculous inversion, its transformation into a land of milk and honey, without struggle.

Dostoevsky observed that the essence of the nineteenth-century revolutionary idea was the negation of honour. This is rancour, the mockery of honour and what it serves—higher law. The Enlightenment, with the late exception of Kant, had neglected honour. But Kant's 'the dishonourable life is not worth living' now fell on deaf ears. Rancour does not usually motivate suicide; it is more likely to drive a systematic programme of destruction, aimed precisely at eliminating everything noble, which shows its personnel up for what they are. Humanism could not hang on to honour, unable to ground it in its own soil. So, in the end, it turned against it. The specific target was the last cultural form with weight, the remaining house in which honour dwelt, if fitfully—the bourgeois one.

It did not need to be like this. There are elements in the revolutionary movement driven by genuine compassion for the poor, and a concern to improve the callous working conditions in many factories—in short, by a concern for justice. The most endearing quality in Marx himself was his kindness to children, and his spontaneous response to suffering. These fine feelings, however, stayed private. They did not feed through into his work. The difference is clear in the empathy with which Dickens and Dostoevsky, for instance, describe the life of the poor, or Simone Weil outlines, in a simple Christian manner, the inhuman conditions of factory labour. She actually worked on a car assembly line—Marx never visited a factory, in spite of invitations from his patron and co-author, Friedrich Engels.

It would be unfair to read the movement Marx inspired, socialism, as solely driven by rancour. It had other roots, and especially the liberal one. Socialism has been part resentment, against the wealthy or those of higher social rank; part compassion for the poor; and part the liberal pursuit of freedom. Its third dimension celebrates the *I* freed from all traditional limits of blood, class and wealth. In itself, socialism does not play a significant part in the story of the rise and fall of humanism. It was too much a subspecies of the genus that did—liberalism.

Liberalism was not rancorous, yet it proved a great destroyer of culture. It was rather naive, in the Enlightenment mode. While it did not itself mock, it cleared the decks for the mockers, as Marx himself perceived. In the cultural battle it played the role of what Lenin would call the 'useful idiot', doing the job for the vandals, but in all innocence. The devil never had a better henchman than liberalism, because its heart was ingenuous.

There were areas in which liberalism was benign, as there still are. Three stand out. In politics, the liberal ideals of freedom and the responsible, rational adult, grafted onto Protestant vocation and aristocratic honour—two real cultural ideals with depth—helped develop the parliamentary democratic system that has remained the political backbone of Western society. Second, experience has shown that the free market, theorised initially in the liberal tradition by Adam Smith, has, for all its imperfections, produced greater prosperity, and with a reasonably fair distribution of goods, than any other form of economic organisation. Third, the liberal ideal of the autonomous individual, articulated by Kant in the imperative to treat all people as ends in themselves, has, in the bourgeois mode, produced an everyday life that is relatively just. These are considerable achievements.

***

Let us now turn to the other side of the scales, and the greatest example of liberal vandalism, at the hands of the most brilliant of all the offspring of Descartes and Newton—Charles Darwin. For Marx, the world is determined by economics and the iron logic of History. For Darwin, it is nature that rules, through the mechanism of natural selection. Biology replaces theology, and indeed it also replaces the humanities. Once upon a time, it was God who created the earth and the species that dwell upon it. Now the creative agent is evolution. Its principle is functional: whatever works, will survive. The existence of things on earth has nothing to do with their truth, their beauty or their goodness. It has simply to do with power. The strongest—in the sense of best adapted—within a given environment survive. Weakness means extinction. The new god, biology, recognises one quality. In the struggle for survival, if it is powerful it is good.

Darwin is the child of Enlightenment science, becoming its greatest exponent—the Newton of the biological sciences. This science has entered a moral vacuum, pursuing its rational ends without heed of wider consequences. Darwin himself was narrow, his whole mind focused like a powerful spotlight on the patient observation of nature, and virtuoso theoretical extrapolation from what he saw. He was cold to art, poetry and music.

The time of the Renaissance man is past. On the other hand, Darwin is not rancorous. His masterpiece, *The Origin of Species*, is written with clear and honest enthusiasm. The argument has a lucidity and systematic elegance quite unlike that of the wildly uneven and thematically jumbled flagship of Marxist science, *Capital*. Darwin is master of the clear and distinct.

It is the cultural consequences of Darwinism that are grave. In question is not the core of evolutionary theory itself, but rather the wider effects of its becoming the queen of modern sciences, where its explanatory tentacles stretch out over ever new territory, from microscopic molecular worlds to the very cosmos. Of concern here are Darwinism's cultural implications for what is 'human', indeed for the entire metaphysics of creation and being.

Darwin joins the mockers with his reduction of humanity to a plaything of nature. Within evolution, humans are merely a passing part of a continuum between the amoeba and some futuristic mutation. Their primal parent is neither Adam nor Brutus, but the monkey. As much as Marx profaned his own Jewish ancestors, Darwin went further, laughing at humanity and its veneration of the past, saying if you really want to know where you come from, go to the zoo, and study that parody of yourself, the great ape. He is your true father. Darwin's mockery is all the more devastating in that it is not grounded in personal prejudice or on a bogus science like dialectical materialism, but on the most powerful and enduring theory produced by modern reason, one which subsequent studies and experiments have only strengthened. Moreover, it is an elegantly simple theory.

The theory that we humans descend from the monkey has delivered two major blows to Western culture. First, it knocked the stuffing out of the humanist *I*. The material determinism of the Enlightenment is trifling next to Darwin, for he teaches that *I* stand on nothing. Humans exist because they do what every creature does—struggle to survive. So far the environment has been kind to them and the species has flourished. This is temporary, as is our position at the top of the evolutionary scale. It is inevitable that the time will come when some chance mutation, or change to the environment, will exterminate humanity. We shall go the way of the dinosaurs.

There is no place for free-will. Nor is there much dignity. In terms of the new sacred, biology, the amoeba has greater distinction, for it has survived far longer than the human species. All that remains of orthodox humanism is that reason allows us to retrospectively plot our own evolutionary path, a path that leads to future extinction. The new science portrays us as no more than supercharged fish endowed with consciousness—physical specimens with profane consciousness—who die accordingly.

'No free-will' is accompanied by 'no responsibility'—only power. Darwin himself argued that our moral code has evolved from primitive forms in lower species, from the social instincts that are necessary for the survival of some species, for example ants and bees. This means that any law is provisional, to be kept while it is useful, entirely relative to the moment of evolution. No such law can be incontestably binding. If such utility is the foundation of the law, humans will soon stop obeying it, for one person's use is another person's nuisance. Everything can be disputed, for everything is relative. There are no absolutes. Darwin thus provides the tank corps for the *blitzkrieg* of modern relativism.

What follows is one of the central axioms of Western nihilism—that life is absurd. Natural selection works through chance variations in a species. The great human individual championed by the Renaissance has become simply the product of a myriad tiny changes from the amoeba. Each one of those changes was random, purely due to chance, before a favourable environment, as second stage, determined that it would survive. In other words, I am the product of a million years of myriad accidents. Another such 'accident' will eliminate me and all my kin, ancestors and descendants. So what is the point of it all?

Darwin provides the answer: struggle to survive. This, however, is the vital spot where we are not animals. For us, the biological imperative is inadequate. Moreover, Darwin himself has so demoralised us by pointing out who our great forefather was, the founder of our race at one remove, that the absurdity has tended to undermine the will, the will to survive.

Darwin protested that his theory was compatible with religion. His hunch was that very few primordial forms existed at the start of evolution—perhaps only one—from which all plants and animals descended. His theory did not explain the creation of these primordial forms. Perhaps God? He misses the point. The theory of evolution was to prove so comprehensively successful that it made the humanist faith in science impregnable. If Darwin himself had not explained the creation of the first form of life on earth, some other scientist soon would, and so on, to the creation of the earth, the solar system, and finally the universe. It would be the scientific explanation that would prevail. After Darwin, all serious Western enquiry into the meaning of things would assume material causation. Supernatural causes were finished for the remainder of the humanist epoch.

The second effect of Darwin on Western culture was deeper and darker. The theory of evolution tapped directly into the unconscious. Darwin received a huge public response due to the association of man with monkey, the 'ape theory' as it was popularly known. The search for the 'missing link' took off, and has continued unabated with the not very successful search for early human forms, for signs of the transitional species between ape and man. The first publication of Darwin's theory roused no popular interest—Darwin became a household name only when the implications for the origin of man became clear.

What was it that riveted the public, stopping it in its tracks, and drawing its interest hypnotically towards this new idea? The answer lies in what features in much of the scientific literature, and even more in the many popular articles and cartoons: the image of the monkey, especially its head, and its family resemblance. What the monkey head resembles is more precise—the human skull. Its lack of long hair, its pronounced eye sockets, its prominent teeth, and its jaw make the skeletal form more obvious. There is some affinity too between the monkey's bulbous jaw and the similarly rounded protruding human cranium, although one is at the lower front of the skull and the other at the upper rear. With eyes half-closed, gazing intently at the monkey's head, one is caught by a dream image, blurred and distorted, of the human skull. We are uncannily transfixed into the shoes of Holbein's ambassadors.

Here is the focus of Darwinian research, under the unconscious equation: ape equals skull. The reference is double, indirectly in the resemblance, directly in that the study of skulls becomes central to the Darwinian enterprise. The thousands of subsequent books on human evolution are full of diagrams of skulls.

Reason bares its fangs. In Darwin, the demonic returns, with the imagery of a medieval hell sublimated into modern scientific forms. The agent was an honest, good and gentle man who would not have stepped on an ant. If there is any personal element, it is in chronic sickness that dogged the second half of his life. Unwittingly, Darwin pioneers the scientific worship of death. This sleight of hand is accomplished by shifting the sacred site from the cemetery to the academy. The horror is kept under strict control, only let loose in the most civil and disguised sublimation, the study of the origin of species, or the *Descent of Man*, as Darwin put it, in another unwittingly loaded title. The invitation to modernity is to join me in the museum, in the laboratory, in the lecture hall, for the scientific study of the skull. Through this study revelation will come. There is no threat, for the supreme human faculty—reason—is in command. Let us worship at the temple of nature; the skull is our holy relic. Science, my science, shall neutralise the fear of death.

This was fraudulent. What Darwin did was to clear the cultural decks for the emergence of the demonic, unchecked. He himself once admitted that his theory was like a murder. Reason lights the tunnel housing Luther's monster, opens the gate, but has no means for taming it, merely providing quaking humans with the delusion that to study its habits is to draw its teeth. Your original father is the gorilla: look again, and see what he represents—death. Once there is Darwin, there is the terror, and apart from it—nothing. Science, as Marx saw, is the agent of nihilism, the destroyer of culture. The celebrated title, *The Origin of Species*, is deep with double meaning. Without God, the ultimate question is on what do we stand, a question now purely about ancestors—given that the death of a fish endowed with consciousness is merely death. Here is Darwin's quest, his search for origins, and he is frank and direct about it, as he is about the simple answer: the skull disguised as the great ape. So it is that in the post-Darwin West, the slightest allusion to the gorilla has sent a hideous shudder through us all.

Natural selection not only knocked the stuffing out of humanism. It eliminated religion. Humanity has no divine origin: we were born, originally, in the primeval swamp. Christ is merely a member of a species, five stages removed from the squid, and further evolution will some day render him obsolete. The Catholic Church made the appropriate, if too timid, reply: let science explain the history of the human body, as long as it does not include the soul. But its reply was to fall on deaf ears, as far as the direction of Western culture was concerned, and Darwin was left with a free hand to degrade the metaphysics of man even lower than Hamlet's 'quintessence of dust'. The twentieth-century, Nobel Prize-winning neo-Darwinian scientist, Francis Crick, would mock the soul as a mere assembly of nerve cells.

The Times in London recognised the new cultural order, welcoming the burial of Darwin's body in Westminster Abbey, 'The Abbey needed it more than it needed the Abbey.' After Darwin, Munch is free to paint the Madonna as neurotic, in a traumatised swirl of reds and blacks, able only to create a dead embryo, itself an image out of a Darwinian textbook.

Darwinism, as total philosophy, is refutable by example. It would hold that there is no essential difference between a group of men abducting a teenage girl, assaulting, raping and murdering her and a pack of wolves attacking a deer. Both acts are driven by violent instincts, with the partial contrast that in the human case the aggression is against the same species, and may contravene some collective survival need. Any self-respecting human community recognises the two cases as fundamentally different. There is a brutality to what the wolves do, but no culpability or guilt: animals are innocent, which gives their behaviour an honest simplicity. In the assault on the teenage girl there is extreme breach of the collective conscience of the community, and Kantian universal moral laws. More significantly, what is sacred in the victim has been violated. The act is a desecration. After the event the entire community is contaminated by spiritual pollution, something wolves do not spread.

The new scientific picture of the world is utterly dispiriting. Darwin himself, in his *Autobiography*, recalled how he was once filled with wonder, when standing in the midst of the majesty of a Brazilian forest. He had been convinced there was more in man than the mere breath of his body, 'But now the grandest scenes would not cause any such convictions or feelings'. The one true belief is in natural selection. In the shoes of Darwin, the joyful bird song at dawn is transformed, at best, into intellectual curiosity about a species sending out warning signals in defence of its territory. Once one starts to think like this—about birds, new-born babies, romance, death—the magic is compromised.

Gone too is the hushed awe at the curtain to *Julius Caesar*, as Antony hymns to Brutus, 'This was the noblest Roman of them all.' Gone is the haunting imperative to human loss of way, Mary Magdalene, as she lies prostrate at the feet of Jesus washing them in her gushing tears. Gone are all heroes of conscience, all images of courage, honesty and fidelity. For, what we see is merely the acting out of social instincts that humans have inherited from ants, instincts that are there because they serve a survival function. The crucifixion is itself a superfluous superstition, a gruesome irrelevancy: we live on in the genes inherited by our children. So all of modern art, literature and philosophy that portrays life as a dismal wasteland, as a sort of living death, worships at the feet of the new prophet—Charles Darwin.

Darwinism harmonised with liberalism. Indeed, the latter's classic text, John Stuart Mill's *On Liberty*, was published in 1859, the same year as *The Origin of Species*. Both were English, and both were blithely ignorant of culture, somehow assuming it unnecessary. The liberal model of society is a benign survival of the fittest, blind to the demonic—in denial of tooth and claw. It leaves all humans free to their own individual devices, under the assumption that all will be well—sweetness, light and progress. Both philosophies saw morality as a sort of awkward encumbrance. Moreover, both played a similar role as cultural destroyers, pitting reason and the striving individual against the forces of tradition, honour, authority and revealed religion. History turned out to be on their side. Their dystopia would be realised.

The benefit of the liberal-humanist order was the conquest of most of the traditional sources of human misery—squalor, hunger, disease and brute labour, but not warfare. Its cost was that life in the palace of reason became typified by the banal bureaucratic routines of the office, and the depressive leisure routines of television and overeating. On the one hand comfort, on the other a disenchanted world emptied of meaning, with the one remaining limit on freedom—death—unanswered, and therefore rising to the surface to cast its cold shadow across life.

In this, the heritage of Marx combined neatly with the liberal-rationalist one. The attack on the bourgeois helped turn him into the Marxist caricature, only interested in material things, believing in science, liberty and progress. The ideal of progress was itself reduced to the purely material, as comfort—what would come to be rationalised as Gross National Product, the key indicator of social well-being. In short, science and liberalism provided the new ideology for the middle class once its Protestant root had withered. The vertex of that ideology was economic progress. Marx had some sense of these affinities, sending Darwin a copy of the second volume of *Capital*, inscribed from a 'sincere admirer'.

We have been considering, in this chapter, one of the darkest episodes in the long and turbulent history of Western culture. It was when humanism turned nasty. There is the sickly, gentle Darwin, in retreat from the world with his large family, like a child in his patient devotion to his studies of plant and animal. In truth, he is another Holbein ambassador, unmusical and with narrower interests, glimpsing an obscure image of his holy grail, the origin of origins, and it is the same one, but this ambassador is going to convert the whole of Western culture to his quest. He is prophet as well as ambassador of death; his book, the most influential in the nineteenth century alongside *Hamlet*. Then there is rancour incarnate, Marx, projecting onto the honourable, pious, middle-class gentleman the low passion to seduce his neighbour's wife. No honour, no trust, no fidelity—nothing but greed.

The cultural consequences of Darwin were—consciously—that religion and honour are irrelevant, we should ignore them and continue on in the enlightened pursuit of comfort; unconsciously, that the origin of origins is death, and it rules. The cultural consequences of Marx were—consciously—that selfishness and economics rule, and culture is merely a cloak disguising base bourgeois motives; unconsciously, the gods of culture have betrayed us, so let us annihilate them.

Gustave Flaubert's dismal and bitter novel, *Madame Bovary* (1857), was merely the leading example among thousands which parody middle-class life as empty and hypocritical, clutching at possessions and status, titillating hysterical women and straight-laced men with Romantic fantasies. The mockers had won the field. Marx and Darwin had developed into a comprehensive victory what had started two hundred years earlier in *Las Meninas*, with the needling away at the old order and its king. Western high culture has, since the middle of the nineteenth century, devoted itself with hardly an exception to the demolition of the traditional order, especially in its bourgeois guise. Marx became the father figure for a tide of intellectual movements through the twentieth century, with a dynamic core that was angrily critical, hostile to the culture of the West and the authority of its institutions.

Chapter Ten

INTO THE HEART OF DARKNESS

Kierkegaard and Nietzsche

So it was that the two high cultural works to preside over the nineteenth century—*Hamlet* and *The Origin of Species*—focus on the skull. That Hamlet is invited to take centre-stage signals that nothing remains to mock. The old order is flimsily wooden. In the chillier air, the spectre of Holbein's corpse saturates the atmosphere. It balefully redirects the mocking drive into the heart of darkness. On the frontier, the wild charge of the vandals is already over. Shelley's Ozymandias, the tyrant doubling as Western culture itself, catches the mood:

> Round the decay
> Of that colossal wreck, boundless and bare,
> The lone and level sands stretch far away.

After the mockers—*nothing*. The West has entered nihilist modernity, humanism's last site. The man who understood its nature best was the German philosopher, Nietzsche. With an unerring nose for first principles he sniffed out the humanist test of finding a place to stand, 'Since Copernicus man has been rolling from the centre toward X.' By his own time the task was hopeless. His Zarathustra exclaims, 'Who will hereafter raise high the image of man?' Nietzsche was the last of the humanist philosophers, knowing the end but still trying to save the order. In his 1882 parable on the Death of God he outlines the implications of life without a sacred beyond. A madman runs into the marketplace screaming that we have killed God. In a series of demented questions he spells out the implications:

> How were we able to drink up the sea? Who gave us the sponge to wipe away the entire horizon? What did we do when we unchained this earth from its sun? Whither is it moving now? Whither are we moving now? Away from all suns? Are we not perpetually falling? Backward, sideward, forward, in all directions? Is there any up or down left?

Without God, life is either horrible or absurd. Then silence!

Next, Joseph Conrad arrived as the new ambassador, carrying the message to everyone with a gift for reading culture who came after Nietzsche—all who were likewise mesmerised by the nihilist challenge. His own 1899 wrestling with the *God is dead* question—*Heart of Darkness*—takes the defining locus of modern civilisation to be the metropolis. Life in the modern city is absurd: people full of stupid importance; some property; meaningless petty routines; the butcher on one corner, the policeman on the other; a healthy appetite and filching a little money; order kept by holy terror of scandal, the gallows and the lunatic asylum. Life is 'that mysterious arrangement of merciless logic for a futile purpose'. Nothing survives Conrad's relentless nihilism. He portrays the highest and the best only to ruin them. And his juicy little tale—which would be retold again and again through the twentieth century—is littered with skulls.

Once the nihilist metaphysics was recognised for what it was, and that its time had come, the first response was to fight. This is the phase of resistance, of dynamic nihilism. It produces the two great pieces of modern theory, ones that got a firm and direct hold on the crisis of late humanism. Their authors were Kierkegaard and Nietzsche.

There had been an earlier phase of resistance, of a different kind, born in immediate response to the French Revolution. This was conservatism, with its founding work, and enduring masterpiece, Edmund Burke's *Reflections on the Revolution in France* (1790). Burke recognised the mockers, correctly predicted the results of their acts, then he chose, rather than wrestling with nihilism itself, to fight against its advance, by restoring the old order. He fancied neither reason nor romance. Conservatism has endured as an opponent to the humanist mainstream, has an achievement or two to its credit, and is worthy of some passing attention.

Burke saw the barbaric consequences of utopian reason applied to politics, of trying to build a new social order on 'clear and distinct' Cartesian principles, founded on abstract ideas about the rights of man. He knew the weakness of intelligence in relation to the demonic outrages of which the human beast is capable when unchecked. He knew its weakness, too, in understanding the nature of the institutions that check such forces—such institutions take generations to build, and thereby embody the accumulated wisdom of myriad forefathers.

Social order depends on custom, tradition, authority and hierarchy. Deep cultural roots anchor things. Burke strove to preserve the aristocracy, and in particular its structural role in the political system of constitutional monarchy. He himself was the grand theorist and defender of the hybrid aristocratic-Protestant English parliament. His guiding principle is caught in advice he gives as to how to approach the faults of the State: as one would the wounds of a father, 'with pious awe and trembling solicitude'.

Long before Marx, Burke saw that Enlightenment modernity was at odds with tradition. His *Reflections* are written with the feverish pungency of wounded rage, of a man fighting for his honour—violated, outraged, and helpless. Conservatism has been largely reaction, futile reaction against the juggernaut of modernity, a series of last ditch stands here and there, on occasion successful for the moment while the war was steadily lost. Its one great success was Burke's own, the preservation of parliamentary democracy. That masterful English creation would prosper for the rest of the humanist epoch, spreading throughout the West, while all around it religion waned, courtesy declined, a law-asserting high culture turned into a rampaging desecrator, and most of the social hierarchy with its complicated tiers of obligation was flattened.

One strand of conservatism was not reaction. It recognised the dogged, narrow-minded virtue of the common people who, in spite of being encircled by celebrated mockers and an educated elite of nihilists, would cling to their traditions and stick to what they believed to be right and wrong. Burke rhapsodised on the English:

> Thanks to our sullen resistance to innovation, thanks to the cold slug-gishness of our national character, we still bear the stamp of our forefa-thers ... We know that we have made no discoveries; and we think that no discoveries are to be made, in morality; nor many in the great princi-ples of government, nor in the ideas of liberty, which were understood long before we were born, altogether as well as they will be after the grave has heaped its mould upon our presumption, and the silent tomb shall have imposed its law on our pert loquacity. In England we have not yet been completely emboweled of our natural entrails.

There is desperation here, knowing the cause is right, but fear-ing it to be doomed. The time calls for extremes—more obvious in the case of Burke's French contemporary, Joseph de Maistre. For de Maistre, the only hope of preserving the old order lay in the aboli-tion of education, and the instating of the sacred altar and the exe-cutioner as the two pillars of society. Jane Austen, too, saw the precarious state of things, describing in her sociological novel, *Mansfield Park*, how one foolish generation under the influence of the new ideas could destroy an age-old great house—its authority tottering. Thirty years later, the French aristocrat Alexis de Tocqueville answered in the negative his own question as to whether democracy and stable culture are compatible.

The problem for conservatism was the tide of modernist humanism—so strong that neither aristocratic nor Protestant cultures could be rescued in their existing form. While a new Reformation was required, conservatism at best staged a series of holding operations, directed by an unworldly vision of the future as a hazy nostalgic recreation of an idealised past. It lacked the colossal initiative demanded by the task, and tended to withdraw into cogent, pessimistic analyses of decline.

Nineteenth-century conservatism would soon focus on a more specific theme—loss of community. It saw the essence of modernity in the steady erosion of strong unified belief and local ties—symbolised in the traditional village. Here, it found the causal dynamic driving the emerging social pathology of lonely individualism; of senseless mobility from place to place, job to job, relationship to relationship, commodity to commodity, and idea to idea; in short, the pathology of a rootless and restless existence, absurd in its busyness. This view would become axiomatic to the mainstream of sociology, theorised most fully by Émile Durkheim, in his study of *Suicide* (1897)—the title itself an unintentional metaphor for the state of Western culture.

***

Both grand theorists of the cultural collapse of humanism, Nietzsche and Kierkegaard, were of Protestant stock. The Luther–Calvin root had gained singular strength in the West.

Furthermore, the orientation of the two exemplars of English cultural conservatism, Edmund Burke and Jane Austen—while being contextually aristocratic—was directed by a Protestant ethos.

It is, however, the Danish philosopher Soren Kierkegaard, coming from a Lutheran milieu, who will recognise with greatest clarity the consequences of failure to restore his religion. If he cannot work a new Reformation, all is over. Kierkegaard dedicates his life to achieving the *death of death*. He returns to the Protestant heartland, by his time its own type of darkness, to search for the faith that eludes him. In the process he finishes the job Rembrandt had started, to confirm whether or not there is a place to stand. We recall that Rembrandt failed, principally because he lost confidence that humanity was up to the divine call. The father of faith, Abraham, lost his mind because of the personal and ethical violation demanded by God.

Kierkegaard takes the next and final step with Abraham. Bypassing the issue of sanity, he questions whether he had faith at all. Kierkegaard was a man of his time, unable to retreat into the secure and unproblematic Christianity of the past, desperate to find a path back to faith that he could take seriously, given what he knew. The result is late humanist modernity's single great piece of religious wrestling, and Protestantism's second crisis.

Kierkegaard argues that human experience in modernity has broken down into three distinct spheres—the aesthetic, the ethical and the religious. They have become stages in cultural decline, with the religious collapsing first, followed by the ethical, reducing life to the aesthetic plane. Kierkegaard attempts a restoration. The major works are *Fear and Trembling* of 1843 and the *Concluding Unscientific Postscript* of 1846, although fragments of the picture appear elsewhere.

What then are the three spheres, or stages? The aesthetic is the sphere of pleasure and the senses, of the individual's pursuit of temporal happiness. Kierkegaard's main example is the love affair. Don Juan is a paradigm of the aesthetic, dedicating his life to the art of seduction. An aspect of this is the psychological observation of mood and motive, in self and other. It is the sphere of Romanticism, of concentrated indulgence in feeling, in aroused passion, in beautiful pleasures. It values artistic expression and individualism.

The second sphere is the ethical, characterised by universals, with behaviour determined by laws higher than the individual. It depends on action, whereas the aesthetic may be conducted in the imagination. If a love affair or flirtation is aesthetic, then marriage represents the ethical. It is not to be ended once individual pleasure diminishes. The ethical places limits on pleasure. One marries husband or wife—a collective category—rather than individual. That a spouse may be interesting, intelligent, beautiful and charming, or not, is irrelevant—for these are all aesthetic categories. Duty and obligation preside over the ethical.

The ethical is the domain of the tragic hero—for instance, Antigone sacrificing herself for the Law. Brutus and Uriah are ethical heroes; Hamlet fails in these terms. The ethical is the sphere of the bourgeois—of marriage, vocation and duty, all in obedience to universal law. Kierkegaard's notion of the ethical is Kantian.

The third and highest sphere is the religious. Like the aesthetic, it is individual-centred. Based on suffering, its characteristics are subjectivity, inwardness and guilt. There are three different modes of religion. There is primitive religion, in which the sacred is pure and direct, a cosmic canopy over all things. Humanity is bathed in divinity. This is the world of the child, of simple guilt, in which punishment works: a smack from the father and all is better, the child enabled to run cheerfully back to play. We have lost this world. What remains is Religiousness A or Religiousness B.

'A' is having faith that faith exists, but not faith itself. God is indirect and invisible. He has no outer presence, unlike primitive religion in which he is entirely external to the individual. Humans are shut up in themselves, locked in subjectivity, in dread yearning for the only escape—revelation. The greater the dread, the greater the person. Neither beast nor angel experience dread, for neither have guilt. In between is humanity. Religiousness A is an absurd condition, in which what humans cannot know, but only believe, is the object of their faith, which necessarily eludes them. This is Kierkegaard's own condition.

Religiousness B is faith. A miracle occurs and there is a *leap of faith*, from 'A' to 'B'. Once again the outer calls. This faith is like being in a ship that has sprung a leak, enthusiastically pumping yet not feeling the need to find harbour. In the same situation the understanding, unlike faith, stretches its arms towards the shore, and sinks. Religion is the relationship within the individual to eternal happiness. The path to it is through dread, distress and paradox. Whoever arrives is higher than the tragic hero. Mary, for instance, is higher than any heroine. Entirely alone in her mission, she foresaw the dreadful fate that would befall her son. 'Was it not dreadful that this man who walks among the others—was it not dreadful that He was God?' And what of the disciples, 'Was it not dreadful to sit at table with Him?'

The problem here, for Kierkegaard himself and modernity with him, is how to achieve the leap of faith. All else is trivial. But Kierkegaard is beside himself with doubt, a doubt we observed in Calvin. Kierkegaard is open about his uncertainty, placing it at the centre of his spiritual quest. It is the monster without whose killing he cannot live. He longs for the simple world of the child, or the Catholic, for whom punishment works. His own guilt is unquenchable.

Further, it is laughable that human suffering should move God—how petty that would make him. There can be no remission of sins. The role of guilt now is to bore into the soul to make a person deeper, more inward, more pitiful—more dreadful. And then the paradox: out of sheer tormenting inwardness comes faith; out of the ashes, new life. Such is Kierkegaard's hope. He even creates a method, a discipline to replace fasting and chastity. His message to the individual is to so burden yourself with inwardness and guilt that the paradox will explode into faith. This is hard-core Calvinism taken to its logical extreme. The only anchor in a chaotic and ephemeral world is my inner self and my conscience. Intensify them!

Kierkegaard devotes *Fear and Trembling* to the question: Is faith possible in the modern world? He poses the question through meditating on the strongest conceivable example, Abraham, the father of faith. Like Rembrandt, he concentrates on the testing of Abraham's faith, through the sacrifice of his only son, Isaac. In Kierkegaard's categories, what God asks of Abraham is that he attain the religious by annihilating both the aesthetic and the ethical. He is required to destroy his own happiness, by murdering his pride and joy, the pleasure of his life, his reason for living, Isaac. Furthermore, he will ruin his marriage, turning his wife in uncomprehending hatred against him. He is also required to break almost every major moral law: thou shalt not kill; thou shalt protect the innocent, especially your own children; thou shalt not betray trust between—here between father and son—not to mention the laws of the tribe and its patriarch, to continue the blood line.

Abraham is neither an egoist pursuing pleasure, nor a tragic hero—he renounces the universal laws of ethics. The knight of faith gives up both desire and duty, unlike the tragic hero who gives up desire for duty, and gains the universal. For Kierkegaard, Abraham is utterly alone with his act, his three-day journey, his setting up of the sacrifice, his response to Isaac's troubled question about the location of the sacrificial animal. No one can understand Abraham. His wife certainly cannot. No one can know what drives him, that intimate private word of God. Abraham is silent, absorbed in what he must do, and the nightmare dread of it, of his own right hand plunging the dagger in, of how he will live afterwards, day after day, night after night, overwhelmed with grief and terror. So it is that God loads his knight of faith with dread, distress and paradox. So it is that he deepens his inwardness. Abraham has 'the terrible responsibility of solitude, of unutterable sighs'. He is the loneliest man.

Again and again through his meditation, Kierkegaard asks whether it is possible to believe in Abraham. Is such faith plausible? What of the enormous paradox which is Abraham's life—that is the question? Think how strong such faith would have to be, to keep him warm at night after the deed, to hold his hand, to keep him sane. Kierkegaard answers timidly, endlessly repeating, 'Abraham I cannot understand.' He laments that he cannot think himself into Abraham's state, for he does not have the confidence of faith. No! It is not possible to believe in Abraham. 'Is faith I wonder to be found on earth?' Kierkegaard swings between adulation and contempt: Abraham offers so much, but he leaves so little. He leaves nothing. But if Abraham did not have faith, he was a simple murderer, a rogue, and of no interest metaphysically speaking.

If faith is not possible, if the father of faith was a fraud, then ethics too soon collapses. All that remains is a debased form of the aesthetic. Such is modern life. Kierkegaard finds it a joke, typifying it by those people in their twenties who believe they have achieved their utmost. There is no inwardness; no seriousness. Dread is interpreted as a disease of the body. People don't call the priest any more lest the patient die of fright. Religion becomes like using a jack in a swamp. Passion too dies, for it has lost its root: faith is the highest human passion.

Kierkegaard pits himself against the times. Unlike the modern hero, whose task is to make things easier, he aims to make them more difficult. His ideal sermon would counter the restless, fidgeting world of entertainment and journalism, by returning every Sunday, with the same originality, to the same theme. So speaks a great Protestant conscience, at its wits' end because it sees clearly the precarious state of its faith, and the increasing frivolity and emptiness of the world in which it dwells.

What then is Kierkegaard's solution? There is a new Protestant agony. Kierkegaard accepts Luther's darkness of faith. He is not interested in the light, for that is at best the plane of the two English lords wagering on the runaway horse, at worst life determined by indifferent pleasures, cushioned in sedative comforts. In the darkness, however, he cannot find faith. He is willing to descend beneath the ethical, like Abraham, but he does not have the firm cord of faith to lead him, only the agitation of unquenchable dread. There is the mental torment of paradox, infinite guilt and no faith. Either one believes in Abraham, or nothing. Therefore it is nothing, and Luther's monster roams in the dark—untamed and untameable.

The core Protestant contradiction—that I have no free-will, but am responsible—became unproblematic once logic had been relegated to its rightful minor place in human conduct. The new contradiction, however, is serious. Kierkegaard's own attempt to reach Religiousness B, to make his leap of faith, is through thinking. It is not just any thought. With peerless ironical wit and ethical-psychological insight, Kierkegaard maps the condition of Western culture and the havoc it is wreaking on individuals doing their best to live within its crumbling structure. On the plane of knowledge, his challenge is to think in the categories in which we live. No more rationalist fantasy about the goodness of humanity, or idylls of social progress; no more otherworldly, fairytale pretence about happiness and virtue; no more Romantic haze! Just the hard facts! For the first time since the seventeenth century, a depth returns to consideration of the central metaphysical questions. Kierkegaard does think in the categories in which he lives.

His solution, which redirects the Protestant contradiction, is to think his way to faith. The hope is to take the path of knowledge in order to reach the path of faith. But Kierkegaard himself knows, as well as Luther and Calvin before him, that this is impossible. Faith and knowledge occupy separate universes. Reason is useless as a means to grace. *Sola fide* is a gift of God. Kierkegaard's attempted compromise is through a certain type of thinking, one designed to accentuate guilt, heighten suffering, intensify inwardness, bring on the loneliness of Abraham, and focus on the paradox which cannot be thought. Indeed, he asserts that, at its core, great thought depends on paradox—that which cannot be thought through. There is truth to this. His next move is to glorify paradox. Faith becomes:

> the objective uncertainty due to the repulsion of the absurd held fast by the passion of inwardness, which in this instance is intensified to the utmost degree.

His logic echoes that of the early Church father, Tertullian, 'Because it is impossible, it is certain.' Kierkegaard puts it:

> A revelation is signalled by mystery, happiness by suffering, the certainty of faith by uncertainty, the ease of the paradoxical religious life by its difficulty, the truth by absurdity.

Here is Protestant modernity's last statement. Faith depends on a miracle, to cut through the paradox to revelation. We do not believe in miracles any more. Kierkegaard does not believe in miracles. Kierkegaard's solution is absurd, pursuing knowledge in order to believe, knowing full well that the mission is hopeless. But he must stick to his mission, for the alternative, what he sees around him, is beneath contempt. At least Kierkegaard has his inwardness to keep him warm, and he has thought in the categories in which he lives, honestly and to the point where there is nowhere left to go. Faith eludes him.

While Rembrandt's doubt was that humans are not up to the divine call—the stuff out of which they are made is of too poor a quality—Kierkegaard's is that they no longer hear the call. They are lost in inwardness; trapped in subjectivity. The monster that they glimpse in the dark, and which they cannot kill, is the Medusa. There is nothing beyond, and therefore nothing under the feet. The shades of the skull start to materialise in front of the eyes. There was to be no serene old age for Kierkegaard, with young kin around him. He died a bachelor, aged forty-two.

***

Nietzsche diagnoses nihilistic modernity from a similar perspective. However, he twists the judgment and inverts the solution. Protestant Christianity becomes the main cause of the problem. It must be killed off completely, allowing a rebirth of the great Renaissance individual. Nietzsche is a humanist—a most unusual one.

Nietzsche's first and finest work, *The Birth of Tragedy* (1872), opens the gambit. Culture is the focus. Human life is lived on the surface, driven by a substratum of demonic instincts, nightmare fears, and a barbaric will to lust and sadism. This is the unconscious, Dionysian basis of reality. Culture's task is to transform or sublimate these Dionysian drives into harmonious and beautiful images that capture the mind and give an orderly direction to how humans conduct their lives.

Nietzsche illustrates this through Raphael's *Transfiguration*. The bottom half of the painting is the dark and turbulent world of humanity, a mad boy possessed by demons, his family distraught and helpless. The top half displays the transfiguration of Jesus, a haunting image of transcendence, a redeeming illusion that only the boy sees. He thereby regains his sanity. For Nietzsche, the greatest example of culture was Greek tragedy—in which the Dionysian is encountered at its most demonic, the individual hero annihilated; but then, out of the ashes, rises an exhilarating sense of the elemental oneness and significance of existence.

In modernity, culture has failed. Either there are the uncontrolled Dionysian excesses of Romanticism, gushing feeling without any ordering principle; or the banal pedantry of rationalism—the dry scholar, the dull priest, the painstaking bureaucrat—eyes closed to the demonic. The result is nihilism.

The second aim of Nietzsche's work is to explain how this came about. One side of the story is that God is dead. Therefore there can be no transfiguration, no faith, no ordering principle from above. Culture depends on a 'redemptive illusion' to sublimate the night demons, to give humans a strong enough sense of a fixed and stable order around them to release the anarchic forces within. Christianity was the last such illusion. It has gone. Hamlet is the new man, without illusion, and he sees the truth clearly and distinctly—not the Cartesian illusion. The truth he sees is that life is either horrible or absurd. Such knowledge can only paralyse. For Nietzsche, Hamlet is the embodiment of modern nihilism.

There is another side to the story. It is developed most fully in the *Genealogy of Morals* of 1887, the work of the 'mature' Nietzsche in which he is at his most pungent, lucid and concentrated. Under the influence of Christianity, the West has experienced a steady disciplining of the instincts, a repression of Dionysus. This has led to an increasingly bad conscience—and mounting guilt. Through this process humans have lost their spontaneity, their gaiety, and their ability to make decisions without laborious inner conflict about what is right or wrong. They have lost their zest for living, to the point of becoming sick of themselves. They have become cautious, timid, bored and boring. Excessive control of the instincts makes for frustration, and the disease of modernity—rancour. The modern individual is malicious irritability wedded to an obsession with comfort. According to the psychology of rancour, the pain of guilt is tranquillised by the letting off of savage emotions against those who are still active and decisive, who retain a place to stand.

This progressive enchaining of the instincts has gone, hand in hand, with growing intellectualism. The pioneering culprit in this history of the deification of reason was Socrates, who rejected Greek tragedy—true culture—as primitive, and replaced it with the first rationalist ethics. Nietzsche pits his psychology against the Enlightenment: the real basis of the modern faith in reason is to allow over-repressed individuals to rationalise their behaviour as good. These are people who have lost the spontaneous ability to act, who find that whatever they do, they feel guilty. We love reason because we need excusing reasons. To have to rationalise every move, out of guilt, makes the sighting of anyone less inhibited trigger virulent envy.

Rancour is the disease of the impotent, made sick by bad conscience. In modernity the sick take over, and the emotion of pity towards those who are worse off, combined with nausea at life, replaces what is healthy and vital—an unselfconscious pleasure in power. For Nietzsche, the contrasting model of an undecadent people was that of the ancient Athenians—with 'hair-raising cheerfulness' their characteristic mood. He posits gratitude, the predominant emotion of Greek religion, as antithesis to the misery of Christianity.

Nietzsche attempted a series of solutions. The first, in *The Birth of Tragedy*, was to urge a return to the metaphysics of Greek tragedy, to myth against reason. Ironically, in this instance he was on the same side as Luther—'this calamity of a monk'—whom he hated. The position could not hold, for it depended on faith in higher order, and Nietzsche had no such faith. With time, he became more and more contemptuous of the darkness of faith, more caustically anti-Christian.

Nietzsche's second and most sustained solution is humanist—the cultivation of great men, of the self-assertive, confident *I*. The Renaissance was the last period of vital culture, in which larger-than-life individuals acted and created at will. Napoleon is the final descendant of this tradition, the last Roman, and Nietzsche lionises him as such, the man unchecked by a bad conscience who proved that we can do anything we will. Napoleon is also exemplar of the incompatibility of freedom and morality. Nietzsche went straight to the flaw in Kantian ethics, highlighting it in the most autonomous man of the nineteenth century—that he was only so because he acted beyond good and evil. The Renaissance for Nietzsche was not reason. It was pure will, the Will to Power. Nietzsche would have found in Velázquez' self-portrait in *Las Meninas*, if he had known it, the incarnation of his ideal humanist, indeed of himself and his own mission.

Nietzsche's 'superman' turns out, however, to be grotesque parody of the humanist ideal, a sign of how close to the end of that culture the West had moved. There is not much difference between Napoleon and the next historical incarnation of the value-creating hero—Hitler. Just how unfanciful these connections are was illustrated in the title of the propaganda film made of Hitler's 1935 Nuremberg Rally—*The Triumph of the Will*. In this Nietzschean phrase is the finale to humanism's opening, 'We can become what we will.'

Dostoevsky was alert to the satanic emanations of late humanism. He delivered a sequence of Christian attacks on humanist monsters. There is his Raskolnikov, who became, significantly, a hero of late nineteenth-century cultural elites—they dubbed him 'the man of the time'. Raskolnikov theorises Napoleon as the extraordinary man who, for the sake of destiny, is permitted to be above the moral law, in his case killing tens of thousands without a blink. There is the nihilist, Stavrogin, a nineteenth-century Hamlet, who out of boredom seduces a twelve-year-old girl and then listens lazily as she commits suicide. There is the revolutionary, Verkhovensky, enacting without conscience the ideals of the French Revolution—he has two passions, eating and destruction. Raskolnikov finds that he cannot become what he will. After committing murder, he is paralysed by his conscience. He is not Napoleon.

If Nietzsche's second solution is horrible, his third is absurd—a mark of his peerless brilliance as diagnostician of culture is that he keeps getting trapped in his own categories. Nihilism is inevitable. Let us then welcome it, embrace it. It will help us get rid of all the moralistic, hypocritical, sanctimonious dross of civilisation. Let us join in the destruction of all values, so that we can start anew. Nietzsche produces his third and last ideal—the value-creating philosopher—and he resurrects Socrates as its first representative. The villain of *The Birth of Tragedy* becomes the hero of the late work.

The mission of the philosopher is to tap the ideals of the time, to see how hollow they ring, as if with a tuning fork. Socrates was the stinging fly, as he called himself, a cultural irritant striking against complacency, unreflected opinion and false belief. The principal task is introspective—Nietzsche calls it 'self-overcoming', whereby the philosopher destroys his own values first. This is a new version, an intellectual's one, of 'We can become what we will.'

There is bad reason, and good reason. The bad is the common modern pursuit of knowledge as rationalisation—a mask enabling the individual *not* to see the truth. The modern intellectual's real fear is to gain consciousness. Good reason has the nerve to endure the awful truth about humanity. It is Dionysian, in method akin to dancing, productive of full-bellied laughter. It forces us to think in the categories in which we live. And indeed, Nietzsche was himself master of his own method—the most insightful psychologist the West has produced.

So Nietzsche's third solution is a fresh Enlightenment—of ruthless psychologising after truth. It hinges on new values. What will they be? Where will they come from? The philosopher is not a man of action, a Renaissance man, nor even a Don Quixote—whom Nietzsche admired greatly for his ability to move in an absurd world. The restoration of culture through mind is impossible—Nietzsche himself stressed as much from the outset by castigating Socrates as the great destroyer. The new values do not come, cannot come, for the reasons that Nietzsche himself made clear. Psychology, however lucid, cannot generate an ethics.

The situation is even more extreme. Hamlet is paralysed by what he sees. The man shouting in the market place that God is dead, is himself mad. And Nietzsche, ever the victim of his own categories—after the coherence of *The Birth of Tragedy*—steadily became more strident and erratic. His last work, *Ecce Homo*, is charged with unrelieved bragging, to the point of delusions of grandeur. Not long after, the author collapsed into a state of catatonic schizophrenia from which he never recovered.

The last words of *Ecce Homo*, the book with a distinctively Christian title, read, 'Dionysus versus the Crucified.' The first letter of his madness was signed, 'The Crucified.' His late works are full of bitter attacks on Christianity, one titled *The Antichrist*. We are back with Luther and Kierkegaard's *sola fide*. Nietzsche knows that if he cannot find a replacement for Christ Crucified, he has lost. He will have turned into Don Quixote at the end, a normal man, whose only wish is to die—Nietzsche hated this ending. Me versus Christ; the humanist *I* as God, or nothing! But who am I? I have tried the mask of Socrates, but I, better than anyone, have seen through the emptiness of reason—'knowledge never creates values'. I have tried

Dionysus, but without Greek tragedy he is a berserk demon destroying all in his path; or, no more than a drunken lout. I myself have to become God, or succumb, like Hamlet, to the all-encompassing horror and absurdity. Nietzsche manages it finally, but only in his demented imagination. His third solution is psychotic.

In madness, he confirms his lunatic identification with Christ, and gives away the source of his rage—he himself cannot become God. The theorist of rancour was himself the most rancorous critic of his own Protestant, Christian roots. His hostility to Luther stems from affinity: the diagnosis is the same, only the path is now barred. Nietzsche takes the alternative, humanist course, seeing Socrates and not Erasmus as its pioneer. What results is that his whole work—modernity's great introspective autobiography in the form of philosophy—demonstrates that the humanist path is a dead-end, one that has now been reached. The philosopher hero destroying values is hastening the very nihilism that Nietzsche has charted as the stagnant hell-pit of the time. There is no way out.

In a footnote to his 'philosopher as hero', Nietzsche launches his last value, *amor fati*—to love fate. From the value-creating great individual—the superman—Nietzsche swings to the opposite extreme. We have no will; we have no freedom; we have no values. All that is left is necessity. So let us worship it. Thus he ends by echoing the instability of Enlightenment thought—in one breath, total freedom; in the next, total determinism. By this stage, the categories no longer edify.

For Nietzsche, no holds were barred. His philosophising with a tuning fork led to the conclusion that truth itself is an illusion. There are merely mental perspectives on reality. What we see are conjuring tricks of consciousness. Emotions govern the eye, and they are subjective. 'Evil' is merely an interpretation; so is 'sin'. Even our assumption about events being caused is a convenient fiction, as for instance in the saying, 'It rains.' What, asks Nietzsche, is the 'it'?

Existence is either horrible or absurd. All is appearance; all is relative; there are no fixed points. Nietzsche drags out the motto of the Assassins, 'Nothing is true; everything is permitted.' He is left with a Darwinian 'will to power' driving the human individual. The real constraint is necessity, not culture. Culture merely inhibits the will, making us sick. Thus Nietzsche shows us where we end if we wed ourselves to the humanist ideals of reason and will, and we are rigorous and honest.

Nietzsche's significance to the story of the rise and fall of humanism is as the last humanist philosopher. He is also significant for introducing the psychology of guilt into the analysis of Western decadence. In particular, he stresses that increasing levels of instinctual repression have progressively reduced confidence in the *I*, have inhibited the will, and have cultivated the intelligence as an agent of rancour. As a consequence, humanity has become tired of itself, hypersensitive to pain, obsessed about comfort, unadventurous, and lacking much desire for anyone or anything. In all of this Nietzsche was persuasive. He was partly right too in blaming Christianity, and especially Protestantism, for radically increasing the cultural war against the instincts.

He was signally wrong, however, not to recognise the other side of Luther's heritage, its serious attempt to address the problem of guilt, reading it as a religious and not a psychological phenomenon—only to be answered by faith, not knowledge. Here Kierkegaard was the truer prophet, even to the point of praising the Reformation for augmenting the burden of guilt in order to focus the spirit religiously.

The crisis for Protestantism came when the theology weakened, leaving the guilt without any cultural forms to sublimate it into images of salvation. While Nietzsche and Kierkegaard provided similar descriptions, their responses were opposed. Nietzsche argued for the glory of the Renaissance without the assault on the instincts, while Kierkegaard, following Luther, dismissed the Renaissance as childish, spiritually speaking. Nietzsche tried to get the last nourishing drop out of humanism; Kierkegaard to turn the tide.

Both paths were closed. The Renaissance man proved not to have the resources to found a new culture on his own. In any case, high levels of guilt had made him culturally obsolete. The value-creating philosopher is a contradiction in terms. It was only in literal madness that the Nietzschean *I* was able to emerge. Nietzsche collapsed in the arms of his own categories: without God, life *is* either horrible or absurd.

Kierkegaard did a little better, in his own wrestling with nihilism. Left to the path of knowledge, as the only way to the summit of faith, he found that he did achieve greater inwardness, deeper guilt, a more tormented solitude, and an all-pervading dread. He failed to reach his goal, but on the tortuous climb he gained a surrogate prize—depth. Kierkegaard is deep. Compared to him, other nineteenth-century figures seem slight—frothily ephemeral. Just put him next to Charles Darwin! There is a type of anchoring in this depth. The paradox, however, failed. He got no closer to the state of grace that is faith.

The path of knowledge leads in circles, spiralling down—into the heart of darkness.

Chapter Eleven

UNCONSCIOUS

Freud

Again it is Hamlet who gives the cue: 'For in that sleep of death what dreams may come ...' After the struggling resistance of dynamic nihilism comes the torpor of resigned nihilism. The humanist I survives as a shadow—lonely, mournful, isolated from community and restless. With no place to stand, it makes its final move, withdrawal into self. Kierkegaardian inwardness rules the world, but it has lost both its religious and its ethical content. It is narrowly psychological. Guilt pervades, and it is a sickness. To be locked in subjectivity means to be dominated by the unconscious. The turn inwards is to embrace the unconscious, hoping for the return of the long lost father, hoping to find a light in dreams. Will and reason have lost their sense. The active life is an absurd waste of energy and time. The last of the great painters, Cézanne and Van Gogh, try to find some order in this retreat from the world. The last of the great humanist theorists, Freud, centres his work on the concept of the unconscious, and tries to find a small part for reason to play.

Freud attempts to reconcile reason and romance. He is a tough realist about the nature of romance, seeing its instinctual basis in the unconscious, driven by the demonic forces Nietzsche called Dionysian. His patients are trapped in unconsciousness, instinct and repressive character becoming the new agents of necessity. It is a psychological necessity that now rules life. Freud pulled no punches in his case studies, liking the shorthand, 'wolf-man' and 'rat-man', to describe two of the definitive ones. The majority of his female patients were suffering from 'hysteria', which he attributed to sexual frustration and analysed without reserve. All proprieties are scrapped in approaching the unconscious: anal compulsion, frigidity, premature ejaculation, and sado-masochism become the stock-in-trade of psychoanalysis. Indeed propriety itself becomes a cause of neurosis; politeness and reticence are symptoms of 'civilised nervousness'. Nietzsche's judgment that 'morality makes us sick' is extrapolated on an imperial scale.

Freud is doctor-confessor to the decadent bourgeoisie, once their lives have been flattened to the psychological plane. His theses echo Nietzsche: the bourgeois temperament has become too severe, producing bad conscience and guilt. The result of over-repression is that individuals become locked in their unconscious, traumatised by fantasies of being chased by wolves or indulging in riotous sado-masochistic orgies. Bourgeois culture in decline produces hysteria, obsession, and depression. Freud himself described the typical middle-class marriage as 'spiritual disappointment and physical deprivation', the frigidity of wives and the impotence of husbands being endemic.

Freud offers knowledge as cure—it can make you happy. The final representation of this stock humanist illusion is psychological knowledge: Know thyself and you shall become well. The objective of Freudian therapy is to discover the origins of neurosis—that is of psychological inhibition—bring them to consciousness, and then hope that awareness will free patients from the bonds of their necessity. Freud was a sober optimist. He did not go as far as the second half of the Socratic credo—that knowledge will make you more virtuous. He had no expectation that his patients might become morally better. Indeed his hopes were at times disarmingly modest, as he put it, 'to turn hysterical misery into common unhappiness'. The movement he founded tended to be more naive, as he was himself at other times, foreseeing a future in which reason had reshaped the instincts. The Enlightenment faith in progress had found one last champion.

The main structure of Freud's work is of little significance for our story. It is hardly more than a dated humanist optimism wedded to Nietzsche. The theory of repression and the unconscious is pure Nietzsche, extended and turned into a system. The main theses are also familiar: repression makes us sick, religion and civilisation are the main culprits in increasing guilt, religion belongs to the childhood of the human race, and morality, history, and philosophy are all reducible to psychology. Even Freudian therapy is the turning into a practical method of Nietzsche's philosophising with a tuning fork, coming to know yourself by destroying your illusions. Both stress intellectual self-overcoming as the way to undermine the last repressive authorities over individuals, and set them free.

Freud's humanism is more simplistic in its half-belief in the possibility of free, autonomous individuals, masters of their own instincts. The conceptualisation of the 'ego'—or in the original German, the I—is its own symptom here. It is uncharacteristically clumsy of Freud to take a word with rich associations in its common, everyday usage, and narrow it. His 'ego' is merely the rational part of the self, the part that uses thought to mediate between the passions, the conscience and the external world. Perhaps this emasculated concept itself represents, in displacement, an unconscious confession about the hopeless failure of bringing reason to bear on the trials of the psyche.

Freud also held to the standard Enlightenment view that science and its truths are adequate replacements for religion and faith, and that secular high culture is capable of serving as a source of moral order. Here Nietzsche was more troubled, his metaphysical

wanderings deeper. He would have granted one of Freud's sceptical themes, that psychological therapy is 'interminable': the patient
is never completely cured, that is, never completely free.
'Interminable' therapy gestures towards the darker Hamlet subtext, that psychological chatter is unable to change anything, or, to
use one of Nietzsche's images, it is like the snake which is merely
capable of turning around and biting its own tail.

The most that can be claimed for Freud as philosopher, in spite
of his rightful status as the most influential theorist of the twentieth
century, is that he systematised parts of Nietzsche, developing a
wide-ranging and penetrating theory with some new areas of psychological detail. His lifelong wrestling with his own inner demons
did give birth to a number of powerful categories and observations,
ones that are indispensable to those who follow—just to list a few:
negation, transference, resistance, the Oedipus complex, the narcis-
sism of minor differences, and instinctual vicissitude.

Freud's urbanity, the stability of his own stoic character and the
high rectitude of his bourgeois life, gave him an equanimity that
made his work impressively clear and distinct, with a masterful
accuracy of insight. But it also blinded him to the emptiness of the
metaphysical world he inhabited. Freud prided himself on his
honesty, but in fact he was far less honest than Nietzsche, who did
not have an urbane bone in his body. Once Freud stepped outside
the confines of psychology he was all at sea, unable to think in the
categories in which he lived.

Where Freud is significant to this story is in playing the Pied
Piper, leading the educated modern middle classes in droves, with
haunting music piping to the rats in the unconscious, leading them
to an illusion of redemptive freedom, but in reality drowning them
in the very unconscious from which they imagine they are being
saved. Freud continues the new, Nietzschean reading of inwardness.
It is no longer the domain of the spirit, of conscience grappling

with wish to produce right action in the world, or when that fails transforming guilt into dread. Inwardness is now neurosis, an instinctual bog in which the modern secular individual is stuck, an entirely psychological bog. The doctor's task is to overpower the gaoler, conscience, by means of reason. In fact, what patients get in their therapy is a beguiling mixture of narcissistic psychic massage and liberal illusion.

The poor patient, rattled with anxiety, suddenly finds that an intellectually gifted analyst, a figure of authority, is willing to spend hours every week discussing his or her every nuance of sordid and petty feeling. Here is the true Freudian sublimation, every repressed instinct may be enjoyed intellectually, in warm and tender talk, as the phalanxes of guilt are disbanded by the ethic of therapy, in which all may be revealed. There is no evil, no bad character, just nasty repressions for which others, notably parents, were responsible. Even when the psychic massage is more severe, exposing raw nerves, leaving the patient distraught and ashamed, even humiliated, its function remains cathartic, for the authority of the analyst is a benignly forgiving one.

Some genuine progress did occur, for psychoanalysis recognised the demonic to which the surrounding liberal culture had remained tenaciously blind. But the method is perverse: one carefully timed hour devoted to polite chat about hideous gothic fantasies—the controlled intellectual tones possible only because of the very bourgeois limits of authority and courtesy the session is meant to explode. This is not at all to do with cure. It is rather Kierkegaard's wager, providing those incapacitated for living—at some levels, everyone in the modern West—with a more stimulating view of themselves. Psychic discomfort is glamorised as a bolting horse and, while the ride was in the past, it was at least an interesting and adventurous past. The irony is that psychoanalysts, who pride themselves on their ability to reveal everything, cannot answer the key question, cannot tell you the simple and important truth: whether you, the rider, have fallen off, let alone whether your neck is broken and you are dead.

Redeeming truths are metaphysical. Psychological truths belong to the lowest, aesthetic order, and, as Kierkegaard observed, they are powerless to contribute to human *well-being*. This ranking deems them trivial. However, once they are brought onto the therapeutic stage, and magnetised by the analyst's authority, they carry such an unconscious charge they appear as ultimate revelations. The whole show is kept on the road by the redemptive illusion that at the end of the analysis there will be no more repression, patients will be freed from their past. They will be liberated.

The legitimating humanist axiom is that trained mind may reform flawed being. The assumption is that character may be rebuilt with the aid of specialist knowledge. The self is like a car engine, with a range of available models starting at the cheap underpowered end, which when thrashed for too long, and run on dirty oil, end up spluttering up the road on two cylinders belching fumes. A Rolls Royce self is also possible, at the end of the process of psychological engineering. A new psychotherapeutic language of 'self-realisation' was launched, perpetually unfolding, to describe the features of such a self.

The question follows: Freed from the past, and from flawed character, for what? There is a simple reply—free to enjoy yourself. Thus reason frees us for romance. At this level, Freud is a relic of the eighteenth century, captivating a philosophically dim and personally desperate West with this obsolete hope fortified by an intellectually commanding psychology.

Patients were not cured. The reality was that typical Freudian subjects simply became more introspective, their lives unchanged apart from the expenditure of more and more time dwelling on self, exactly the opposite of what might make them better—a more active involvement in life. Freud's updated Socratism, that guilt is a failure of self-understanding, was proved a lie in practice.

What happened through interminable talk was that the guilt was articulated, provided with conscious hooks on which to tie its grievances. Brooding absorption in self was given shape. At best, there might be modest gains at the margins. A patient might gain some intermittent detachment from being sunk in a tortured relationship, through coming to understand that unresolved feelings from the past towards parents—of insecurity, dependency, anxiety, and anger—were being displaced into the present. This might ease some of the weight of false or neurotic guilt. The analyst might also be able, by holding a mirror up in front of behaviour, to help make it more honest. But one does not need a grand edifice of psychological theory to play this role; it is that of the frank and perceptive friend, using a bit of Kantian practical reason.

The central problem remained. Modest gains in the negotiating of daily conduct seem to make little difference to the constitution of the patient. Being is not malleable. The devastating example of this was the wolf-man, whose case study is the most important in the whole Freudian canon. In 1980, lengthy conversations with the wolf-man himself were published. He describes his sessions with Freud as enjoyable discussions with a cultivated man, ones that had no long-term effect on his character whatsoever. He came across, late in his life, as an engagingly urbane man—honest and sane.

Here was comprehensive empirical falsification of the foundation axiom of Kantian ethics: reason does not control will. You can know what is wrong with you, but being able to act on what you know, setting yourself free, is another matter. Character is destiny, or, more precisely, necessity. The figure we are reminded of is, of course, Hamlet. Modern culture is Hamlet writ everywhere. Freud would have been closer to the truth, unwittingly so, if he had followed one of his impulses and rather named the Oedipus complex after Hamlet. Hamlet is far more hopelessly neurotic than Oedipus, more guilt-ridden in a modern way, and his attempted self-cure is through endless talk, a 'cure' that makes him worse, serving as a rationalisation for impotence—as theorised by Nietzsche, but not in the case of Hamlet.

We should not understand the *Hamlet complex* as the problem of a man who wants to kill his father and marry his mother, but as that of one whose last passion is to think himself sane and free, who tries it and fails, and is left with a solitary felicity, unconsciousness—which, as he rightly perceives, means death. Here is one of the many reasons why Freud had the greatest of all humanists, Shakespeare, as his favourite writer.

So, Freudian patients became more and more in love with their own embattled unconscious, proud of their sickness. They were not alone. All of the educated middle classes who have read Freud with held breath, but not invested in therapy, all those who have watched quasi-Freudian films, scanned quasi-Freudian newspaper articles, or bought books titled *How to Become a Better Person*, all have come under the thrall of the new authority. In fact, the cultural air the twentieth century breathed was inescapably Freudian. As Philip Rieff put it, the therapeutic had triumphed.

The key is unconsciousness. The ancient Greeks, who were wiser, called it oblivion—*lethe*—which they postulated as the normal human state, one of permanent forgetfulness. The English derivatives 'lethargy' and 'lethal' carry some of the original charge. Freud was himself wiser than his English translator: in the original German, the unconscious is named the 'unknown'.

Take the rat-girl. Herbert Hendin describes her in his 1975 book, *The Age of Sensation*. She is a 1960s American college student. She dreams of a glass of water, clear and calm on the surface, with a rat at the bottom, bleeding at the tail. She is the dream, with her life well organised and successful on the surface. She fears that her inner self is rapacious, a rodent that if set free will gnaw to death anyone close to her. The demon is her femininity, the female erotic, symbolised by the bleeding at the tail. In reality she broke off any relationship with a man once it threatened to become intimate, fearing that if she opened herself to her instincts what would come out would be the rat. She vowed never to marry. However, she was finding less and less pleasure in the safe area of her life—her studies.

The rat-girl is a case of modern repression, trapped in inwardness to such a degree that the outside, her active life, is cut off from feeling, and brings no pleasure. What could an analyst do for her? A lot of talk about vermin, and where they come from psychologically speaking, is not going to give her the one thing she needs, faith in a stable world predicated on a fixed higher order strong enough not to come tumbling down if her rat starts to run amok. In order to risk living, she needs confidence that other humans are secure enough in where they stand not to panic when they meet what she fears is her true self. Freud, and for that matter Nietzsche, could tell her all about her demonic unconscious, but they have nowhere to lead the rat once it is out—Nietzsche lamented exactly this in his Death of God parable. She is right not to trust them. But she cannot live the way she is. She is the victim of humanism. Indeed she may even be beyond the Freudian illusion: her unconscious is so horrible that she may refuse the invitation to study it, to look into the glass.

The cultivation of the unconscious is explicit. Patients lie on a couch, invited to relax and put themselves in a trance or dream state. Daydreaming aloud is the approved method. Furthermore, the most prized subject matter is night dreams. Patients are encouraged to dig into the caverns of their sleep, to find the gold nuggets. 'To sleep perchance to dream ...' Life is richest in sleep. In sleep the true meaning is revealed. During the day one puts up with sterile bourgeois routines, drab and frustrating marriages, but at night life comes alive. This is the heart of darkness tamed: even nightmares become bearable, ultimately precious. Daytime may, at best, be 'common unhappiness', but there is compensation.

So the last glorification of the humanist *I* is psychobiography, pieced together from dreams, the one story left that has meaning, kept safe and intact in the unconscious. It provides a sort of place to stand, if only in the imagination, giving sense to the quest of knowing the unknown. Hamlet's dying request to Horatio, 'tell my story', expresses the same hope, that there must be some logic hidden there to make sense of the mess I have lived, to give sense to the *I*. But Nietzsche had already exposed this empty hope.

By the end of the twentieth century, psychoanalysis had seeped out in myriad popularised forms across the entire culture, a banal global whimper that would have appalled the founder. Therapy was taking over from living. One only had to step out one's front door and slip over on a banana skin to be offered counselling. Kierkegaard's joke had turned into the truth of the time—its advice, 'Don't dare to live.'

Freud was not alone in piping modernity towards the river of the unconscious. Painting had preceded him. In the chaotic fall from the great tradition of the Old Masters that is nineteenth-century art, enough of the authority of the past survived to make possible in the 1880s and 1890s a brief recandescence. On the edge of the plunge into rank nihilism stand two great painters, Cézanne and Van Gogh. Both, however, had made the fatal concession, and sought to embrace the unconscious, as solace. They stood, oblique to each other, on the same precipice, but with a different outlook. They instruct us of an important conceptual distinction between two kinds of unconscious, one sublime and one demonic.

Cézanne represents the sublime unconscious. With unusual self-awareness for an artist he stated two ambitions: to redo nature in the shoes of Poussin; and to make Impressionism more solid and enduring like the Old Masters. He achieved both. Cézanne starts the breakdown of form, with a deliberate purpose not found in Turner or the early Impressionists. Nietzsche's relativism—that truth is illusory, that there are merely perspectives on reality—was concurrently being worked in art. Cézanne experiments with fracturing forms, breaking reality down into abstract components. However, he always put it back together again. He was no relativist. In the long tradition of Western culture there is little to match the intensity with which he concentrated on the re-establishment of order. It is as if Cézanne were one of the citizens of Poussin's Ashdod: having contributed to the devastating plague, he now dedicates his life to finding the hidden order of forms. In his greatest works, the landscapes, the forms are so precariously built up from dabs of paint, smudges of colour, snatches of shape, so delicately and accurately placed, that the viewer can feel the wind in the trees, the warmth of the sun shimmering on the houses. Things lack solidity: there is none of the heavy rectilinear architecture that Poussin deprecates in his buildings. Things are fleeting, but so sensitively vivid that the fear that there is no substance to reality is transmuted into an illumination about an underlying order.

Just as Poussin has the fresh-faced boy tiptoeing into *The Plague of Ashdod*, establishing powerful lines of force to anchor the scene, Cézanne managed through great labour so to proportion and place his forms that they tapped an underlying, invisible order. There is no terror here, just the sublime intoxication of an idyllic dream.

But Cézanne is not Poussin. He has removed the people. Humans do not inhabit his natural utopia. His world is sublime, but it is abstract, excluding all moral content. The Old Masters painted scenes of human crisis, of temptation and disaster, stories which instructed us how to behave, which Law to obey, and through tragedy provided visual intimations of grace. Cézanne withdraws from all of this. He invites the frazzled modern soul to dream with him, to escape from hard reality into an unconscious world made conscious. His genius was to reveal an elemental order to the unconscious. This revelation enabled a flight from the dismal, profane world of ugly and nasty people to a sort of Western Nirvana. It is another couch, but one with a more uplifting outlook than that provided by psychoanalysis. Here is romance's last great moment, its swan song, and it is a truly beautiful death. In the *Lac d'Annecy* of 1896, for instance, one is wooed into a complete and perfect order, which is almost a state of grace.

The argument is starker in the lesser painters. In Monet there is not the intensity, the rugged ascetic wrestling with forms. What results is an easier, more relaxed and sentimental beauty. In Monet's *Rouen Cathedrals*, *Westminster Bridges* and *Water-Lilies* the images are pleasantly dreamy. With half-closed eyes viewers can swoon away. Monet helps them retreat into the sublime unconscious, as with a light hypnotic tune, and linger awhile in the smoky blurred forms of harmonious inwardness. Monet too had his iridescent moments, the extraordinary luminous light of *Verteuil in Summer* (1880), brilliant moments which, however, burn out, leaving no trace. In literature the same retreat was worked by Proust who, writing from his sickbed and without an ounce of active life left in him, envisioned life as a continuing sequence of beautiful dreams. The source of felicity is again the sublime unconscious.

There are two ways on from Cézanne. There is the wallpaper effeteness of Monet and other Impressionists. Then there is the more radical continuation of the breakdown of forms. Cézanne himself initiated the move with his late *Bathers*. Picasso and Braque followed, one step further over the edge, Braque retaining the beauty of line and colour, but with the meaning gone. Finally came the intellectually rigorous Duchamp. Duchamp's 1912 *Passage from Virgin to Bride* deliberately takes one of the two moments in a woman's life that should be most rich in ethical and religious emotion, and abstracts it into an incomprehensible muddle. Here, however, we are straying into the territory of the demonic unconscious.

Van Gogh represents the demonic unconscious. In his great works there is a terrible intensity, the forms with jagged edges, rickety planes and swirling shapes at the moment of disintegration. The painter just holds them together, and in that *just* is a breath-taking cultural force for order. Van Gogh makes clear what a life-and-death struggle is culture, and what its breakdown means. It is through his own work that he clings on to sanity, furiously resisting the waves of psychosis. The parallels with Nietzsche are obvious, the dates almost identical.

Van Gogh, however, is not on the side of nihilism. He is a lonely knight of resistance. It is a compromised resistance, for, as with Cézanne, there are no people, no communities, no human ethical domain. The battle is conducted on the plane of perception, and it is the world of nature and inanimate objects that provides the powerful subject matter. Nevertheless, Van Gogh finds an order in the mind, out of the unconscious projected onto thatched cottages, poplars and cypresses. This time the unconscious is demonic, threatening madness, a tormented horrific madness, which can be felt in the major works, for they take a direct look into the eyes of that Medusa, and just manage to hold their footing.

A procession of modern artists follows in the shadow of Van Gogh. There is Munch with his hysterical women and depressed men—his *Madonna* a sister of the rat-girl entangled in her own neurotic nightmare lifelessness. There is the Austrian, Schiele, and the harsh, violent world of German Expressionism. In literature there is Kafka, taken over by paranoid guilt fantasies of being turned into a bug, or depressive guilt feelings at not bothering to turn up at his own wedding. Guilt has shed its explicit Greek sublimations, and turned itself into a huge, shapeless and all-encompassing chamber—the demonic unconscious. This is the modern hell. Freud theorised it, Brecht dramatised it, and most contributors to twentieth-century high culture drank in its shadows.

The climax was Picasso. The man whom the twentieth century celebrated as its greatest genius revealed, through his long life and vast work, what scavenges around in the wreckage of humanism. Picasso incarnated the Nietzschean superman. His egocentricity was mammoth—driven by a tempestuous will to power, and especially over his women. His *Weeping Woman* portraits, for instance, show the reality of the demonic unconscious free from all limit. The subject is one of his mistresses, Dora Maar, whom Picasso often beat, and into unconsciousness. He felt compelled to destroy the very things in Dora that he admired. In the end she lost her mind. The portraits are typical of Picasso in their flatness of feeling, apart from a horror that lurks in the faces. The abstracting of the subject kills off any normal projection of female grief or sadness, a repressive distortion that likely indicates the painter's own guilt, his need to blur the reality of why the woman is at her wits' end with despair. What comes through is his own terror at the emptiness of existence.

Picasso lived 'beyond good and evil'. He lived 'freely', obeying only his pleasure, and especially a brand of capricious sadism. His response to the one woman who ever escaped from him, Françoise Gilot, was to burn a lighted cigarette into her cheek and ensure that no art dealer handled her pictures. He was not only mean-spirited, and resentful of the success of any of his friends, but also a coward. In court he disowned his friend, Apollinaire; he refused to intercede with the Nazis to save the life of an old Jewish friend, Max Jacob; and during the war when a pot exploded he dived under the table, leaving his wife and daughter unprotected. The rationalisation was the modern nihilistic one, 'I am against everything.' The artist is the great man, whose genius allows him beyond all petty, moral constraints. The notable thing here is not that someone should have lived out Nietzsche, Dostoevsky and Conrad's 'everything is permitted', but that Western elites should have bowed down at his feet for having done it. Picasso is emblematic.

Picasso is reminiscent of Marx, in his satanic character and mission of destruction. He is also reminiscent of Velázquez, of the triumphant value-creating artist—Picasso was, by the way, obsessed by *Las Meninas*, painting his own versions again and again. The difference is that the twentieth-century genius had very little to say and no values to create. In the end, it was a curse for him to be born with such a prodigious technical talent, and such a drive to paint, for apart from occasional moments of childlike gaiety his vision was merely of disintegration—rampant cubism. At the time of the *Weeping Woman* portraits, he painted a crucifixion in which Mary, the mother, drinks her son's blood, and Magdalene clutches his genitals.

In the aftermath of humanism, with all cultural barriers smashed, 'We can become what we will' is simplified back to the jungle, in which lust and sadism rule—Hitler's *Triumph of the Will*. Yet even here humans are not just animals, for they have consciousness, which means ultimately, consciousness of death. Free-will has no answer to the skull, and so out of an odd mixture of childish exuberance and anxiety the genius of the twentieth century churns out fifty thousand works. To live freely, by one's own will, means to be drowned in one's own unconscious, spewed out in its demonic form.

What happens to society once individuals become submerged in their own unconsciousness? The modern experience has been bureaucracy. As romance degenerated into caged subjectivity, reason degenerated into the sterile order of the office, and what Max Weber called 'mechanised petrifaction'. With individuals in total retreat from the world, their private lives all, the public world was rendered profane, losing first its traditional spiritual and ethical underpinnings, as Kierkegaard predicted, and second losing its emotional ones. The caricature of the bourgeois became reality, as Freud found out. Thus the outer did become absurd, as Nietzsche and Conrad had seen, as Hamlet had experienced it. Or it became persecuting, as Kafka imagined it in the paranoid imagery of his *Castle* and *Trial*. The rationalisation of life also swept through art, in surrealism, in Bauhaus, in the arid geometry of Mondrian, and later in even more brittle banalities.

In short, the heritage of the death of culture in the humanist mode has been a routine public life, and a retreat into the individual unconscious in the hope of staving off madness or melancholia. That unconscious itself becomes more and more an inescapable pit, a devouring demon. There are the occasional consolations of the sublime, with the help of a Monet, or of intellectual clarity, with the help of a Freud. There are sorties to idealise the demonic itself, in order to recapture lost vitality, as in D.H. Lawrence, for instance, gushing lyrical enthusiasm over charging bulls, rearing stallions, homosexual wrestling or female fecundity. The rat-girl is, however, the reality, the true child of modern culture.

The deceit of Freud was that he made things worse, becoming a far more influential prophet of nihilism than his more perceptive, more satanic and more tragic predecessor—Nietzsche. Freud's concern was individual health, what he called normality, the pursuit of pleasure his criterion of value. According to his disenchanting psychology the child is under the thrall of its genitals and its anus, there is no difference between Napoleon and Christ—both were 'father figures'—and a story like the transformation and redemption of Magdalene is a piece of primitive, irrational delusion. Magdalene would have been better off undergoing psychoanalysis to cure her guilt. Munch's Madonna could easily have been a patient of Freud, a fate no doubt, to which she would have remained indifferent. Why not, she might have said, if it helps to pass the time—after all, the wolf-man said no less, in praise of his pleasant and inconsequential talks with Freud about Russian literature.

Freud, in his own personal life, was much better. In response to the slings and arrows of life's hardships, he aspired to a state of resignation. He held resignation to fate in the highest ethical regard. But this residue in him of an earlier culture—one with depth—provided the equilibrium which enabled him all the more virulently to play his role as leading prophet of resigned nihilism.

All is silent. All is still. Coleridge's earlier guilt imagery has become the reality on the frontier of Western culture:

> Day after day,
>
> day after day,
>
> We stuck, nor breath nor motion,
>
> As idle as a painted ship
>
> Upon a painted ocean.

That ocean is flat, grey and boundless. That ship is ghostly, ghastly. It is Holbein's blurred skull. In a late shift in his theory, Freud introduced a notion that worried and baffled his followers: rather than counterpoising an 'aggressive instinct' to the life-creating erotic one, he chose the term 'death instinct'. Freud postulates an impulse within us all towards death, a desire for extinction. Was there not some obscure inkling here of the truth of his own mission, that in cultivating Hamlet's 'to sleep perchance to dream' he was acting in the service of the forces of destruction, that to turn the unconscious into god was to paralyse humanity, seducing it with psychological knowledge, turning it—through interminable sophisticated chatter—to stone?

Freud's 'talking cure' completes the humanist trajectory, the last glow of the flaming meteor before disintegration. It spotlights, care of its own futility, the five-hundred-year fateful misreading of the

West's founding axiom, 'In the beginning was the word.'

There can be no surprise that after Cézanne, Van Gogh and Freud, Western high culture—its art, literature, music and philosophy—was to portray life as a sterile promontory, as worse than death. The coat-of-arms of this culture displays a rat bleeding at the tail under an owl's face doubling as a skull—the motto *nothing*. The humanist epoch ends with Hamlet, Hamlet, and more Hamlet.

Part Four

DEATH THROES

Chapter Twelve

SACRED RAGE

Henry James

The story of the rise and fall of humanism is not complete without consideration of two later attempts to build anew within the wreckage. They use what was there, introducing no new materials. They take us over the frontier into a post-humanist domain. Both come from the New World, America, and they draw their strength respectively from a Protestant and a hybrid Protestant–Catholic root. While most that passed for High Culture in the twentieth century merely shone a spotlight on different corners of the ruin, mounted a fragment or two, perhaps touched it up a bit, or chipped some more pieces away, there were two grand trials at reconstruction—those of Henry James and John Ford.

I am not taking account of other moves towards a new religious vision, notably those of Rilke's *Duino Elegies* and Simone Weil's essays, for neither cast significant ripples in the wider culture. Martin Heidegger is also of significance in the twentieth century. He sought to switch the focus of modern philosophy onto *being*. Taking his cue from Nietzsche, whom he designated the last of the Western philosophers, he accepted the 'death of God' case against humanism, that the Kantian ethical order would not stand on its own. He attempted to ground a new metaphysics, beyond good and evil, on the essence of *being*. In his later essays, he gestured towards a mystical dimension, drawing on the German poet, Hölderlin. Heidegger's work remains a suggestive byway, perhaps waiting to be developed through less abstract, narrative representations of the 'I am'.

Henry James has been applauded as the last of the great novelists, his work the high-point of Western fiction. John Ford is the most important contributor to that major genre, the Western, within the new art form of the twentieth century, the film. His main work spans almost exactly the twenty years between 1940 and 1960 that mark the classical period of the cinema, its great Hollywood era. Both Henry James and John Ford create visions that are realistic to their own time and have metaphysical weight. Both were in search of a place to stand.

The work that is definitive to the vision of Henry James is *The Ambassadors*. Although it was the second published of his three great last novels, it was the first written (1900–01). James himself assessed it as 'quite the best, "all round", of my productions'. It stands in relation to our story here as the second Ambassadors, a reply to Holbein, as to much else with which we have been engaged. Put simply, *The Ambassadors* is an examination of what happens to a middle-aged gentleman, a pure New England type, when he is thrown into the most seductive humanist milieu of old Europe, situated in Paris. The two poles are Calvinism and aristocratic humanism.

Europe is culture and civilisation. It is scintillating, subtle intelligence. It is courtesy and refinement. More concretely, it is people who know how to live their lives as works of art, fashioning their movements with delicacy and charm, and then subjecting them to analyses, so that they gain the additional pleasure of seeing the pattern of things—understanding. In the same year that Freud published his *Interpretation of Dreams*, Henry James was giving his Europeans a rare capacity for psychoanalysis, one better integrated into their living, being a vital part of their social talk, rather than displaced onto the doctor's couch.

The main representative of Europe is the beautiful Madame de Vionnet. She has immense reserves of style, from the skill with which she presents herself, the physical woman, through the taste of her apartment and its inherited accumulations, to the virtuosity with which she speaks so as to touch the sensitive spots with a mixture of allusion and concealment. She is likened to Cleopatra. She has a score of different characters, in her magnificent opulence of interest. The local category for her is *femme du monde*.

In Paris, language is used with a spare and directed precision, with a technical elegance reminiscent of a master violinist, so that each note is a strictly controlled hint. Such culture takes a lot of time to develop. Like the Europe with which both Henry James and his hero have fallen in love, Mme de Vionnet is not young. She is near the time when her physical graces will no longer draw men so irresistibly to her. But then, the charm of Europe lies in its ruins, their mossy antiquity offering the depth and permanence that only great age can bestow: nothing flashy; nothing vulgar; nothing clumsy; nothing naive. All is polish, the profound interior illuminated as if by light penetrating through the surface of a precious stone. In Paris, the ideals of freedom and romance find their highest aesthetic realisation.

Lambert Strether is from Woollett, New England, in the vicinity of Boston. Woollett is undiluted Puritanism, without either aristocratic or humanist trace. Duty, piety and bourgeois rectitude are the rule. On the one hand, it is innocent, lacking refinement and social grace. Its inhabitants live by principle. They are without understanding. On the other hand, Woollett's failure lies in its dearth of enjoyment. There is so much propriety and control that pleasure is stifled. The main representative is Mrs Newsome, a wealthy widow, Strether's patron and fiancée, who has sent him to Paris as her ambassador to convince her son, Chad, to return to Woollett, marry and take over the prosperous family business. Mrs Newsome is Queen of Woollett. In Kierkegaard's terms, Mme de Vionnet and Paris are pure aesthetic, indeed the aesthetic at its finest, more engagingly painted than by Kierkegaard himself. Mrs Newsome and Woollett are purely ethical.

Chad Newsome has been in Paris for years. In effect he has been educated there. Strether meets a young man whom he does not recognise, who has acquired the polished cultivation of Europe. His principal teacher over the last three years has been Mme de Vionnet, with whom he is having an affair, although Strether in his innocence does not realise this until late in the piece. Strether's first response to Chad and his challenging question, 'Do I strike you as improved?' is that of the loyal ambassador, 'I haven't the least idea.' He can still stick to his New England principle. However, his own education is already well underway with the help of a Europeanised American, the 35-year-old Miss Gostrey, who has become devoted to him, and he to her. Strether has seen immediately that Chad is much improved—a man who has learned the art of living, of getting real pleasure out of life, a man who is always at his ease, with a happy blend of the cordial and the formal.

Strether, in his own undemonstrative way and hardly knowing it, falls in love with Mme de Vionnet. His love is generalised from Mme de Vionnet to all she represents. As his mission as ambassador becomes increasingly difficult, he tries unsuccessfully to avoid her. He sees how she has transformed Chad and shows indirect signs of jealousy. His advice to another young American is, 'Live all you can', unlike himself, who has let it all pass by, until it is too late. 'If you haven't had that what *have* you had?' Freedom and romance have him in thrall. Yet not completely, for his wise fatalist self follows up, 'Still, one has the illusion of freedom; therefore don't be, like me, without the memory of that illusion.'

The Ambassadors is tightly constructed, written in twelve books of similar length, with a series of symmetries that liken its structure to that of a classical temple. Technically it is without flaw. The architecture is, however, deceptive, as in a Poussin painting. The true lines of force, concealed, divide the story into four stages, all of them determined by Strether. The mild-mannered hero, hitherto dominated by the Queen of Woollett, a lamb as his Christian name intimates, a hesitant and bewildered New Englander in awe of Paris, it is he who controls events. Stage One takes up the entire first half of the novel. Strether arrives and delivers his ambassadorial message to Chad. Then he hesitates. The sheer poise of aristocratic humanism has got to him, as it did to those Protestant middle-class boys once they entered the English public schools. The young American disciples of this aesthetic religion also influence him. He likes what it has made of them. Because of his hesitation events stall. He pauses not simply because he has been seduced by new gods, but also because something eludes him. There is a truth he has to discover before he can move, 'an obscure truth lurking in the loose folds.' To continue as ambassador, given his blind and uncertain state, would be foolish. His inner voice tells him: 'Wait, you have more to learn.'

Stage Two: the second half of the novel opens with new ambassadors arriving from Woollett. Strether has been sacked. His immobility has rightly been interpreted as betrayal. The arrival of the new ambassadors changes nothing. It does, however, provoke him into action. He urges Chad not to go back to America for he, Strether, needs more time. The pressure from Woollett is wrong. Strether has become the main opponent of the Queen of Woollett.

The third stage is his turning, at last, to gain a clear sight of Europe. It is summer and he travels at random away from Paris to take a day in the country by himself. By coincidence, he bumps into Chad and a very embarrassed Mme de Vionnet. He realises that the pair are spending a few days together. What he had taken to be a virtuous friendship is in fact a liaison, as Mme de Vionnet's clumsy attempt to cover up makes plain. He now sees her for what she really is beneath the sophisticated facade, a woman tragically in love with a partner ten years younger, who is becoming restless. She is doomed. Strether is hurt. He has been used. He feels cold and lonely.

In the last meeting between Mme de Vionnet and Strether she confesses that she has changed his life, separated him from Mrs Newsome and turned him against her, closing that door. She hates herself for upsetting his mind—and for her selfishness. It has not even brought her happiness. He leaves. Humanism, for all its cultivated allure, is founded on the selfish pursuit of pleasure—all else is calculated appearance, that is deceit. He worked hard to delay Chad's departure, in part for her, yet all she has given him in return is an obscure dream of happiness, now exploded. Strether rejects Paris and Europe.

The fourth and final stage is with Maria Gostrey, the other woman with whom Strether has been half in love. A true and loyal friend throughout, she was the only one to whom he could talk openly, the only one who was honest. She is like what he has become, a Europeanised American, enjoying the understanding and manners of Europe but having retained the conscience of America. They belong together, with their rare harmony of virtue and knowledge. Strether, however, says No. It would not be right. His only logic is to have got nothing out of the affair for himself. He has betrayed Woollett in not fulfilling his mission as ambassador. His honour requires that it cannot have been for selfish reasons, rewarded with the happiness of companionship with Maria. So he must return to Woollett, although there is nothing, and no one, there for him. He does not believe in Woollett values any more—he no longer belongs there. He does not belong anywhere. By the end, the three main characters are all left gloomily alone.

Once Strether's eyes are opened, he sees Paris and Woollett for what they are and forsakes both to save his honour. As a higher product of Puritan New England, his Calvinist conscience does not allow him to suppress within himself what he knows. The Calvinist God, however, is no more, and Strether has no perception of a higher order. So what drives his conscience? It is what Henry James calls 'sacred rage', a term which has its roots in Homer. This force is bestowed on the least attractive character on stage, Waymarsh, a boorish, narrow-minded New Englander who finds Europe an ordeal. 'The sombre glow just darkened in his comrade's eyes', and Waymarsh, early in the piece, commands Strether to 'Quit it!'—his mission—for there is trouble brewing. In Waymarsh, the rage is a rather crude cannon, with poor sights, tending just to blast away. He is the opposite of Mme de Vionnet, whose sights are set exactly where she wants them, but who has no sacred rage, no force.

The rage is never directly attributed to Strether, but it is there, simmering under the surface, while he is being trained, until by the end it has a perfect precision and accuracy of fire. What Europe does for Strether is school him, provide him with a context in which to apply his immense capacity for concentration on what is, so that he can get his response right.

Strether has his extraordinary intensity of concentration. He is taut, he is tense, and, as his name hints, he is stretched. When the male in the new ambassadorial party observes that Strether has come to Paris to have a good time, he is quite wrong, for it is not in Strether's nature to relax and enjoy himself. He is on a mission, a Captain Ahab in Europe, driven to find the truth however vile and monstrous it may turn out to be. The only one who is relaxed is Chad, for he has little at stake now that he has taken all he can—plundered Paris so to speak, and he has too limited an imagination to be seriously troubled by his debts. Mme de Vionnet, the ambassador of aristocratic humanism, is no more at ease than Strether. Beneath the superbly constructed manners, she is always on edge.

She is helpless. She is powerless. Without the sacred rage, she has nothing to save her.

Only the innocents can act, in their moments of sacred rage. Without a raw and instinctive sense of honour driven from within, the best alternative is humanist Europe, in which paralysis and emptiness are dressed up in finery, interrupted by fitful passions and moments of pleasure, and softened by evenings of gilded understandings. There is some doubt about the pleasure, in spite of Strether's advice, 'Live all you can.' Mme de Vionnet is living all she can, but she finds herself trapped and anxious. She is gradually turning into another Hamlet. The message is close to that of Don Quixote, although his reincarnation here is as an uncomic pilgrim—born 'portentously solemn' as Strether describes himself—a Puritan Brutus left alone on the field of battle, surrounded by corpses, with only his honour and his sacred rage. In his innocence, he is outraged at reality. The difference from Don Quixote is that Strether is not dreaming, and *that* is due to his Protestant conscience. Chad also can act, but it is the action of a man strolling through life without serious engagement, and it becomes both arbitrary and uninteresting what he might or might not do.

By the end, humanism is finished. Mme de Vionnet is deflated, disgusted with herself, dishonoured, and not even happy. She will soon lose Chad. Humanism's fall is not, however, without some glory. Strether has a new capacity for understanding—as Maria Gostrey puts it to him, 'Wasn't what you came out for to find out *all?*' In addition, Henry James himself has developed a style of writing which, in its exquisite precision, its subtle virtuosity, is his debt to civilised Europe. And after all, if the novel is a bourgeois form, then James is its greatest exponent. Set against this is the deeper truth, that the Bostonian pilgrim in Paris had set out to unite humanist and Puritan in one soul and thereby escape the clutches of nihilist modernity. This was not to be. Trying to move beyond, and failing, he ended up moving backwards, narrowing the options by reducing the bourgeois possibility to its Protestant core, eliminating the humanist extensions and refinements.

Henry James goes to Europe to encounter the humanist ideal, the high-point of the civilised, and he rejects it in favour of innocence, conscience and sacred rage. Luther would have been proud of him. However, the American cannot tear himself away from the gracious drawing rooms with their honeyed conversations. In his great final three novels he fully develops only one character who can dominate centre-stage—that is Lambert Strether. James turns him, through his suffering, into a fine man, then sends him back to Woollett, something James himself refused to do. A fine man, for what? That is the question. One does not need to ask it of Achilles at the end of *The Iliad*, or of Oedipus once he has blinded and banished himself. The true tragedies were complete. *The Ambassadors,* by contrast, is unfinished. It is not free from the humanist epoch, therefore it cannot attain the rank of tragedy. Henry James has returned to the metaphysics of the Reformation, and before that Greek tragedy, but there are open issues to be resolved. To what order does Strether now belong, once he has proved his honour?

The problem is not the traditional one of the hero finding himself in bad times with his task to restore order. Once blind Oedipus leaves Thebes, balance returns—the lonely hero, through his own suffering, has sacrificed himself for the sake of the community. Antigone has her family—she sacrifices herself out of loyalty to kin. In *The Ambassadors* there is no community worth saving. Paris is present only as a test for Strether, not in itself. In any case, he rejects what it stands for. He also rejects the other community, Woollett. So where is the resolution, except in Strether himself. Here is James' stark Protestantism: the individual and his or her conscience is all. But as Kierkegaard warned, the theology and the faith have gone. While Strether is inwardly driven by sacred rage, what Kierkegaard called dread, the question remains, where and for what?

Strether is saved by his conscience. It tells him there is a law he must obey. He does not yet make it out, so he must persevere. It tells him that there is a truth to human behaviour. That too he does not yet know. Throughout, his natural desire is to find out what things 'really' are. Paris, which lives off appearances, mocks this 'really'. Once Strether knows the truth, he will know the law. Listening to his conscience he tiptoes along, cautiously, ever so cautiously, lest he take a false step. It is an art this listening, to hear in order to be able to act rightly. In the same position Woollett blocks its ears and stubbornly marches to its old principles, which leaves its inhabitants, as Strether puts it, playing at life, a parody of bourgeois rectitude. Humanist Europe does not have such a problem, for it obeys the pleasure principle, with its own clear logic. What Strether learns, aged fifty-five, is the old Calvinist lesson, wait until you hear your conscience, then act accordingly. This is his real education.

The Ambassadors is the great Kierkegaardian novel. It attempts to reverse the stages, starting with the aesthetic, moving into the ethical, and hoping to attain the religious. The categories are slightly revised. The religious is inborn, in the form of sacred rage. Waymarsh loses his sacred rage because it is not integrated into the ethical and the aesthetic. Once he starts to enjoy himself in Europe he becomes lost in the aesthetic, and is finished—indeed he comes to embody what Woollett fears happens to its members once they surrender to Paris.

For Strether all is one: all stages have to work together. He ends up an ethical hero, but alone, knowing he has done the right thing in sacrificing his pleasure for duty. For this he must pay dearly, losing all possibility of happiness. But genuine Protestantism does not operate on a theological calculus of sin and punishment. He must pay simply because that is his condition. He is born the one who is stretched, just as Oedipus is born to kill his father and marry his mother. Strether is not Abraham. He does not have faith. He is lost in his inwardness—an inwardness that drives him through life enabling him to act, but which cannot bring faith nor project a canopy of belief. This is why Strether and his author are so tempted by humanism, for they have no explicit attachments, so why not 'Live all you can', for indeed 'If you haven't had that what have you had?' In practice, they try out this humanism but their Puritan consciences stop them in their tracks. If Strether were to follow his 'Live all you can', a reworking of the 'We can become what we will', he would end the novel with Maria Gostrey. Why not? It is because of the sacred rage, shouting at him 'Quit it!' He is not free. He has to say No.

He thus condemns himself, as he had prophesied in Book Seven, if the living were to smash, to a fate worse than death—'It will make me old.' Later on, as the climax approached, he had intuited 'I shan't live long.' So, the man from Woollett, true to type, has proved incapable of pleasure.

The problem is pinpointed in the case of the great German sociologist Max Weber. In his major work, *The Protestant Ethic and the Spirit of Capitalism* (1904–1920), Weber attempted to redeem the bourgeois from the Marxist caricature, showing that the success of capitalism depended on the new ethical integrity upon which the modern middle class was founded. That integrity was Protestant, a Calvinist derivative. Perceiving that the ethic was being diluted into a degraded materialism, Weber closed his book on a note of extreme pessimism.

Late in his life, in a lecture delivered in 1918 entitled 'Knowledge as a Vocation', Weber went further. The subject was the contemporary university. Weber accepts Nietzsche's diagnosis of modern culture as nihilistic—having killed God, it finds itself believing in nothing. He asks, how can the university function in such a disenchanted world? The university in its modern form has evolved from its Renaissance forefather, stipulated on the humanist ideals of a trained mind, culture, and the benefits to both individual and society of applied knowledge. But those ideals are dead. The main consequence is that students now come to university in search of answers to the great metaphysical questions—what to do and how to live. In other words they seek prophets. Weber's retort is that prophets do not belong in the university. The lectern is not a pulpit. He finds three functions left for the modern university: the advancement of knowledge; the teaching of methods of thinking; and the imposition of a clarity and consistency of thinking within the framework of already given ultimate values. Under the pall of Nietzsche's scepticism about the value of knowledge, Weber is only enthusiastic about his third function, but it depends on already given ultimate values, the lack of which stimulated his enquiry in the first place. His argument thus collapses in futility.

The one thing Weber can salvage is the virtue of 'intellectual integrity', that individual teachers should obey their consciences and fulfil their vocation. The hope is that rigorously disciplined scholars, dedicated to their own branches of knowledge, will communicate enough moral authority to their students to fill the metaphysical void. This is caricature Calvinism, the university as a conglomerate of single-person sects each obeying his or her individual conscience, while all around the institution decays into an aimless and moribund bureaucracy. Weber described with devastating accuracy the post-humanist university of the twentieth century.

Weber's individuals with intellectual integrity, and thereby vocation, are Strethers. They are descendants of Vermeer's geographer, astronomer and lace-maker, except the securing bourgeois milieu around them has faded away to nothing. Weber knew the game was over. He clung to the only root that still could hold him, if temporarily, the Calvinist one. So did Henry James, once he had tried the alternative, the humanist root with aristocratic trappings, and found it to be rotten. The sociologist at the end of his tradition, like his great teacher Nietzsche, was no more than a gloomy diagnostician. Henry James was more. Strether is not confined to the lecture hall, nor to the psychoanalyst's couch. He actually manages to live. Hence his quixotic appeal. But in the end he has added nothing new to our story. America, the New World, is simply a purer form of Protestantism; it is quite familiar to us, failing to offer a way out, a new direction. We have not advanced from the predicament that Kierkegaard analysed with unmatched prescience. Some detail has been filled out, projecting from America a late Protestant salvo, but one that misses the target for already familiar reasons. Kierkegaard had set the terms for the post-humanist interregnum. The one change is that dread is redrawn as sacred rage. Internal anguish may clothe a religious drive. James does not go further.

A society cannot survive which is so fragmented that, at best, it contains a few individuals with intellectual integrity, while the rest go about their profane routines. There has to be a unifying social ethic—as will be explored in the next chapter—and an over-arching higher conscience. Kierkegaard's categories fit Strether. His sacred rage in alliance with new understanding drive him up out of the aesthetic into the plane of the ethical. Rejecting his own advice, 'Live all you can', he triumphs over nihilist humanism and becomes an ethical hero. He does not, however, attain the religious. His loneliness is not that of Abraham in the midst of the darkness of faith; it is that of the honourable man, the Puritan gentleman who has lost his community. It is thus a partial victory with no future. Humanism has helped him, giving him understanding; but it is his Puritan conscience, with its undercurrent of sacred rage, that has saved him. That is not enough. What Poussin did with his own sacred rage is again necessary. He used it to inspire a religious vision of the beyond, while tying that back to the here and now on earth.

Chapter Thirteen

LAST STAND

John Ford

America represents what has to be built from scratch, out of nothing. That is how John Ford saw it. His life-task was to create the myth that would give America a place to stand. Without the myth it would fail, and relapse into a condition worse than that of old Europe, which at least had its memories of a great past and some surviving vestiges of tradition. America had to make its tradition. It was essential it be the right one. By the twentieth century all Western countries were in the same basic predicament—of rickety foundations, the old ones having loosened through their long affair with humanism. It was thus of far wider significance whether America succeeded. If America could do it, then the others might follow its path.

For Ford, America is both the New World in itself, and the place with a future where exiles from the decaying Old World flee in hope, to build anew. Ford knows that if America is to work it needs a foundation myth, a sacred story imprinted on its collective being. He worked in practice to solve the problem for all modern societies—that of legitimacy. In what can I believe? Whom shall I obey? In her book *On Revolution* (1963), Hannah Arendt argued that America had secured its legitimacy through its political Constitution, which it had successfully turned into a sacred text, and embodied in a number of central institutions, notably the

Supreme Court. This is the civic religion of 'God bless America!' We shall see that Ford considers the same answer, tests it and rejects it. His search was to take him over an immense stretch of territory. From *Stagecoach* of 1939 to *Seven Women* of 1966 he made thirty-three films of significance, with a prodigality of themes and images, all directed at finding a secure place to stand.

Axiomatic to the entire enterprise is the contrast between myth and history. Ford is in the tradition of Greek tragedy, as articulated by the young Nietzsche, that history, being the rational and dispassionate account of the past, is a sign of the death of culture. Culture is rooted in sacred sites, sanctuaries built out of *mythos*, and it is merely a symptom of the weakening of the foundation myths when the humanist deification of reason gets going, when logic replaces blood, and myth is deprecated as superstition. Forget history, disinter the myths, for it is from within their mystery that you may find out who you are. It is through them your ancestors speak. The rest is flotsam.

'I will plant companionship thick as trees along all the rivers of America.' So stated John Ford. Companionship is the key—at the heart of his ideal of community, being both what community makes possible and what justifies it. This, at least, was Ford's early, Catholic vision, his opening gambit. There is more to it. For companionship and community there has to be an ethic independent of them. It is that of honour, which means individuals each taking an oath to which they are faithful above all else. Companionship, trust, loyalty and honour combine to form the magic circle. Where and under what circumstances is it to be found? Ford gives different answers at different points of time, on his own journey wrestling with the angel with whom he could never completely settle accounts. They are represented respectively in three paradigmatic films—*Rio Grande* (1950), *The Searchers* (1956), and *The Man Who Shot Liberty Valance* (1962). Fragments of them are to be found throughout his work, sometimes with different inflections.

Ford's first major attempt at a foundation myth is *Young Mr Lincoln* of 1939. The subject chose itself, the American Abraham— father of the chosen people. Interested in origins, Ford concentrates on the young Lincoln, before the start of his political career. The hero, like his country, has no past. He appears from nowhere, without father or mother, out of nothing. He finds his own anchoring point in the grave of his fiancée, Ann Rutledge, beside a river. At times of great decision he returns to the river to talk to the grave. It is the most authoritative image in the film. Ford's Lincoln is a man of the people, with a popular touch, saving a helpless, fatherless family from evil bullies by making the legal system work. Rational justice championed by the gifted secular pilgrim will make America, securing its families and small communities. *Young Mr Lincoln*, however, does not succeed at the high level of ambition at which it was pitched. It lacks mythic force.

Ford takes another decade of varied experiments to find the community through which he can work his vision to the full. He finds it in the United States Cavalry. The third of a trilogy of cavalry films, *Rio Grande*, is the fulfilment. The principal characters are members of a broken family: Colonel Kirby Yorke, the father and head of the cavalry community based in an isolated fort on the frontier; his estranged wife, Kathleen; and their son, Jeff, who has failed at West Point officers' academy and has just been posted to his father's unit.

Early in the film the Colonel tells his son that 'an uncompromising devotion to your oath and your duty is required'. The oath is to the army. Kathleen, who arrives unannounced soon after, counters with, 'All this danger to serve people as yet unborn— and probably not worth serving.' She has hit the target, although she unwittingly tramples on the justifying ethos of her own aristocratic class, that of noble service. The desolate and dangerous frontier is being tamed for the future, so that decent communities can settle and build. This is the making of America. The oath is to America, past, present and, most importantly, to the unborn. Moreover oath and duty can forge a higher, exemplary community here and now, the cavalry itself. This is a good place for families; it is the best place for the initiation of young men into responsible adulthood. But is honour and community enough?

Through the story, North and South are united and the American Civil War atoned. The vertical, which is hierarchy, is brought into harmony with the horizontal, which is community. Indian scouts are decorated for bravery. The innocents—children—are saved. Most importantly the right balances at the heart of community have been found. But Yorke's wholehearted devotion to oath and duty came at a price. He had sacrificed his family—the destruction, as his wife puts it, of a beautiful thing. One of his punishments was a gruelling loneliness. By the end of the film, cavalry and family are of equal importance, nurture and honour integrated. Similarly, Kathleen had put the mother–son tie ahead of family, and the exaggeration of nurture had blinded her to the fact that the dishonourable life is not worth living. The second imbalance is corrected. In fact it takes a son with a very fine character, including the pride and stubbornness of both parents, to effect this restoration, with the help of companionship and the community.

Rio Grande is perfect in its accuracy and economy of image, in its pacing, in its balances—in its form, the film equivalent to Jane Austen's *Pride and Prejudice*. The reward to those inducted into community is twofold. First, there is the experience that life is full. It has its cycle of birth, growth, decay and death. Over and above that cycle there is the duty to uphold one's oath and to ensure that the unborn enter a world worth joining. There is the redemptive experience of doing what has to be done. The code of honour and what it serves, the New World, are underpinned by a religious order intimated by a series of Christian icons. Second, there is the spirit that follows. One of the greatest gifts is cheerfulness. The men, women and children of *Rio Grande* are buoyed up by a zest and humour, an enthusiasm and camaraderie. It is to be found in songs that accompany the action, full-blooded songs, the songs of the community. It is in the deep tones of the bugle and in the ringing of bells—school bell at the start, church bell at the end. There are more songs in *Rio Grande* than in any other John Ford film. Out of this cheerfulness comes gratitude. It is quite an achievement.

Ford could not rest with *Rio Grande*. It was as if, in response to what might withstand the annihilating gale of modernity, he knew he needed a stronger, more deeply rooted *mythos*, and therefore a tougher one. He turned to tragedy, and to a much harsher Protestant view of things than the more Catholic cavalry community had allowed. Significantly, between *Rio Grande* and Ford's masterpiece, *The Searchers*, is the painting of an idyllic Catholic utopia in an Irish village—the Academy-award winning *The Quiet Man*, Ford's fantasy withdrawal from reality before he takes on his great epic.

Kirby Yorke's 'uncompromising devotion to your oath and your duty' is now put to violent test. The background to *The Searchers* is also the Civil War, which Ford once referred to as his principal interest in life, ahead of movies. It is odd that he made only one full film on the Civil War, *The Horse Soldiers* of 1959, in which he fails to show much enthusiasm for the story-line. *The Searchers* is epic tragedy, a modern *Iliad*. The hero is Ethan Edwards, played by John Wayne, and for almost the entirety of the two-hour film he journeys in fury seeking revenge. Like Achilles, he is a big man. He has not been seen since the end of the Civil War, three years earlier, when he refused to surrender his Southern sword. He asserts that one oath in a lifetime is enough for any man, and he took his to the Confederacy. The film opens with his arrival at his brother's homestead in remote Texas country where community is new and fragile, and where the struggle to survive is daunting in a harsh, arid nature. The backbone of the family is the mother, Martha, his brother's wife, who welcomes Ethan with a barely suppressed intimacy. Women love men, and he is the man.

Then comes the outrage. All that is intimate and precious is violated and killed. Ethan has ridden off with a posse in pursuit of rampaging Comanche Indians. It is a decoy. While they are away, the Indians massacre his family and kidnap his two nieces. The search begins with an impatient Ethan storming off before the funeral service has ended. The Reverend Samuel Johnson Clayton, who doubles as both spiritual and military head of the community, leads it. After a punishing journey in pursuit, the white people are attacked, and just manage to survive. They decide to give up.

Ethan goes on. Nothing will stop him. For seven years he rides through the snows of northern winter to the scorching desert summer. He is super-human. He is also a very violent man, at any point as likely to add to the moral havoc as restore order. He is alone with his duty to his kin, and above all to Martha, in his avenging torment of will. There are rumours of crime in his past; he arrives with freshly-minted gold and wearing Union soldier's trousers. There is intimacy with his brother's wife which might have wrecked the family if fate had not intervened. At the start of the search, in a blind fury, he shoots out the eyes of a dead Indian, so that according to Indian belief his soul will never rest. This violates the law of respect for the dead, an immediate allusion to Antigone, and signals the affinity of this story with the metaphysics of Greek tragedy. Ethan curses himself with this act, for it is his own soul that will never find peace. Later he massacres buffalo just to reduce the food stock available to the Indians, a transgressive excess against Nature reminiscent of Achilles. Ethan Edwards is a berserk, demonic man with little sense of limit. He is irritable and snappy. Even when he sits down with his family to dinner, before the massacre, he infects the domestic harmony with tension. However, given what the Indians have done, to the limit of horror, only such a man will prevail.

The part-Indian, adopted son of Martha, Martin Pawley, accompanies Ethan—Martin is 'poly' in blood and culture. Also there is Brad, the teenage boyfriend of the captured Lucy. Brad's mother had pleaded with Ethan not to waste the lives of their boys in vengeance, a noble and entirely justified assertion of the female ethic of nurture against the male ethic of honour, the ethic of the hearth against that of politics. In the circumstances she is right, but wrong. Politics is a necessary evil. The community will not survive unless the violated order of things is restored. This requires retribution, and for retribution the logic of politics—power—applies. Brad loses his mind, being only human, when he realises Ethan has found and buried the raped and scalped body of his teenage beloved. He sees the agony in the contorted face of Ethan, who shouts at him never to ask him to describe what he found. Ethan is the only one who can take a direct look into the horror of existence. Part of his task is to hide the eyes of normal men from the terror they cannot bear. The Comanches kill an unhinged Brad.

Scar, the Indian chief, acts by the same code as Ethan. White people have killed his sons, so he takes revenge. His own community has been violated, and unless he can restore order it will fall apart. Restoring order requires vengeance, and on a large scale, until the ledger is balanced. Two cultures are at war through their two big men, each under oath, driven by honour. Only one can survive, and history determines it will be the Europeans. Ford is no relativist. Neither Ethan nor Scar has any choice. The obligation is to the culture into which one is born. There is no compromise, for in between is a cultural no-man's land. We are shown detribalised Indians—they have lost all dignity and self-respect. We are shown white people captured by Indians then rescued. They have all lost their minds. Ethan knows this, spitting out that it were better they were dead.

Finally Ethan and Martin catch up. Debbie, the surviving niece, now a teenager, tells them it is too late, for she has become an Indian. Ethan wants to kill her—in addition, she is one of Scar's squaws, and therefore sexually dishonoured. He knows her mother would have wanted it that way. Martin intercedes and an Indian arrow wounds Ethan.

They retreat to their community, from where an expedition is mounted to wipe out Scar's tribe. Martin sneaks into the Indian camp the night before and finds Debbie, who changes her mind. After the dawn assault, Ethan catches her as she flees from him. He grabs her, but on the point of carrying out her dead mother's wish, he relents, taking her up in his arms. He carries her back to the community—restored. Martin is free to marry at last, thereby rejoining the living chain, so that the unborn may be born, and into a secure and worthy world. The film ends with its theme song, 'Ride Away', as Ethan leaves. No human community can incorporate him; he has transgressed far more than can ever be atoned. Like Achilles, there is far too much blood on his hands. He has done what he had to do, under oath, but in the process cursed himself to endless wandering. His life is as good as over. There is an old saying that he who seeks vengeance should dig two graves.

The crux of the story is a double paradox: the change in Debbie, and even more the change in Ethan. Ford supplies the answers, prefiguring the entire action in the opening ten minutes of the film. Calvinist predestination broods over the drama. There is special intimacy between Debbie, then a girl, and her uncle Ethan. He gives her a 'gold locket'—which is not the cursed gold (everyone in the film who takes and keeps gold dies), but silver, a war decoration in the form of a Maltese cross. The cross protects Debbie. She is unbaptised, which means culturally flexible. Furthermore, when her parents send her out of the house to escape the massacre, she shelters next to her grandmother's grave, in the cemetery in which her family will soon be buried. She draws strength from the spirit of her ancestors.

Above all, she has a rare character, with sure, uncanny instincts. When Captain Clayton, on first arrival at the Edwards' home, swears in new deputies he is interrupted in the middle of the oath, at the words 'faithfully discharge'. Forgetting where he left off, Debbie, sitting at the dining table drinking her milk, pipes in with 'faithfully fulfil'. It is now an oath set by her, with stronger wording. The moment she speaks, her uncle appears in the rear doorway, the two figures visually linked. Without knowing what she is doing, she has stipulated the terms of Ethan's true oath, which will include saving her. Ethan does not swear with the others, but it is he who—also unconsciously—accepts the obligation. This young girl is like the Ashdod boy—she knows.

Debbie is fortified enough to survive the two cultures, to cross over and to come back. Ethan's wounding at the key moment, as teenage Debbie stands on a bridge over a river, is an act from above, stopping him. Ford's favourite song, which repeats in *The Searchers*, is 'Shall We Gather at the River'. It is only Poussin's Matthew who himself does not need to cross over—for he is guided by an angel. Debbie does. So does Ethan.

The journey in retribution—the 'search'—is gruelling beyond any normal human endurance. It is Homeric, and not pleasant to watch. Of two driving causes, the concrete one is the massacre—resulting in violation of the moral order. The opening scenes of the film are devoted to painting the virtue that is family with a fore-doomed intensity. Then it is ripped to shreds. We see the truth indirectly, in the torment in Ethan's face and the mania with which he knocks Martin unconscious, to prevent him seeing the mutilated bodies of his adopted family.

The other cause is the destiny of Ethan himself, who carries the mark of Cain, and is cursed never to settle. He is saved by his oath—

THE WRECK OF WESTERN CULTURE

Martha caresses his Confederate coat, sealing the unconscious bond, although his deeper commitment is to Debbie. 'Uncompromising devotion' is put to much severer test than in the benign world of *Rio Grande*. To avenge, Ethan must transgress, and at every turn the burden of his guilt increases. He is the true pilgrim in our larger story, the Kierkegaardian hero, making his life harder, guilt upon guilt, spitting out contempt at every comfort, every temptation of ease. He is inwardness and dread, but seizing hold of his own caged subjectivity in order to act, to do what he has to do. His character has tragic grandeur, and thereby so does his 'search'.

The gruelling remorselessness of the story is offset by comedy. The buffoon is an old fool, Mose Harper, who, in the Shakespearean tradition, mimics his masters, yet in his simple-mindedness sees the truth. Mose is battered by life, but he retains an impish vitality lacking in Rembrandt's old men. His one remaining wish is a rocking chair by the fire—the old bones are cold. Here is Ford's leading symbol of restored community, a homeliness which can provide the hearth and the rocking chair. The film ends in homecoming—except for Ethan.

It will be a long time, if ever, before Ethan is permitted to settle—in an early scene in his brother's house, it is he who sits in the rocking chair. That would require another story, an *Odyssey*, which by the way Ford tells in his next film, *Wings of Eagles*, and self-consciously, for a copy of Homer's second work appears on the screen. Ethan's own emblematic saying, contrasting with the fool's 'rocking chair' and 'Thank you kindly', is 'That'll be the day!' The rhetorical assertion is that of indomitable power. No one and nothing will bring down the man Scar nicknames 'big shoulders'. Fate can throw everything at him but he will endure. Yet he is damned, so fallen that nothing can hurt, or redeem.

Ethan's will is not that of the humanist, 'We can become what we will.' It is not free, nor is it guided by reason. John Wayne's character is not particularly interesting—he is merely a big brute under oath cast in a predetermined world with a mission. We are back with hard-core Protestantism, and in a raw, rough vein unfamiliar in Henry James. Ethan carries out his mission. He is a pilgrim warrior, another Cromwell. He is insensitive and inhuman, not likeable, except in his tenderness to the girl Debbie, and his forgiveness of the woman Debbie. Martin fears and hates him, although if the mission had been left to Martin, with his more feminine compassion, it would have failed.

Ethan's motive has nothing to do with his own happiness. It is pitched at two levels. One is middle order, the ethical obligation to kin. What he does is for the good of family and community, to neither of which he belongs. Although demonic, he is selfless.

His higher order motive, which is unconscious, is geared to his own nature, his 'I am', and with it to his fate. He appears in part as a male Magdalene, steeped in fallen worldliness, but this is still not the right category for him—not wild enough, although there is metamorphosis, in the late, conscious recognition of his kindred spirit, Debbie. Ethan Edwards is rather a mighty embodiment of 'sacred rage', the last in a line in American culture whose great predecessors include Captain Ahab, Hester Prynne, William Faulkner's Joe Christmas, not to mention the real-life figures such as Stonewall Jackson.

What then does it mean to be American? The challenge lies in the establishment of a community in the wilderness, a decent place in which children can grow up. We are back with foundation. The task is much tougher than in *Rio Grande*. It requires tragic suffering, followed by a colossal enactment of vengeance. We start with a precarious order, without roots, the ground shifting. It is, metaphorically, both the modern West and the New World—fresh born. This order is annihilated and the test begins. What *The Searchers* establishes is a sacred site in the wilderness, around a burnt homestead and the cemetery in which the mutilated bodies are buried, the site to which Martin can return after his long ordeal to marry the sister of the boy who went mad. There is blood in the soil. There will be singing and dancing at the wedding. Clayton will officiate, and Mose Harper will look on, beaming from his rocking chair.

The threat has gone for the time being. The Indians are dead and the founding father, the agent of retribution, has ridden away taking the pollution of all the blood-guilt with him, on his big shoulders. Companionship abounds, or does it? It does for the ordinary members of the community, but not for he on whom their well-being has been dependent. Debbie is the next generation, and will remain in the background, with her own indomitable will, until she is needed. She is Ethan's true child—accordingly, it is hard to imagine that she will marry, have a family, or in any real sense come to belong. She is too big, too much like her uncle. Modern Westerners who grow up in thrall of this myth might hope that, if they are boys, they may one day occupy the shoes of Ethan, if girls, those of Debbie. When they pause to reflect, however, they may well reconsider. By the law of tragic *mythos*, duty to community, sacrifice for the good of America, is merely a surface rationale. Ethan and Debbie, driven by sacred rage, are caught up principally in being faithful, both of them, to their own singular, inherited 'I am', and the destiny into which they have been cast.

***

The American hero, in the towering bulk of John Wayne, is wounded in the chest in *Rio Grande*, in the shoulder in *The Searchers*. In *The Man Who Shot Liberty Valance* he dies. The last of the paradigmatic trilogy is a requiem to Ethan Edwards, made six years later. Now he is Tom Doniphon. His time, that of the Old West, has passed, with the arrival of the railroad, irrigation, towns, law and education. The America he struggled to found no longer needs him. He dies a forgotten man, and lies without his boots in a pauper's coffin, in his town of Shinbone. John Ford takes a direct look at the peaceful and prosperous town for decent folk, the ideal that has directed his earlier films, and turns against it with bitter satire. Tombstone has become Shinbone, a prosaic farce of a place where the ancient heroes die unknown, buried ignominiously.

What has gone wrong? Friends arrive in town for the funeral, an old couple, Senator Ransom Stoddard and his wife, Hallie. The Senator then goes off to tell the Shinbone story. Again it is foundation, how they made America when they were young.

Stoddard had come to Shinbone straight from Law School in New England. His coach is held up by Liberty Valance, a bad man of medieval proportions, without conscience and driven by explosive sadism. In one of his manic furies he whips Stoddard half to death. The only man in town strong enough to stand up to Valance is Tom Doniphon. Tom hopes to marry Hallie, and is building an extension on to his house with that in mind. She is the daughter of the family that runs the main eating-place in Shinbone, Peter's Place, the noisy, bustling heart of the community. Father and daughter are played by the same actors who appear in the main family in *The Searchers*.

Stoddard sets up in town as a lawyer, vehemently arguing that Liberty Valance must be arrested and tried according to principle of law. The theme music from *Young Mr Lincoln* accompanies him. Stoddard also starts a school, teaching reading, writing and the principles of the American Constitution, above all the workings of democracy.

Hallie, fed up with the lawlessness of Shinbone, is swept away by the enlightened ideals championed by Stoddard. Valance goads the lawyer into a gunfight, but it is Liberty who is shot—from the shadows by Tom. Tom realises he has lost Hallie, gets drunk, then rides home and burns down the extension.

Hallie is the key character. In her young womanhood, working in the noisy heart of a bustling community, rough and uncivilised but vital, she was seduced by humanist dreams of education, democracy and freedom—she represents everyone, male or female, born into the modern West, condemned by their culture to make the identical choice. The old community had worked in its own sort of way, although its law was that of the gun. Tom had kept Liberty in some sort of check; even Liberty took note of public opinion. But Hallie is restless, a part of her called by the tune of civilisation, as was Lambert Strether.

So she gives up the man she loves for her fantasy, and ruins her life. Her husband as agent for the inevitable march of progress, history as necessity, destroys the place where her roots and her heart lie. The new Shinbone has law and order; education, democracy and freedom; but it is dead, with silent and empty streets. What has Hallie to return to in old age? There is one root—Tom is buried there. She has something to tend. In fact she plants a cactus rose, symbol of the untamed frontier wilderness of her youth, on top of Tom's coffin in its bare soil, without a pot so that its roots will feed directly off the body underneath. Apart from this extraordinary act, Hallie is hardly more than a shade coming back to haunt a place from long, long ago.

Yet Ford has put the case for progress in its most attractive light. Its champion is a hero, with his lawbook and his inviolable principle. Stoddard is a courageous man, more so than Doniphon, pitching himself into battles he cannot possibly win. He is a modern Quixote in his fearless idealism. Moreover, he is a man of action, and he succeeds. He dedicates his life to a brilliant political career, to serving the nation, to planting and tending the mythology of Abraham Lincoln.

Liberty Valance has valour built into his surname: the only character with true freedom, he forces all those who cross his path to prove themselves. His signature challenge, 'What kind of man are you, Dude?', is directed at Stoddard and the new order. Stoddard is courageous, but he has no weight. All the gravity in the film is with Tom, in the shadows, in a backstreet undertaker's room. One authority presides—his coffin. All the important action in the film takes place at night. In the fight scene, Liberty orders Stoddard to get into the light. He does so for an instant. This is the light of reason. The schoolroom had been flooded with light, as were the film's political conventions. Valance belongs in the dark, as does Tom. The truth belongs in the dark. John Ford is back with Luther, and Holbein. More specifically, he proves that it is not courage but gravity that is at the core of *honour*, and it is tied to an authority based on power, harnessed to right judgment.

Hallie is a modern woman, who with foolish inevitability falls for the shiny phantasm of the free, rational individual, and pitches her life into the dark, a directionless dark in which there is no death of death. Her Ransom husband is Jean de Dinteville reborn—no one, in his time, more seductively eligible—no one more lethal.

Kirby Yorke's oath to the cavalry and America depended for its sense on the future, on the towns and gardens that might spring up in the tamed wilderness. Ethan Edwards is driven to avenge his kin, but 'faithfully fulfil' loses half its sense if there is no future, the obligation to ancestors always linked to an obligation to the unborn. *The Man Who Shot Liberty Valance* undermines the future. The new America, that of democracy and the Constitution, of education and development, depends on a different myth than that of the old West. It is the Lincoln myth. It lacks gravity. Stoddard discovers that even he needs a legend from the old West on which to build his career. People want to be led by him because they have heard a story, not about how he used his lawbooks, but how he used his gun. He has failed the Liberty challenge. Furthermore, in a bitter irony, 'What kind of man are you, Dude?' combines with the first name of the challenger to scorn an America that believes in the Statue of Liberty.

The old West makes the new America possible, but the new does not work. All is clear and distinct, but the streets are dead. The Lincoln myth is superficial; the 'man who shot Liberty Valance' myth is a lie. There is only one sacred site, the coffin of the old West, but it is abandoned and forgotten. *There* was a 'kind of man', indeed a far more admirable one than Brutus. After him, there is nothing under the feet, the ground taken over by pompous chatterbox politicians and scavenger journalists.

Ford has come to agree with Kathleen Yorke, 'All this danger to serve people as yet unborn—and probably not worth serving.' His late pessimism runs through a trio of films, *Two Rode Together* (1961), *Liberty Valance* (1962) and *Donovan's Reef* (1963). The first is a dark story in which the community is not worth saving; worse, it has so little sense it murders the innocent, and the hero is a dandy egocentric marshal devoted to making money and living well. *Donovan's Reef* pictures a South Seas utopia, entirely split off from America. It is Ford's *Tempest*, with hope withdrawn into a fantasy world at a distance. America is lost.

Ford is hardly easier on himself. His life-work attempting to forge a binding myth has been no less quixotic than Ransom Stoddard's Enlightenment. And like Don Quixote, he renounces his vision at the end. In *Liberty Valance* he turns on his own legend and prints the truth. The truth is that the past, which was heroic, has gone: the legend is dead. The goal it fought for, the new America, proved false. The founding and the making was itself great, but the result was a whited sepulchre, the companionship fizzling out. History has won, determining that Ethan Edwards will be replaced by Ransom Stoddard, and that a lively honest woman, the salt of the modern Western earth, having to choose, will make the wrong choice. The America that imagines it can do without a formidable foundation *mythos*, that thinks the civic religion of 'God bless America!' and the Constitution is enough, finds its new man. He is merely a twentieth-century copy of a Holbein ambassador.

The discipline of modern sociology has produced two enduring theories. First, there is Max Weber's thesis about the formative role of the Protestant Ethic in the rise of the modern West and its own decline in the nineteenth century, leaving a disenchanted and nihilistic world. It is a theory examined in this book in its deeper and more encompassing form in Kierkegaard and Nietzsche. The second theory is that of Emile Durkheim, most extensively developed in his 1897 work, *Suicide*. Durkheim saw the determining feature of modern society as the decline of community, and the commensurate growth in the cult of the individual. The assumption is that humans gain their sense of purpose, direction, and meaning in life from being integrated into a group, with which they share a collective conscience, a common culture. Otherwise they will suffer from the characteristic modern pathologies of egoism and anomie, restlessness and rootlessness. John Ford makes similar assumptions in his early to middle work. *Rio Grande*, without knowing it, is a brilliant formulation of the sociological ideal of community, with an analytical precision and concreteness not to be found in the intellectual model. Similarly, *Liberty Valance* is an account of the decline of community in the particular modern manner, at the hands of noble humanist ideals.

The reason sociology has never gone beyond Weber and Durkheim is that the modern West has not taken a new turn since 1900. If anything it suffers progressively more from, on the one hand, weak community and a lack of companionship and, on the other, the disenchantment of a rationalised world without unifying sacred belief or attachment. Individual vocations, secular ones, provide the last place to stand; Ethan and Debbie are the only counter to Holbein's ambassadors.

John Ford's own final word is very close to that of Henry James. In his last film, *Seven Women* (1966), community is a cage within which celibate nuns retreat from living into an absurdly pointless venture in China. In fact, their Christian Mission is set up just like a fort, in deliberate mockery of the principles of *Rio Grande*. The hero is a nihilistic woman doctor, smoking and boozing freely as she derides the brittle hypocrisies of the community into which she has exiled herself. With an earthy, nonchalant charisma she is a modern Magdalene, saved from a clear-eyed, brutal cynicism by her vocation—a true one unlike that of the unworldly nuns. Ford himself later commented that, 'She was a woman who had no religion, but she got in with this bunch of kooks and started acting like a human being.' The doctor's oath to her profession, the one thing in which she believes, anchors her. She sacrifices her life for it. She is Debbie ten years on, or Max Weber's individual alone in the world with his 'intellectual integrity'. This is Lambert Strether's honour.

Henry James tried to fit his pilgrim into the refinements of taste and feeling of humanist Europe, but had him flee in order to preserve his honour. John Ford tried to build and defend Catholic community through the sacred rage of a rugged Protestant hero of the old West. Like Poussin, with whom he had much in common, he managed a plausible alternative Reformation, but once he took a close look at what the New World had become he turned away in disappointment. The place he had created to stand in America would not hold, for history was too much on the side of a profaning humanism. He is reported as saying late in life, 'Our ancestors would be bloody ashamed if they could see us today.'

It is also true that his vision was too secular, no doubt forced on him by the place and the time. Its earlier goal was a city of man on earth. But working by means of his own stories, Ford discovers the old wisdom that no city of man is enough. So he abandons the ideal of secular community. His own last stand then turns to the tragic hero and his heir, Debbie. In the modern West Debbie turns into the cynical doctor who still believes enough in her vocation to move, but who remains so sunk in world-weary resignation that sacrificing her life seems hardly to matter to her. In short, Ford's own relentlessly gruelling 'search' led him straight into the arms of Kierkegaard's truth that the ethical hero—Kantian moral law embodied in even the most admirable of individuals—is not enough.

Chapter Fourteen

THE END:
SEPTEMBER 11, 2001

On September 11, 2001, the test came. Demanding both practical and metaphysical responses, it defied the military law of never fighting a war on two fronts. The man on horseback this time was not humanism ascendant—the Gattamelata— nor the Homeric hero reborn—Ethan Edwards. The Western media provided the unconscious cue to what had struck—its own nightmare from within. It blurted out the symbolism in the month following the destruction of the World Trade Center in New York— the pair of 110-storey skyscrapers reduced to a pile of rubble a mere 100 feet high, spread across a sixteen acre site, the death toll three thousand.

Who, or what, had done this? One man, shown alone on horse- back, riding through the wastes of Afghanistan, tall and handsome, with clear skin and full lips, sun-tempered, with a mocking smile and invincible aura, nonchalantly looking the West and all its might straight in the eye. Usama bin Laden challenged, 'What kind of man are you, Dude?'

Liberty Valance was back, this time cast as a bad man with brains, stealing the West's most potent modern myth, inverting it into the stranger riding into the frontier town to destroy it. The traces were chilling. The more common, previous English spelling of the name 'Usama'—and accurate transliteration from the Arabic pronunciation—was replaced instantly, on September 11, by 'Osama'. The opening three letters had understandably spooked America. To the elites—intellectual, media, corporate and political—it was vital that the man who had done this was an outsider, an alien personification of evil. For then, to kill him, would fix the problem. Once again, all would be well.

If, on the other hand, Bin Laden were America's shadow self, then this nightmare would take on an entirely different complexion. The practical solution to the problem of terrorism—hunting down and killing its leadership—would not work, except at the shorter-term, material level. A cultural or metaphysical showdown operates by its own logic. Further, to contract the name one more notch, the shadow self became that of the entire modern West—'Us'. Here was *nemesis* of a quite unprecedented order.

One month on from September 11, Usama released a speech decreeing that his terrorist war was that of the 'camp of belief' pitted against the 'camp of unbelief'. This speech—in its precision of rhetoric, its poetic mobilisation of theology combined with moral invective, its potency of image—struck the raw nerve of the West like nothing since Martin Luther. And it was backed by action. Which Western organisation could match the brilliance of hijacking four passenger jets in unison, flying them skilfully, three of them proceeding to hit their targets—given the potential for the unforeseen in such an intricate mission, carried out in secrecy without trial run, and under formidable pressure?

A range of personae was surfacing. It was as if Luther's satanic *alter ego* had been reborn, half-a-millennium on. In the same speech, Usama stated that his God had 'elevated the skies without pillars'. The subtext, like phosphorus in the dark, taunted the West: All you believe in is the modern metropolis created by humanist will and reason, bathed in clear light, as on a sublime, sunny September morning in New York—efficient, opulent, and comfortable! If the pillars of your culture are the Twin Towers of the World Trade Center then I can bring them down, using disciplined men unafraid of death—you who are cowards, terrified by death. Moreover, I can do it in your most cosmopolitan and dynamic city, targeting its tallest skyscrapers, home to Western capitalism's leading finance and bond traders, buildings themselves symbolic of the might of your civilisation. All that will remain will be a gigantic hole. Moreover, if I so choose, the Statue of Liberty will follow.

We are compelled to ask ourselves: What are the true twin towers of Western culture? Not humanism's free-will and reason, for they narrow down to the World Trade Center in New York—such is one of the theses of this book.

Over the portal to Apollo's ancient temple, high up in Delphi on the side of the sacred mountain, Parnassus, two sayings were carved into the stone. 'Know thyself!' and 'Nothing too much!' presided over the Greek foundation of Western culture. Humanism has transgressed both. The *I* it sought to know was the wrong one; and the insecure *me* that finally emerged took to gorging itself on excesses generated abundantly by its civilisation.

The judgment should not be misunderstood as moral—it is metaphysical. That the modern West has become excessive in the mode of greed is, to be sure, an ethical reading, but the message from Delphi places the blame on a failure of culture. *I* become obsessed by *me* when, in the shoes of Holbein's ambassadors, I no longer believe in anything beyond my self.

As illustration, Bin Laden's single driving motive was destruction—destruction of the West. He showed no inclination to follow in the footsteps of his fundamentalist predecessor, Ayatollah Khomeini in Iran, and rebuild Islamic societies. He takes his, presumably unwitting, cue from the humanist West's definitive shadow self, Hamlet. Usama bin Laden appeared at the opening of the twenty-first century as the melancholy Prince's agent—both under the same oath, to death. Hence the instinct of the media, in unconscious shock at the attack on New York, to imagine him cast in a John Ford film. Little wonder that throughout the West, many were, in the same breath, both terrified and titillated.

Usama is half insider, too, when viewed from a historical perspective. Much about him is familiar from within the twentieth-century West—of what remained scavenging around in the ruins of humanism. That century's first catastrophe, World War One, was in good part a product of the 'death of God' crisis of meaning, with the cultural elites on both sides in favour of the war on the grounds that it might give them something in which to believe. The result was not revitalisation and a new faith—in nation—but the carnage of a generation of European men in the wastelands of northern France and Flanders. By 1918, Holbein's skull had the West comprehensively under its spell. Its next emanation was totalitarianism.

The totalitarianisms of the Right and the Left—fascism, or Nazism, and communism—obeyed the same formula. They took the technological genius of humanism, its industrial and organisational power, and wedded it to fundamentalist rancour. The fundamentalisms varied—with Hitler, an ideology of nation fusing culture, race and land; with Stalin, the ideology of the French Revolution fused to a paranoid demonisation of democratic capitalism. The end in both cases was belief in nothing, a militarist society run by the secret police, and death camps.

This lineage is not a scatter of aberrations on the margin, but central to the twentieth century, an era split between totalitarianism and liberal humanism. The great cultural critic Georg Lukàcs is a case in point. Lukàcs had taken Nietzsche and Kierkegaard's diagnoses to heart—teaching himself Danish in order to read the latter's work in the original. He had been a regular visitor at the home of Max Weber. No one in the second decade of the century had his finger more squarely on the cultural pulse. He understood that by

1900 the bourgeois order—the last to remain standing and provide some higher meaning—was in terminal decline, a decline Lukàcs saw charted in the novels of Thomas Mann. In December 1918, the 32-year-old Lukàcs returned to his native Budapest and made his own Kierkegaardian leap of faith—he joined the Communist Party. He did so, not out of sympathy with the poor, but out of the need for something in which to believe—the need for ideology. This prodigiously intelligent man, schooled in the range and depth of Western culture, turned into a fundamentalist, defending Stalinism for the rest of his long life.

From Lukàcs and Stalin it was a direct step to Usama. He engineered the same totalitarian formula. Not an Islamic scholar, his university education was in economics and management; likewise, the leaders of his organisation trained as technocrats. His targets on September 11 came straight out of a Marxist textbook on power elites. If this were a holy war, as he claimed, one would expect attacks on centres of religious authority such as the Vatican, Westminster Abbey or an American synagogue. Usama's rancour bears the stamp of Marx, and envy at the success of the West, now led by America. For, the half millennium that saw the triumph of humanism also marked the commensurate, steady decline of the Islamic Middle East into chronic stagnation.

The one difference that makes all the difference was that Usama included Luther's scalpel in his saddlebags, alongside the Koran and a 7,000-page training manual for guerrilla warfare and terrorism. The West was always going to defeat communist societies, for that was a war of competing materialisms—over who could generate the most wealth—a battle fought within capitalism's field of strength. The West's metaphysical nerve, the nucleus of its vulnerability, was quite another matter, now exposed to the hot knife gouging into raw tissue.

What remained in New York after September 11, 2001—once

100,000 truckloads of rubble had been excavated—was a hole of vast discomposure. How might relatives and friends, the city of New York, indeed the entire West, mourn the loss of the three thousand who perished, and of threads in the cultural spine that had been severed? What fitting monument might be constructed, in remembrance, in the sixteen-acre chasm? At stake, once again, was the need to achieve a death of death, in order to Rest In Peace. Otherwise, the site would fester as the unconsecrated graveyard of the humanist West.

In fact, the hole would be filled with more skyscrapers, as if to say we have to get on with our lives, put it behind us—business as usual. The metaphor of choice would brazenly proclaim: we know it all, and we have nothing to learn. So, Usama had won, his own world's social inertia mirrored by the West's cultural freeze. The Twin Towers' replacement would have none of the sublime soaring elegance of what disintegrated on September 11, the new aesthetic mediocrity signalling that New York itself wanted to merge into the crowd of minor cities—another Miami, Frankfurt or Manchester. Four new, diminutive skyscrapers were planned, a single 'Freedom Tower', with the other humanist pillar, to reason, excised. As Apollo looked down in bemusement, the ultimate question remained: Rebuild around what—a void of embarrassment? A popular song had earlier put it, 'Freedom's just another word for nothing left to lose.'

Five hundred years on, and Luther's warning light was still flashing: a choice between the darkness of faith where the light of reason does not shine, the realm in which it might be possible to achieve a death of death—or the skull. An equivalent to the Cross would have to be erected in the American hole, an absolute work of art tapping into the Western tragic *mythos*, one that spoke to the times, one achieving the stature of a Poussin *Last Supper* or a Bach *Passion*. Failure would mean that Duchamp's *Urinal* still presided in New York.

***

It is all a question of a place to stand. Nothing else really matters. Donatello found his in Padua, inside the cathedral. Poussin found his in the thick of the *mythos* stories that engage all people at critical times in their lives—and with redemptive figures such as the Ashdod boy and Mary Magdalene. Luther found his in a vision of the darkness of faith and the death of death, for which it was necessary to find the monster and kill it. Shakespeare attempted it in a heroic portrait of the man of honour, shadowed the image and found himself left with Hamlet, skull in hand. Cervantes resorted to the fierce idealism of Don Quixote, a ludicrous solution. For a period, the bourgeois managed to stake a humanist egoism to the Protestant rock and find a reasonably gratifying way of life. Kierkegaard, at high personal cost, achieved a substitute, a certain stability in his own inward depth. It was not satisfactory, for faith eluded him in his master works. Henry James, buoyed up by his sacred rage, keeping afloat in the heaving fathomless ocean of modernity, tried to find a harbour and failed. John Ford just found his footing then abandoned it, in despair at his times.

In this pantheon, there were two singular *mythos* precedents to September 11. Poussin uses the Ashdod plague—laying total waste to the old order—to ask what is necessary to build culture anew, and thereby provide lost souls, once again, with the capacity for life. John Ford initiates his modern search for bearings with a violation of higher order that has left his human community stranded in a boundless void.

Then there were the other protagonists, those who rather than take on the monster denied its existence and fled. No angel visited and whispered in their ear, no enchanted boy pointed the way. So they set out to destroy everything that was solid. Their modern founding father was Velàzquez, their most insightful prophet, Nietzsche. There was the naive utopianism of Descartes and the moral intelligence of Kant, a good man with the misfortune to be born into a failing tribe in a bad time. He did consolidate the middle-order humanist platform of liberal democracy and universal human rights, but it was a platform not a rock. There was the rancorous vandalism of Marx and the genteel but deceptively virulent nihilism of Darwin. Lastly, there was the beguiling introspection of Freud, the drowning of self in its own unconscious, with its wretched precursor in Hamlet. Let us not even consider all those who hoped that comfort could suffice.

Humanism failed because its *I* is not the centre of creation, in the sense of being creature and creator in one. It was a different species from the 'I am' taught by Jesus. Honour on its own is not enough. There is no free-will in any important sense of the term, and human reason is powerful only on a narrow front within strict limits. What is of nearly infinite capacity in the human individual is imagination—fancy. Humanism flourished here, with its fantasy of freedom and reason, that I can become what I will. It was this fantasy, represented as it was in the Gattamelata, Velàzquez' self-portrait, Descartes' 'I think' and Nietzsche's 'Me versus Christ', that emasculated the existing real cultures—the ones that provided the Archimedean rock. This fantasy set the demonic free, in its modern form, which meant privately Munch's Madonna and the rat-girl, and publicly the French Revolution and, later, the Twin Towers.

At the same time, the domain in which the humanist imagination became concrete, that of science and technology leading to the industrial revolution, produced an opulence of material power and comfort that allowed humans to think, as long as they narrowed their consciousness down to their animal needs and repressed their conscience, that they *had* become what they wanted. Moreover, Darwin told them they were animals. Thus, while the humanist castle was tumbling down in the face of the psychological and spiritual reality, it was cemented together at the level of material comfort. It had found the key, in the capitalist model, to a resilient economic dynamism—again, in itself, no small achievement.

Here was the modern context for Jesus' dictum, 'It is easier for a camel to go through the eye of a needle, than for a rich man to enter into the kingdom of God.' Jesus, by the way, was not critical of those who were rich, but of those who were attached to their wealth, dependent on it for their sense of self. The predominant thinking of the twentieth century was that of an animal, that the good life is to consume, to procreate and to sleep, and in those terms there was giant progress. Most Westerners *had* become corpulent.

The twentieth century turned into a parody of humanism. While the confident *I* of the Renaissance had been *me*-centred, it had been geared to a higher end. It strived to use reason and free-will to create the human world anew—Michelangelo his *Moses*, Newton his laws of motion, Kant his ethics, and the cumulative development of the modern metropolis. After Nietzsche, this collapsed into *me* the last man, in a rootless mania of consumption, stimulated by the consolations of regular therapy, massaging the insecure self, telling its diminutive being how great it is.

Kierkegaard proved the master diagnostician with his hierarchy of spheres, rising from the aesthetic, through the ethical to the religious. He predicted that a culture centred on the ethical order would inevitably collapse into the self-centred pursuit of pleasure. Humanism's greatest achievement was a liberal-democratic kingdom of ends, a society based on universal human rights governed by Kant's absolute moral laws and guided by civic common sense—practical reason operating in its fitting place. This social model was superior, in moral terms, to the range of tribal intolerances that had preceded it—tribal cultures being inherently hostile to outsiders.

The vital spot here was an appeal to the 'human' in everybody, that it was invested with enough passion that its own cultural core—the body of universal moral laws—become an Archimedean rock. Henry James put it to the test, giving his ethical hero, Strether, in addition, the sacred rage to drive him—but found this still not enough to save him, or anyone else, in the absence of some higher Truth. John Ford also put the humanist vital spot to the test, focusing on an idealised moral community in which families gather together cheerfully to work and to celebrate, where children are born, and rocking chairs are provided for the old. But he too came to agree with Kierkegaard that good community, while essential to human well-being, was a middle-order reality, however buoyant its families, however strong its clubs and associations, and all its other tissues of belonging. It lacked enough vitality and fortitude to survive on its own. When the heat is on, as in *The Searchers*, and *being* is put to the test, the members of an ethical community are not up to redeeming the human world. Moreover, without the sacred *mythos* manifest in an Ethan or Debbie, they are doomed.

Not only is the human individual not creature and creator in one. He is not, as Darwin would have us believe, a highly evolved and super-charged fish. True, endow a fish with consciousness and what you get is the modern individual whose material life is spent in terror of the inevitable future, which is death, an unconscious terror which poisons the pleasure. The creature is turned to stone. Indeed, Spinoza's mocking image of free-will equated humans with stones endowed with consciousness, imagining that they were rolling downhill of their own free choice—Spinoza cold-bloodedly honest about the facts, two centuries before Darwin.

Under the humanist constellation, Death rules. But this metaphysics of man, a fish endowed with consciousness, sets him too low. It is the dregs of humanism. Consciousness is mind, it is intellect, it is reason—it is Descartes. It is not the fragment of divinity, the soul. The soul creates the guilt that ruins Brutus, countermanding his freedom to kill Caesar. In fact, it makes him human, although Shakespeare may not realise this, so blurred has his consciousness become by the curse of humanism. Kant was under the same curse, very close to a breakthrough, aware that it is the shamefulness of vice not its harm that counts. But he too had been so comprehensively seduced by the 'Devil's whore' that he retreated into his sterile rationalist logic. Holbein's *Corpse of Christ* and *Ambassadors* are fish endowed with consciousness, but Holbein, early in the day, was not yet so entranced. He could still speak the unholy truth. At the end of this road, humanism would come to be symbolised by its final work of art—Duchamp's *Urinal*

***

All has come before, yet we need to start again. To go back, to the fateful spot where the three roads meet beneath Delphi, is to find the signpost. It was inscribed, two thousand years ago, by John. He opens his Life of Jesus, 'In the beginning was the word.' These cryptic six words, as rendered from the Greek by William Tyndale, overthrow the metaphysics of the Old World of the Hebrew Bible, which had its foundation *mythos* in God creating the universe. The old God had stipulated the nature of being as centred in his own identity, 'I am that I am.' John responds by telling a story which inexorably leads to the new *logos*, or knowledge. Jesus narrows the central truth down to two words, 'I am.' In effect, the human individual, exemplified by Jesus, has replaced God. Here was to be humanism's cue for centring its own cultural revolution on redefining the *I*.

John sets up a range of categories that will prove decisive to the future path of Western culture. A few verses into his first chapter he elaborates on the *word*, 'In it was life, and the life was the light of men, and the light shineth in the darkness, but the darkness comprehendeth it not.' Here is the source of Luther's 'darkness of faith' and 'death of death'—no more than footnotes, shrewdly extracted from the foundation story. Unsurprisingly, Luther valued John's Gospel as supreme.

The story of the rise and fall of humanism signals to us what will be needed if a new culture is to succeed. There is the enthusiasm for man and his works that the Renaissance attempted to enshrine. This is, 'I like him!' It has nothing to do with the rocket that launched the humanist Icarus, 'We can become what we will.' It is rather the simple zest for life, the buoyancy of existence that John Ford caught in his *Rio Grande*. It is the sublime balance of a man in form guided by his own concentrated mind—the Gattamelata. It is the beauty of the clarity and completeness of Euclidean geometry that between Descartes and Darwin becomes cold and rank. Its defining emotions, as Nietzsche observed, are cheerfulness and gratitude. Ford believed they needed a certain robustness of community.

Nietzsche chose to identify these emotions with the ancient Greeks rather than the Renaissance. He thought they needed harsher soil in which to grow, one fed by suffering, one that might give birth to a tragic *mythos*. He knew all about 'Alas, poor Yorick', and Luther's monster, as did Rembrandt, and Kierkegaard with his own Abraham. Whether there is a place to stand would be decided here, whether the human target, as the dread mounts, will be turned into stone, like Holbein's ambassadors and Hamlet, Munch's Madonna and the people of Ashdod. Roots sunk into this harder Greek soil feed off the demonic, close to the evil of which humans are capable. The challenge is exemplified by Ethan Edwards with his, 'That'll be the day!' This big, berserk man, who is more than a fish endowed with consciousness, snorts derisively, 'What kind of man are you, Dude?'

Renewal will also depend on shame and the possibility of the righting of being, as with Mary Magdalene. It is on this front that humanism floundered, and proved that to celebrate the glory of humanity on its own is not enough; worse, it unwittingly nurtures one of the nastiest of all monsters—rancour. John had established the Western archetype of rancour in his telling of the Last Supper. The narrative reaches its climax with the exit of Judas, the only one who has received bread dipped in wine, in his case the poisoned gift of 'I am not'. Not-being is inwardly propelled into destroying the one who shows him up, the one who exposes him as incapable of finding his own radiance, in the *word*. For Judas, the light goes out as he leaves the room. The episode ends with three starkly simple Greek words, *en de nux*— 'And it was night.'

The exit into endless night eternally threatens. The *word* pressures being, exposing the stature of the *I*. It was on this threshold that modernity faced its greatest test, and even in the case of the few who understood the full momentousness of the challenge, and went out to meet it, their action failed. From the blurred skull, painted in sixteenth-century London, the path leads directly to that black hole of vast discomposure in the centre of twenty-first century New York. And when the time comes for it to lead on from there—whither? The culture of the West will not be renewed until the moment it kills Luther's monster, and once again achieves a death of death.

There are eternal laws—moral and metaphysical—and at its deepest level, the human conscience is born understanding them: Calvin's notion of conscience as that which does not allow us to suppress within ourselves what we know. So, however much a particular period may distort and repress true conscience, it will not eliminate it. The great articulations of that conscience endure: *The Iliad*, *Agamemnon*, *Oedipus the King*, Mark and John's Lives of Jesus, the works of Donatello, Raphael, Poussin, and Bach. The markers of the central way of a culture, of our culture, survive, and are there for each new generation to read, if it will. That way is ever firm under foot.

Our story is told. Its purpose has been simple, to shout that humanism is dead, and has been so since the nineteenth century. It is time to quit it. Let us bury it with appropriate rites, which means honouring what was good, and understanding what went wrong and why. We do not want to fall for its charms a second time. We are peculiarly vulnerable, in that over many generations it has developed in us a sweet tooth for knowledge, an endemic weakness for its own narcotic, the exercise of intellect. Its rallying illusion is bred deeply into us by now—that knowledge will make us better and happier, and that we are free, free to improve ourselves. New York continues to erect Freedom Towers. Here is the reason that the corpse has been in our midst for so long without the appropriate response. Our healthy instincts have been rationalised virtually out of existence by this sickness, this illusion—by now un-redemptive—that mind can reform being.

We need to recover our capacity for spontaneous and unselfconscious revulsion. We need to recognise just how fed up we are with this heritage—fed up in a way that frees us to move on. This story has been told to arouse the disgust. For that, it has been necessary to show just how good the alternative was, the one exemplified by Poussin—what a sublime reality was forsaken, one which could have firmly anchored the West. This story has also aimed at making a contribution to the funeral service. To say it once again, it is time to bury the dead, and to start the difficult business of restoring our capacity for life. In the beginning, at the foundation, where all truth roads meet, was the *word*.

THE WORKS

Donatello: *The Gattamelata*, c. 1447
Padua High Altar, c. 1450
Shakespeare: *Julius Caesar*, c. 1599
Hamlet, c. 1602
Cervantes: *Don Quixote*, 1604+1614
Holbein: *The Ambassadors*, 1533
Luther: *On the Enslaved Will*, 1525
Calvin: *Institutes of the Christian Religion*, 1536–59
Raphael: *Deposition*, 1507
Sistine Madonna, c. 1513
Caravaggio: *Call of Matthew*, 1600
Poussin: *The Plague of Ashdod*, 1631
Matthew and the Angel, 1640
Penance, 1647
Eucharist, 1647
Velázquez: *Las Meninas*, 1656
Rembrandt: *The Sacrifice of Isaac*, 1636
Bach: *St Matthew Passion*, c. 1727–44
Descartes: *Discourse on Method*, 1637
Mozart: *Così Fan Tutte*, 1790
Kant: *Groundwork of the Metaphysics of Morals*, 1785
The Critique of Practical Reason, 1788

Marx: *The Communist Manifesto*, 1848
Darwin: *The Origin of Species*, 1859
Kierkegaard: *Fear and Trembling*, 1843
                Concluding Unscientific Postscript, 1846
Nietzsche: *The Birth of Tragedy*, 1872
Freud: *The Interpretation of Dreams*, 1900
Henry James: *The Ambassadors*, 1903
John Ford: *The Searchers*, 1956
                The Man Who Shot Liberty Valance, 1962

INDEX